Praise for

EXTREME CHURCH MAKEOVER

Extreme Church Makeover is a book for which many of us
have been waiting. It addresses many of the most strategic needs being
faced by the Church today. The message of the second chapter alone
could be used of God to transform many churches.

PAUL CEDAR
CHAIRMAN, MISSION AMERICA COALITION
AUTHOR, *A LIFE OF PRAYER*

The Setting Your Church Free process described in
Extreme Church Makeover has been a significant and strategic experience
for our congregation. It was significant in that it helped us resolve
some conflicts that we had because of the untimely death of our senior
pastor. The strategic principles of this book have allowed us to turn
the corner into the twenty-first century—an important event for a
95-year-old church. I would highly recommend this makeover process
for any church that has more than a few years of history.

DAVID JENKINS
PASTOR, CALVARY BAPTIST CHURCH
SOUTH BEND, INDIANA

The process outlined in *Extreme Church Makeover* is one
of the most effective weapons in my arsenal of resources to assist
churches that are experiencing spiritual bondage issues. I have used
the process outlined by Neil Anderson and Chuck Mylander to assist
severely conflicted congregations regain their spiritual and moral
direction. I eagerly anticipate using this new edition to see still more
victories over the evil one as I work with churches in transition
that are seeking spiritual recovery and wholeness.

JOHNNY E. ROSS
CERTIFIED INTENTIONAL INTERIM MINISTER
BY THE CENTER FOR CONGREGATIONAL HEALTH
NORTH CAROLINA BAPTIST HOSPITAL
WINSTON-SALEM, NORTH CAROLINA

Extreme Church Makeover deals with one of the basic elements in church growth: the spiritual releasing of a church for the power of God. While many are writing about the principles and programs to make a church grow, and others are featuring the user-friendly aspects of marketing the message to the general public, Anderson and Mylander have dealt with the spiritual factors that prohibit the church from revival and the power of God.

DR. ELMER TOWNS
DEAN, SCHOOL OF RELIGION
LIBERTY UNIVERSITY
LYNCHBURG, VIRGINIA

Just as individuals bring emotional and spiritual baggage with them into the Christian life, whole congregations can carry such baggage from events in the history of the congregation. Freedom for the individual to grow in maturity depends on dealing with the personal sin and emotional baggage, and freedom for a church to grow often depends on dealing with the corporate sin in its history. *Extreme Church Makeover* provides the guidance a church needs to do that.

TIMOTHY M. WARNER
FORMER DIRECTOR OF PROFESSIONAL DOCTORAL PROGRAMS
TRINITY EVANGELICAL DIVINITY SCHOOL
DEERFIELD, ILLINOIS

You hold in your hands one of the best resources available for churches and pastors who are desperate to experience God's healing and transforming power. The Steps to Setting Your Church Free, based on the seven churches in Revelation, provide a refreshingly biblical and exceptionally practical framework for cultivating a spirit of genuine repentance and renewal in the local church. Having tested these truths in the real world of pastoral ministry, I can vouch for their validity, and I am thankful for the opportunity to share these timeless principles with a new generation of pastoral leaders.

DAVID O. WILLIAMS
ASSISTANT PROFESSOR OF PASTORAL MINISTRIES/CHAPLAIN
BARCLAY COLLEGE
HAVILAND, KANSAS

EXTREME CHURCH MAKEOVER

NEIL T. ANDERSON
CHARLES MYLANDER

Regal

From Gospel Light
Ventura, California, U.S.A.

PUBLISHED BY REGAL BOOKS
FROM GOSPEL LIGHT
VENTURA, CALIFORNIA, U.S.A.
Regal PRINTED IN THE U.S.A.

Regal Books is a ministry of Gospel Light, a Christian publisher dedicated to serving the local church. We believe God's vision for Gospel Light is to provide church leaders with biblical, user-friendly materials that will help them evangelize, disciple and minister to children, youth and families.

It is our prayer that this Regal book will help you discover biblical truth for your own life and help you meet the needs of others. May God richly bless you.

For a free catalog of resources from Regal Books/Gospel Light, please call your Christian supplier or contact us at 1-800-4-GOSPEL *or* www.regalbooks.com.

Originally published as *Setting Your Church Free* by Regal Books in 1994.
Revised and updated edition published by Regal Books in 2005.

© 1994, 2005 Neil T. Anderson and Charles Mylander
All rights reserved.

Library of Congress Cataloging-in-Publication Data
Anderson, Neil T., 1942-
  Extreme church makeover / Neil T. Anderson, Charles Mylander.— Rev. and updated ed.
    p. cm.
  Rev. ed. of: Setting your church free. c1994.
  Includes bibliographical references.
  ISBN 0-8307-3794-4 (hardcover) — ISBN 0-8307-3795-2
  1. Church renewal. 2. Pastoral theology. I. Mylander, Charles. II. Anderson, Neil T., 1942- Setting your church free. III. Title.

BV600.3.A53 2005
250—dc22   2005015781

1   2   3   4   5   6   7   8   9   10   /   10   09   08   07   06   05

Rights for publishing this book in other languages are contracted by Gospel Light Worldwide, the international nonprofit ministry of Gospel Light. Gospel Light Worldwide also provides publishing and technical assistance to international publishers dedicated to producing Sunday School and Vacation Bible School curricula and books in the languages of the world. For additional information, visit www.gospellightworldwide.org; write to Gospel Light Worldwide, P.O. Box 3875, Ventura, CA 93006; or send an e-mail to info@gospellightworldwide.org.

CONTENTS

FOREWORD

In the early 1990s, I was pastoring a church in Ames, Iowa. My associate pastor was a former student of Neil's at Talbot School of Theology. He had contacted Dr. Anderson about the possibility of conducting a Living Free in Christ conference in our church. When I was informed that the conference included topics on spiritual warfare, I was at first opposed to the idea. I had grown very skeptical about anyone teaching on this topic. I called Neil with my concerns, but what I heard sounded quite different from what I had encountered in the past. So we invited Freedom in Christ Ministries to come to our rural university community.

During that week, I saw lasting change take place in the lives of many people. I personally gained a more biblical and balanced understanding of spiritual warfare, but more importantly, I gained a deeper understanding of who I am in Christ and how to abide in Him. I had a greater appreciation of what Jesus meant when He said, "You will know the truth, and the truth will set you free" (John 8:32).

Not long after the conference, I was called to be a district superintendent with the Evangelical Free Church of America. I encouraged the pastors in my district to give careful consideration to the truths Neil was bringing to our attention. I was working with many pastors and church leaders trying to help them become healthier by respecting Jesus as the head of our churches. Then Neil released a new book coauthored by Dr. Charles Mylander, who was also a district superintendent, entitled *Setting Your Church Free*. This book was like a gift from God.

In the ensuing years I led several churches through the Steps to Setting Your Church Free. Most of those churches experienced significant change. When the leadership prayed and asked the Holy Spirit to guide them, the Lord revealed their strengths, weaknesses and corporate sins. Painful memories surfaced during the process and the leaders forgave those who were part of the problems in the past.

The Lord has given us a tool to actually resolve personal and spiritual conflicts. In the churches that were significantly helped, the leaders took seriously the truth regarding sin, forgiveness and repentance. There was a sense of relief for those churches that took this repentance process seriously, and the leadership experienced a greater degree of freedom in their personal lives and ministries. Those churches began to experience more of what it means to "grow with a growth that is from God" (Col. 2:19).

Yet, these truths must be taken seriously. I have seen pastors and leaders go through the motions outlined in this book with little impact, because they didn't enter into the experience with their whole hearts. Jesus said to the seven churches in Revelation, "He who has an ear, let him hear what the Spirit says to the churches" (Rev. 2:7). Jesus also said, "Everyone who hears these words of mine and puts them into practice is like a wise man who built his house on the rock" (Matt. 7:24). This process of corporate conflict resolution doesn't work if people simply and mechanically go through the Steps. It works when spiritual leaders are earnestly seeking God and desire to be all that He created them to be.

Working through Neil's personal Steps to Freedom in Christ and the corporate process of conflict resolution outlined in this book is not an end. It is a new beginning for believers and churches that are stuck in the past due to unresolved issues, which can only be resolved in Christ through faith in God and genuine repentance. Neither Neil Anderson nor Chuck Mylander is the Wonderful Counselor or the ultimate church consultant, but they know that Jesus is, and they have given us a tool that connects us to Him. God is being glorified, churches are healthier, and believers are experiencing greater joy and freedom for giving careful attention to the truths delineated in Neil's books. I highly recommend you read this book with the spirit of the Bereans (see Acts 17:11).

Dean Johnson
Former District Superintendent of the North Central District
Evangelical Free Church of America

INTRODUCTION

Pastor Mark was a gifted evangelist who led many people in a nominally Christian fellowship to salvation. Opposition to Mark's message and leadership style began to surface, and the inevitable struggle for power resulted in a church split. Along with the conservative core, Mark started Community Bible Church, which he pastored for 10 years. Tragically, he had a moral failure, which led to a bitter departure.

Mark's successor was a young man named Jerry, who was attempting to pastor his first church. He didn't last long. In guarded language, the calling committee at Community Bible Church admitted they had run him off. Jerry probably made a lot of mistakes that inevitably accompany every pastor's first ministry experience. When Community Bible Church extended a call for yet another pastor, John accepted with the understanding that the primary culprits of the original problems were no longer players in the church.

It was a joyful experience for several months, but before long the honeymoon was over. Resistance to John's leadership increased at every board meeting. Gossip was rampant, and rumors floated around the church. John spent most of his time putting out fires instead of leading in a responsible way. A spiritual pall hung over the church like a brooding vulture. Worship was an arduous task when it should have been a joyful celebration. People responded to his messages neutrally at best, and there were no visible signs of anybody bearing fruit.

In the past, John's identity had been wrapped up in his role as a pastor; that identity was now being threatened. He would normally have doubled his efforts, but somehow he knew that this was not the answer for him or for Community Bible Church. So, John first sought help for himself, and through genuine repentance and faith in God, he rediscovered his own identity and freedom in Christ.

Having a new sense of security in Christ, John wanted to help others resolve their conflicts and be established alive and free in Christ. He began preaching from the book of Ephesians, teaching his people who they are in Christ and helping them realize that their "struggle is not against flesh and blood, but against the rulers, against the authorities, against the powers of this dark world and against the spiritual forces of evil in the heavenly realms" (6:12). At the same time, John began to pour through the minutes of previous board and church meetings. He discovered that the church had not dealt fairly with their previous pastors, nor had they dealt adequately with other moral issues.

John shared his observations with the current church board. Although the primary players were no longer in the church, the same pathology seemed to continue—which is almost always the case. Getting rid of a pastor or ungodly lay leaders doesn't solve the problem by itself. A host of unresolved problems and pain are often left in the wake of departing dysfunctional leaders. Being a small church, the board decided to bring the matter before the whole Body. This brought up a lot of painful memories, and it was obvious that past issues had only been covered up and not resolved.

The church sensed some release after acknowledging their sins and seeking forgiveness from one another, but Pastor John felt that more needed to done. He encouraged the board to contact Jerry, the previous pastor, and ask him if he would be willing to come back to the church for a special service of reconciliation. They discovered that Jerry was still hurting from the devastating experience and had not returned to the ministry. He declined the invitation at first but finally agreed to come back for the good of both his family and the church that he was asked to leave.

As Jerry stood before the church Body, the board read a list of offenses the church had committed against him and asked for his forgiveness. They waited patiently as he painfully considered the choice. Finally Jerry responded, "Jesus requires that we forgive others as He has forgiven us. So I choose to forgive you for what you have done to me and my family, and I want to acknowledge the mistakes I made as well." There wasn't a dry eye in the house.

Mark, the founding pastor, refused the invitation, but the board had done all they could to resolve their issues and bring their church into a right relationship with God. Jerry has since returned to the ministry. The spiritual pall left the church and the congregation sensed new life in Christ.

Community Bible Church, Mark, Jerry and John are fictional names, but the story is true. As we have traveled across America and around the world, we have had the privilege of talking to many denominational leaders and missionary executives. Based on their observations, about 15 percent of our churches are functioning like living organisms and substantially bearing fruit. However, many are spiritually dead and bearing no fruit at all. In the United States, there are 1,600 forced resignations of pastors every month. Many of these pastors make up the 1,500 who are leaving the ministry every month due to interpersonal conflict, burnout and moral failure. Most denominational leaders are overwhelmed with church conflicts. They find themselves like pastor John, spending most of their time trying to put out fires instead of offering visionary leadership. Most of these leaders and church consultants are aware that hurting churches must come to terms with their past and genuinely repent, or there will be no future.

How can churches repent and resolve their conflicts on a corporate level? This was the subject of our book *Setting Your Church Free* (Regal Books, 1994). In the following years since its publication, we have led many churches, missionary agencies and parachurch ministries through the process of corporate conflict resolution. We have gained a lot of experience through the process, and we now offer this work, *Extreme Church Makeover*, to help revitalize your ministry through repentance and faith in God.

CALLING FOR REPENTANCE AND RENEWED FAITH

When new Christians or members join a church, they likely bring with them a fair amount of "baggage" left over from unresolved conflicts and lack of repentance. In addition, many pastors leave bad church experiences hoping for a better ministry somewhere else. Unless these pastors make a conscientious effort to overcome their hurts and disappointments, what do you think they will bring to their next church?

Accumulate enough of this in your church and you will have corporate bondage. By corporate bondage, we mean unresolved personal and spiritual conflicts that inhibit churches from being redeemed and liberated fellowships of believers who love one another and reach their communities for Christ.

Paul wrote, "If one part suffers, every part suffers" (1 Cor. 12:26). The sins of some individual leaders in the church will cause the whole Body to ache. If the leadership lacks an adequate theology of resolution, they either lower their standards and expectations or live in denial and continue to muddle along with business as usual.

We have learned that individual freedom must come to the leadership before organizational freedom can be accomplished. The church Body cannot rise above its leadership. Additionally, if you have a church full of people in bondage to sin, you have a church in bondage; and if you have a church full of bad marriages, you have a bad church. The whole cannot be greater than the sum of its parts.

What is not lacking are opportunities to grow in our faith. In America, we are glutted with competing churches and Christian books, audiocassettes and radio and television programs. What is lacking is repentance and the knowledge of how to repent. Faith without repentance results in stagnation. What is needed is a way to help people resolve their personal and spiritual conflicts so that they can be established alive and free in Christ, which is what Neil has been working on for years—helping Christians experience their freedom in Christ through genuine repentance and faith in God.

ENCOURAGING RESEARCH RESULTS

Several exploratory studies have shown that if people are given the chance to resolve their personal and spiritual conflicts, there are promising results. Judith King, a Christian therapist, did several pilot studies in 1996. All three of these studies surveyed participants who attended a Living Free in Christ conference and were given the opportunity to process the "Steps to Freedom in Christ" (or "Steps"). The conference covers the core message of Neil's first two books: *Victory Over the Darkness* (Regal Books, 2000) and *The Bondage Breaker* (Harvest House, 2000). The Steps to Freedom in Christ is the tool used to help Christians resolve their personal and spiritual conflicts.

The first study involved 30 participants who answered a 10-item questionnaire before completing the Steps. The questionnaire was re-administered three months after their participation. It assessed levels of depression, anxiety, inner conflict, tormenting thoughts and addictive behaviors. The second study involved 55 participants who answered a 12-item questionnaire before completing the Steps. It was readministered three months later. The third pilot study involved 21 participants who also answered a 12-item questionnaire before completing the Steps and who then completed the questionnaire three months later. The following table illustrates the percentage of improvement for each category:

	Pilot Study 1	Pilot Study 2	Pilot Study 3
Depression	64%	47%	52%
Anxiety	58%	44%	47%
Inner conflict	63%	51%	48%
Tormenting thoughts	82%	58%	57%
Addictive behaviors	52%	43%	39%

Additional research was also conducted by doctoral students at Regent University under the supervision of Fernando Garzon, Doctor of Psychology, on the message and method of Freedom in Christ Ministries. Most people attending a Living Free in Christ conference can work through the repentance process on their own using the Steps. However, in our experience, about 15 percent of people can't go through the Steps alone or within the allotted time provided in a conference setting because of the difficulties they have experienced. The results below are from those participants who received a personal session with a trained encourager. They took a pretest before the Step session and a posttest three months later. The following table illustrates the percentage of improvement for each category:

	Oklahoma City, OK	Tyler, TX
Depression	44%	57%
Anxiety	45%	54%
Fear	48%	49%
Anger	36%	55%
Tormenting thoughts	51%	50%
Negative habits	48%	53%
Sense of self-worth	52%	56%

The encouragers who led the participants through the Steps were well-trained laypeople. Since there are not enough pastors and counselors to help more than five percent of our people even if that is all they did, equipping and using key laypeople has to happen if we want to see the needs of our people met. We must see the need to equip laypeople to do the work of ministry. They can do the work of ministry if we understand that Jesus is the Wonderful Counselor (see Isa. 9:6) and the only One who can set the captive free and bind up the brokenhearted. The theology and process of helping others resolve personal and spiritual conflicts are shared in Neil's *Discipleship Counseling* (Regal Books, 2003).

Individual freedom must be established before corporate freedom can be realized, but resolving individual problems alone doesn't resolve corporate conflicts. The church leadership must address those problems. In this book, we attempt to share the theology and process that can lead to corporate conflict resolution. The Lord Himself is the ultimate "Church consultant," because nobody knows His own Body as He does and nobody but Jesus can bring resolution.

DISCOVERING SPIRITUAL UNITY

Neil is the author of the first part of this book, which deals with principles of leadership. Talbot School of Theology, where Neil taught for 10 years, extensively researched its graduates for the purpose of revising its curriculum. As suspected, the results showed that the problems involving leadership were first interpersonal and second administrative. At the time, there were no required courses on leadership and administration for Master of Divinity students, a deficiency that has now been corrected. Many other seminaries are also seeing the need to better equip their students for spiritual leadership.

Poor leadership and administration lead to interpersonal problems and spiritual bondage. Trying to resolve personal and spiritual conflicts in a church or mission group without correcting leadership problems is an exercise in futility. It is like trying to help a rebellious 14-year-old boy and then sending him back into the same dysfunctional family. One must ask why he rebelled in the first place.

Chuck is the primary author of the second half of the book, which discusses specific steps of corporate conflict resolution (see appendix A). We will refer to these steps throughout the book. The procedure we are suggesting is a comprehensive process of personal and corporate assessment and cleansing. An adequate answer must also take into account the reality of the spiritual world. Every organized church has personal, spiritual and leadership problems. A biblical answer must be balanced and must address all three areas.

Finally, we believe that the unity of the true Church is essential to accomplish our mission on planet Earth. The Lord prayed that we would all be one (see John 17:21). The only basis for that unity is our common heritage in Christ. All Christians are children of God.

Most Christians are ignorant of their spiritual heritage. In helping Christians all over the world resolve their problems, we have found only one common denominator: None of them know who they are in Christ, nor do they understand what it means to be a child of God. Why not? If the Holy Spirit bears witness with our spirit that we are children of God, why aren't they sensing it? They did sense God's presence after they repented and found their identity and freedom in Christ. Paul implores us:

Walk in a manner worthy of the calling with which you have been called, with all humility and gentleness, with patience, showing tolerance for one another in love, being diligent to preserve the unity of the Spirit in the bond of peace (Eph. 4:1-3, *NASB*).

According to Paul, we are to preserve the unity. When people are established alive and free in Christ, a discerning Christian can sense the unity. But it won't be sensed if Christians struggle with unresolved issues or with finding their identity in their natural heritages. In addition, the Western church has often stressed its personal relationship with God at the expense of its corporate relationship to Him. This has been increasingly more evident since the rebellious '60s. The consequence is a self-centered cult of individualism where rights are emphasized over responsibilities.

Part of the problem in the English-speaking world is our language, which has no provision for a plural "you." (Some parts of the country say "y'all" or "youse," but the rest of the country frowns at this use of the King's English.) Many passages in Scripture where the Lord addresses the corporate Church Body are translated as "you," but the "you" is plural. He is addressing the Body of Christ. From God's perspective, there is one Church, one Spirit and one Lord.

This book in itself is a statement of spiritual unity in the midst of diversity of gifts, talents and perspectives. Chuck was theologically educated at an evangelical Friends college and leans toward the Wesleyan doctrine. Neil was taught reformed theology and leans toward Calvinism. We both hold to the authority of Scripture and believe that the original manuscripts are infallible. The issues we address do not pit the Wesleyan against the Calvinist or the evangelical against the charismatic. This is not to say that these are not important issues, because they are and will remain so until the Lord comes back. But they are not issues that we are going to allow Satan to use as a point of division.

The primary battle is not between differing theological positions held by committed Christians. The primary battle is between the Christ and the Antichrist, between the Spirit of truth and the father of lies, between the true prophets and the false prophets, between the good angels and the demons, between the kingdom of God and the kingdom of darkness. The Body of Christ is in that spiritual battle, and we dare not be ignorant of Satan's schemes, which are intended to divide us.

The Lord wants His children to be alive and free in Christ (see Gal. 5:1) and for His Body to be righteous and fruit bearing. We're sure that you want the same for your people and your church Body. May the good Lord grant repentance and knowledge of the truth that will set you and your ministry free in Christ, just as He did for the following church, as told by its interim pastor:

In 1993, I purchased a set of Neil's tapes, *Resolving Personal and Spiritual Conflicts*. After listening to these tapes, I began applying his principles to my problems. I realized that some of my problems could be spiritual attacks, and I learned how to take a stand and won victories over some of my problems in my life.

But that was only a tip of the iceberg. I'm a deacon and preacher in a Baptist church. My pastor was suffering from depression and other problems that I was not aware of, and in 1994 he committed suicide. This literally brought our church to its knees. I knew of some of the problems of the previous pastors and felt it was spiritual, but I didn't know how to relay it to the people since the devil or a demon cannot affect a Christian. *Right*.

The church elected me as their interim pastor. While in a local bookstore, I saw a book of yours entitled *Setting Your Church Free*. I purchased and read it. I felt with all the spiritual suppression in our church this was the answer. There was only one problem: how to get the rest of the church to believe. After a few weeks of preaching on spiritual issues, I knew we had to do what you instructed in your book. The previous pastor who killed himself would not believe your material; he would never read or listen to your message.

Slowly, very slowly, the people accepted my messages and I was able to contact one of your staff. He flew to Houston in August 1994 and led the leaders of our church through the

Steps to Setting Your Church Free. The leaders loved it. I felt step one was past. Next, I wanted to take all the people through the Steps to Freedom in Christ. Six weeks later, I was able to do so. I really don't understand it, but we were set free from the spiritual bondage of multiple problems. I can't put it all in a letter or I would write a book.

During all of this time, one of my middle-aged members, an evangelist, was set free. He learned who he was in Christ and is back in ministry—praise the Lord. I saw the daughters of the deceased pastor set free and able to forgive their father, and they were able to go on with their lives. At one point, one of the girls was contemplating suicide.

This is a new church; God is free to work here! In September, we founded our pulpit committee. Our church voted 100 percent for our new pastor. This has never happened in our church before, and this is an independent and fundamental Baptist church. Well, when you do things God's way, you get God's results.

I also work one night a week in our county jail, which is the second largest in the country. I work with the homosexual men, and I have seen many set free.

All biblically conservative schools of theology have a common core of belief that they find essential for each of us to live and grow by. You may not agree with all we have to say, but would you agree that we all need to find our identity and freedom in Christ, and be "diligent to preserve the unity of the Spirit in the bond of peace" (Eph. 4:3, *NASB*)? It is our prayer that this book will help the Church come closer to fulfilling the prayer of Jesus in John 17, which is where we begin.

PROTECTED FROM THE EVIL ONE

I am coming to you now, but I say these things while I am still in the world, so that they may have the full measure of my joy within them. I have given them your word and the world has hated them, for they are not of the world any more than I am of the world. My prayer is not that you take them out of the world but that you protect them from the evil one. They are not of the world, even as I am not of it. Sanctify them by the truth; your word is truth. As you sent me into the world, I have sent them into the world. For them I sanctify myself, that they too may be truly sanctified. My prayer is not for them alone. I pray also for those who will believe in me through their message.

JOHN 17:13-20

I was beginning a conference by preaching Sunday morning in the host church. Between the two morning services, I asked the pastor if he would care to share with me what was going on in the church. The atmosphere was so thick that I could cut it with a knife. My wife had already retreated to the balcony to pray that God would be merciful and grant repentance. "Is it really that obvious?" the pastor responded. The pastoral staff was deeply divided, and no amount of acting and cover-up could disguise the spiritual climate of that church. Personal animosity and bitterness had given the enemy an opportunity to wreak havoc.

At a denominational yearly meeting, I asked a district superintendent to share his experience with helping churches resolve their corporate conflicts. The previous weekend, he had led the leadership of one of their churches through the Steps to Setting Your Church Free. He spoke at the same church the following Sunday morning. The congregation had no idea that the board and staff had gone through the corporate Steps, but after the Sunday morning services, two different individuals shared with the district superintendent that they sensed something had happened in their church. The spiritual climate had changed, and people could sense it.

The high priestly prayer quoted in the passage at the beginning of this chapter reveals the concern our Lord has for His people. Jesus' first concern is related to our spiritual vulnerability. He knew that Satan would take advantage of our sinful attitudes and actions. Jesus is returning to the Father, but the disciples and the soon-to-be established Church will remain on planet Earth where "the ruler of the world" (John 14:30, *NASB*) "your enemy the devil prowls around like a roaring lion looking for someone to devour" (1 Pet. 5:8). Unlike concerned parents who may be tempted to isolate their children from the harsh realities of this world, Jesus does not ask that we be removed. His prayer is that we be protected from the evil one.

The spiritual nature of this fallen world is a sobering reality, but Jesus has not left us defenseless. First, "You have been given fullness in Christ, who is the head over every power and authority" (Col. 2:10). The Church is established in Christ and seated with Him in the heavenly realms (see Eph. 2:6). Because of our position in Christ, we have all the authority we need over the evil one to carry out the delegated responsibility of fulfilling the Great Commission (see Matt. 28:18-19).

Second, "Having disarmed the powers and authorities, he made a public spectacle of them, triumphing over them by the cross" (Col. 2:15). "His intent was that now, through the church, the manifold wisdom of

God should be made known to the rulers and authorities in the heavenly realms, according to his eternal purpose which he accomplished in Christ Jesus our Lord" (Eph. 3:10-11).

THE ETERNAL PURPOSE OF GOD

Knowing our purpose is what defines our mission and directs our efforts in a meaningful way. The "eternal purpose of God" is to make His wisdom known through the Church to the rulers and authorities in the heavenly (i.e., the spiritual) realms. Satan thought he could stop the plan of God by inciting the rulers of the day to put Jesus to death, but he was wrong. The rulers and authorities in the heavenly realms are seeing salvation come to all those who call upon the name of the Lord. God was able to unite both Jews and Gentiles into one corporate Body.

"The Son of God appeared for this *purpose*, to destroy the works of the devil" (1 John 3:8, *NASB*, emphasis added). Should you be tempted to think (wrongly) that these rulers and the authorities in the heavenly realms are mere human governments and structures of earthly existence, let me encourage you to read Dr. Clinton E. Arnold's *Powers of Darkness: Principalities and Powers in Paul's Letters* (InterVarsity Press, 1992).

If the ultimate spiritual battle is between the kingdom of darkness and the Kingdom of Light, and if God's eternal purpose is to make His wisdom known through the Church to spiritual rulers and authorities, how are we doing? The belief in a personal devil has always been a doctrine of the true Church. Many Christians in the Western church attempt to live as though the devil does not exist, having little understanding of how the spiritual world impinges on the natural world. A few believe no interaction is taking place. Some, out of fear, make a conscious choice not to deal with the reality of the evil one. In liberal, "Christian" circles, belief in the devil is not academically credible. Consequently, we are like blindfolded warriors who do not know who our enemy is, so we strike out at ourselves and at each other.

The Church is filled with so many wounded individuals that some people in the world see it as a hospital for sick people. But that is not what Christ established His Church to be. The Church is more like a military outpost that has been called to storm the fortresses that are raised up against the knowledge of God (see 2 Cor. 10:3-5). Thankfully, within that military outpost is an infirmary. I have spent a lot of my time in the infirmary, because this war has a lot of casualties. Yet the Church does not exist for the infirmary; the infirmary exists for the Church. The Church is "the pillar and foundation of the truth" (1 Tim. 3:15), which is supposed to be salt and light in this fallen world (see Matt. 5:13-14). Since "we are more than conquerors through him who loved us" (Rom. 8:37), why are we limping along in defeat and unbelief?

THE ENEMY'S AGENDA

If I were the enemy, I would try to divide your mind, since a double-minded person is unstable in all of his or her ways (see Jas. 1:8). I would then try to divide the home, because a house divided against itself cannot stand (see Matt. 12:25). Finally, I would try to divide the Body of Christ, because united we stand, but divided we fall. Thankfully, all Christians are single-minded, all Christian marriages are experiencing a oneness in Christ, and the Church is one big happy family of unity and love! Does that sound right?

The Lord has not left us defenseless. We have a sanctuary in Christ, and He has equipped us with the armor of God. We have all the resources we need in Christ to stand firm and resist the devil, but if we do not assume our responsibility, those resources will go unused. He has instructed us to put on the armor of God (see Eph. 6:10-18). What if we haven't? We have been told to "put on the Lord Jesus Christ, and make no provision for the flesh in regard to its lusts" (Rom. 13:14, *NASB*). What if we have made provision for the flesh? It is our responsibility to "resist the devil" (Jas. 4:7). What if we don't? God's provision for our freedom in Christ is limited only to the degree that we fail to assume our responsibility.

The most common and naive response in the Western world is to ignore the battle or to make the fatal assumption that Christians are somehow immune. Just the opposite is true. Ignorance is not bliss; it is defeat. If you are a Christian, you are the target. If you are a pastor, you and your family are the bull's-eye! It is Satan's strategy to render the Church inoperative and to obliterate the truth that we are "dead to sin but alive to God in Christ Jesus" (Rom. 6:11).

The divorce rate and disintegration of the Christian family roughly parallels the secular world. Sexual activity among Christian singles is only slightly less than their secular counterparts. The distinction between a Christian and a pagan is no longer obvious. The tragic fall of many visible Christian leaders indicates that something is dreadfully wrong. Having an intellectual knowledge of Scripture obviously is not enough, because I am sure these leaders were educated. "Christianity does not work" is the message sent into the world when we fail to live a righteous life.

John identifies little children of the faith as those who have come to know the Father and have had their sins forgiven (see 1 John 2:12-14). In other words, they have overcome the penalty of sin. Satan loses the primary battle when we trust in Christ, but he does not curl up his tail, pull in his fangs and slink away. His strategy is to keep the believer under the power of sin.

Twice in this passage in 1 John, the young men of the faith are identified as having overcome the evil one. How are we going to help people reach their full maturity in Christ if they have no idea how to overcome the evil one? The unfortunate truth is that many Christians, including leaders, have seemingly uncontrollable appetites and behaviors. The sin-confess-sin-confess-sin-confess-and-sin-again cycle does not deal with all of reality. It should be sin, confess, repent and resist.

If you think you are immune, consider three pertinent questions:

1. Have you experienced any temptation this week? Biblically, who is the tempter? It can't be God (see Jas. 1:13). God will test your faith in order to strengthen it, but Satan's temptations are intended to destroy your faith.
2. Have you ever struggled with the voice of the accuser of the

brethren (see Rev. 12:10)? Before you answer, let me ask the question in another way: Have you ever struggled with thoughts such as *I'm stupid,* or *I'm ugly,* or *I can't,* or *God doesn't love me,* or *I'm different from others,* or *I'm going down?* I know you have, because the Bible says that Satan accuses the brethren day and night.

3. Have you ever been deceived? The person who is tempted to answer no to this question may be the most deceived of all. If I tempt you, you know it. If I accuse you, you would know it. But if I deceive you, you do not know it. If you knew it, you would no longer be deceived.

Now listen to the logic of Scripture: "If you hold to my teaching, you are really my disciples. Then you will know the truth, and the truth will set you free" (John 8:31-32). Jesus said, "I am the way and the truth and the life" (John 14:6). In the high priestly prayer, Jesus prayed, "Sanctify them by the truth; your word is truth" (John 17:17). When we put on the armor of God, the first thing we do is put on "the belt of truth" (Eph. 6:14).

John wrote, "For all that is in the world, the lust of the flesh and the lust of the eyes and the boastful pride of life, is not from the Father, but is from the world" (1 John 2:16, *NASB*). The tendency is to read this passage and assume that the only enemies of our sanctification are this fallen world and the flesh, but that is not true. The three channels that John mentioned are the exact same three channels the devil used to tempt Eve (successfully) and to tempt Jesus (unsuccessfully). We see the channels but not the spiritual force behind it, and we forget that Satan is the ruler of this world and that "the whole world lies in the power of the evil one" (5:19, *NASB*).

THE BATTLE FOR OUR MINDS

Consider the conflict that required God to intervene dramatically in the Early Church when He struck down Ananias and Sapphira. Peter asked, "How is it that Satan has so filled your heart that you have lied to the

Holy Spirit and have kept for yourself some of the money you received for the land?" (Acts 5:3). The message could not have been made more clear. If Satan (the father of lies) can operate undetected in your church, your home, your marriage or yourself, convincing you to believe a lie, he could gain a measure of control over your life. The Lord had to expose the battle for the mind as soon as Satan raised his ugly head in the Early Church. The strategy is not new. Satan deceived Eve, and she believed a lie (see Gen. 3:1-7). The sobering reality is that Eve was spiritually alive and without sin at the time she was deceived. To assume that a Christian who is spiritually alive and struggling to overcome sin can't be deceived is hopelessly naive!

A few years ago, we surveyed 1,725 professing Christian teenagers. Of those who were in high school, 70 percent said that they heard voices in their heads, like there was a subconscious self-talking, or that they struggled with really bad thoughts. Twenty-four percent had impulsive thoughts to kill someone. I don't think this is just a natural phenomenon. I believe 1 Timothy 4:1: "The Spirit clearly says that in later times some will abandon the faith and follow deceiving spirits and things taught by demons." Is that happening? It is happening all over the world.

No matter where I go, the problems are basically the same and the answer is always the same. In the last 20 years, I have counseled more than 1,500 adults who hear voices or struggle with tempting, accusing and blasphemous thoughts. With very few exceptions, the problem has been spiritual. It takes an average of about three hours to help a person find their freedom in Christ. Most will experience for the first time "the peace of God, which transcends all understanding" (Phil. 4:7). One pastor wrote to me after reading *The Bondage Breaker*: "I have been in the pastorate for 15 years struggling with three compulsive addictions: workaholism, overeating and my private thought life. Praise God for the freedom in Jesus Christ. I have just experienced this freedom and I am looking forward to enjoying it until death or Christ's return."

Why don't believers know about this battle for their minds? For one reason, we can't read each other's minds. We really do not have any idea what is going on in the minds of other people unless they have the courage to share it with us. In many cases they won't share, because in our culture they would likely be labeled as mentally ill. People will tell others about their abuse or what has happened to them, but they may not share what is going on inside. Are they mentally ill, or is a battle going on for their mind? The lack of any balanced biblical contribution to mental health has left them with only one conclusion: Any problem in their mind must be either psychological or neurological. Consequently, we have been taught to look for natural explanations and cures, and when none is found we conclude, "There is nothing left to do now but pray." The Bible teaches a different order: "Seek first his kingdom and his righteousness" (Matt. 6:33).

I have great respect for the medical profession, and I had the privilege to coauthor *The Biblical Guide to Alternative Medicine* (Regal Books, 2003) with Dr. Michael Jacobson. In the book, Dr. Jacobson and I reported that 30 years ago, few (if any) medical schools offered any electives or showed any interest in spirituality. Today, there are over 70 medical schools that are open to spirituality, but the contribution comes mostly from Eastern philosophies. For instance, a major issue in medicine is the connection between the brain and the mind and the resolution of psychosomatic illnesses. The number one spokesperson for this issue is Deepak Chopra, who espouses Hinduism. These are illnesses the Church should be addressing, and the Christian community should be the primary contributors to wholistic health.

The natural world assumes that someone who hears voices or struggles with blasphemous and condemning thoughts has a chemical imbalance. How can impersonal brain chemistry create a personal thought? How can our neurotransmitters randomly fire in such a way as to create a thought that is foreign to what we would choose to think? Such a possibility can't be explained any more than I can explain how Satan puts thoughts into our minds. It is much easier for me to believe the latter because of 1 Timothy 4:1, 2 Corinthians 11:3 and other passages, especially because I have found it to be true in thousands of people worldwide.

A FALSE DICHOTOMY

Asking whether personal or corporate problems are spiritual or psychological assumes a false dichotomy. Our problems are always psychological. Psychology by definition means the study of our soul, and our soul is always a part of the process. On the other hand, our problems are also always spiritual. At no time is God absent or irrelevant. He is right now "sustaining all things by his powerful word" (Heb. 1:3), and there is no time when it is safe to take off the armor of God. The possibility of being tempted, accused or deceived is a continual reality. The Bible teaches that the unseen world is just as real as what we see: "For what is seen is temporary, but what is unseen is eternal" (2 Cor. 4:18). If we could just accept this truth, we would stop polarizing into psychotherapeutic ministries that ignore spiritual reality or jumping into some kind of deliverance ministry that ignores developmental issues and human responsibility. We must take into account all reality and strive for a balanced answer to our problems.

The basic answer for conflict resolution, whether personal or corporate, is to "submit yourselves, then, to God. Resist the devil, and he will flee from you" (Jas. 4:7). Trying to resist the devil without first submitting to God can be a dogfight. This is often the error of deliverance ministries that confront demons directly without having the person in bondage first submit to God. On the other hand, you can submit to God without resisting the devil and stay in bondage. The tragedy is that many recovery ministries are not doing either one.

Submitting to God requires us to deal with the sin in our lives. Sin is like garbage; it attracts flies. Naturally, we want to get rid of the flies, but the answer is to get rid of the garbage. If you get rid of the garbage, the flies will have no reason or right to be there. Repentance and faith in God has been and will continue to be the answer throughout the Church Age.

I did not ask for my first encounter with the powers of darkness; it was thrust upon me. My feeble attempt was based on the confrontational process of calling up the demon, getting its name and rank, and then casting it out. I found this process to be ugly, exhausting and potentially harmful to the victim. Often it had to be repeated, and the results did not seem to last. In this procedure, the deliverer appears to be the pastor, counselor or missionary, and information is obtained from demons. Why would we believe them? The nature of these demons is to lie.

Scripture teaches, "There is no truth in him [Satan]. When he lies, he speaks his native language, for he is a liar and the father of lies" (John 8:44). Now, I find it unnecessary to know the name of the demons or their ranks. I don't dialogue with demons, nor do I advise others to interact with them. We shouldn't want demons to manifest. We should desire that the Lord be manifested and thereby glorified. We should never let the devil set the agenda, nor should we ever say "the devil made me do it." We are responsible for our own attitudes and actions, both personally and corporately.

Jesus is the deliverer, and He has already come. We should get our information from the Holy Spirit, because He is "the Spirit of truth . . . he will guide you into all truth" (John 16:13).

The shift in my thinking began when I realized that truth sets us free and that Jesus is the truth. In John 17, Jesus prays that we be kept from the evil one by being sanctified in the Word of God, which is the truth. This is why I prefer to think of our battle as more of a truth encounter, as opposed to a power encounter. I know of no place in the Bible that instructs us to seek power. We are to pursue the truth and come to understand our identity and position in Christ (see Eph. 6:10). We already have all the power we need, because of our position in Christ.

> I pray also that the eyes of your heart may be enlightened in order that you may know the hope to which he has called you, the riches of his glorious inheritance in the saints, and his incomparably great power for us who believe. That power is like the working of his mighty strength, which he exerted in Christ when he raised him from the dead (Eph. 1:18-20).

The power for Christians lies in their ability to believe the truth, while the power of the evil one lies in his ability to deceive. When we expose the lie, the enemy's power is broken. Often when Christians struggle, they wrongly conclude that they lack power. The temptation is to pursue some experience that will give them more power—it will be a false trip. Satanists pursue power because it has been stripped from them. Christians are to pursue the truth and carry out their ministry in the power of the Holy Spirit.

We have the spiritual authority to carry out our ministry because of our position in Christ, and we have the power because of the indwelling presence of the Holy Spirit. These are operative only as we live dependently upon God. We are to "be strong in the Lord and in his mighty power" (Eph. 6:10). If we operate in the flesh, independent of God, we will be defeated and ineffective. An unregenerate Jewish community sadly found this out:

> One day the evil spirit answered them, "Jesus I know, and I know about Paul, but who are you?" Then the man who had the evil spirit jumped on them and overpowered them all. He gave them such a beating that they ran out of the house naked and bleeding (Acts 19:15-16).

I once worked with a young lady who was extremely abused in her youth. She briefly lost her mental control and a vile voice said through her, "Who the (blank) do you think you are?" If that happened to you, how would you respond? I said, "I'm a child of God," and I told the spirit to be silent in the name and authority of the Lord Jesus Christ. The lady returned to her right mind, and that day she found her freedom in Christ in a quiet and controlled way.

Another time, a large lady, who had been severely abused, slowly got out of her chair and started to walk toward me in a menacing way. What would you do? Based on 1 John 5:18, I said, "I'm a child of God and the evil one cannot touch me." She immediately stopped and returned to her seat. Authority does not increase with volume. We do not shout out the devil. We calmly take our place in Christ. We have lost control if we end up screaming and shouting. In such cases, fear is the controlling issue, not faith. Fear of anything other than God is mutually exclusive to faith in God. The same holds true for parenting. We are not exercising our God-given authority when we scream and yell at our children. We are undermining that authority, because we are responding according to the flesh.

The "power encounter" or confrontational approach to confronting and dealing with demons was primarily developed from the Gospels, because they are the only New Testament historical books that show how the Lord confronted the demonized. Prior to the Cross, Satan had not yet been defeated and the Holy Spirit had not yet come in His fullness. Therefore, accomplishing deliverance required a specially endowed authority agent. This is why we read in Luke 9:1, "When Jesus had called the Twelve together, he gave them power and authority to drive out all demons." If we are to continue driving out demons in the Church Age, where are the instructions in the Epistles? The Epistles contain no instructions for how to cast a demon out of someone else. Why not?

A GREAT HOPE FOR FREEDOM

After the Cross, deliverance for Christians is no longer the outside agent's responsibility; it is the individual's responsibility. I can't put on the armor of God for you, or confess for you, or repent for you, or believe for you, or take every thought captive to the obedience of Christ for you. I can't even resist the devil for you. Those are your responsibilities, but I can help you. With that in mind, there is a very definitive passage in the pastoral Epistles for helping Christians find their freedom in Christ:

> And the Lord's servant must not quarrel; instead, he must be kind to everyone, able to teach, not resentful. Those who oppose him he must gently instruct, in the hope that God will grant them repentance leading them to a knowledge of the truth, and that they will come to their senses and escape from the trap of the devil, who has taken them captive to do his will (2 Tim. 2:24-26).

This is not a confrontational model; it is a kind, compassionate and teachable model. It requires a dependency upon the Lord, for only He can grant the repentance that gets rid of the garbage. This model identifies truth as the liberating agent and implies that the battle is for the mind. It requires a lovingly mature servant of the Lord who knows the truth. We have had the privilege of training thousands of pastors, missionaries and laypeople all over the world who are at this time setting captives free in Christ. To illustrate how transferable this model is, let me share with you a letter I received from Dr. David Finnell, director of the International Network of Church Planters and a teacher at Columbia Bible College and Seminary:

> I came across your materials a couple months ago and really sensed that they expressed the truths that I have been struggling with concerning power encounter. I have been involved with power encounter on the mission field and as a teacher here at Columbia Bible College and Seminary. I have really been concerned with the lack of personal involvement of the counselee in power encounter. I have utilized your materials in counseling situations over the last few weeks with dramatic and powerful results.
>
> All of my students in my Prayer and Evangelism class are reading *The Bondage Breaker* and going through the "Steps to Freedom." I am spending personal sessions with those whose bondage is too great for them to deal with on their own, with very positive results.

I had to do the same when I taught at Talbot School of Theology. It would be a tragic mistake to believe that every Christian and every Christian leader is living a liberated life in Christ. Does Christ want His children and churches to be free? Of course! "It is for freedom that Christ has set us free. Stand firm, then, and do not let yourselves be burdened again by a yoke of slavery" (Gal. 5:1). The context reveals that we are free from the law and legalism, but freedom is not license to sin:

"You, my brothers, were called to be free. But do not use your freedom to indulge the sinful nature" (Gal. 5:13).

Does this process work for nonbelievers? No, we have to lead them to Christ first. Our evangelistic effort will be far more effective if we understand how Satan holds unbelievers in bondage. According to Paul, "Even if our gospel is veiled, it is veiled to those who are perishing. The god of this age has blinded the minds of unbelievers, so that they cannot see the light of the gospel of the glory of Christ, who is the image of God" (2 Cor. 4:3-4). When the children of God take their rightful place in Christ and pray against the blinding of Satan, we will see a greater harvest of souls.

Individuals and church bodies are often caught in the paralysis of analysis. We have a pretty good idea of what the problems are, and researchers like George Barna keep reminding us through their polling how sick we really are, but what is the answer? If you were lost in a maze, would you want a "mazeologist" to explain to you all the intricacies of a maze and give you coping skills so you could survive in the maze? Would you want legalistic pastors scolding you for getting into the maze in the first place? No, you would want to know the way out of the maze—"the way and the truth and the life" (John 14:6). There are many ways to go wrong, but only one path leads back to God. There are many types of abuse, but you will need to forgive if you want to be free from your past. You can sin a million different ways, but the biblical answer is the same. People in bondage need a clear road map to show them the way out. If they already knew the way out, they would have taken it long ago. Nobody likes to live in bondage.

I believe God has made some people smart and others not so smart. I do not believe that God's plan for salvation or living the Spirit-filled life is available only for the smart. Those who think they are smart should make God's answer simple enough so that the simplest of His creation can understand it. However, in keeping our message simple, we dare not be simplistic or naive.

The Steps to Freedom in Christ are just a tool to help people resolve the issues that are critical between themselves and God and then resist the devil. No tool will set you free. *What* sets you free is complete repentance and faith in God. *Who* sets you free is Christ. We have the privilege of being the Lord's bond servants whom God works through to accomplish His purposes. It is almost impossible to hurt anybody by leading them through the Steps. Being ready for communion the following Sunday is the worst that can happen. You have nothing to lose, but much to gain.

When you see a doctor, he or she may prescribe some tests to try to determine the cause of your illness. When these tests do not reveal a problem, you don't get mad at your doctor, do you? In the same way, shouldn't people be able to attend our churches and ascertain whether or not their problems are spiritual? Don't be disappointed by the secular world when they don't take into account the reality of the spiritual world. It is not their responsibility. It is the Church's responsibility to resolve spiritual conflicts and offer biblical answers to "psychosomatic illnesses."

We can't totally resolve conflicts in the Church without taking into account the reality of the spiritual world. We are spiritual beings, and the Church is a spiritual Body united together by the Holy Spirit. When we sin personally or corporately, we leave ourselves vulnerable to spiritual corruption.

I got a call from a pastor after he and his staff attended my conference. He shared with me that he discerned an oppressive spirit that seemed to grip his church. Efforts to move the ministry forward were challenged. A lot of personal prayer and much soul searching had little, if any, effect. From the congregation's perspective, the church's programs were continuing to function as usual, but John believed something was not quite right.

The founding families of the church were a faction that had split off from another church, which had been a bad witness in the community. The pastor wondered if this could be an opening for Satan to keep this church in bondage, even though the charter members were no longer attending. He talked it over with his board, and they decided that the church should confess their corporate sins and the rebellious nature of their beginnings. It was a moving experience for the church Body. The pastor reported that the oppressive spirit wasn't present anymore, and neither was the resistance to his leadership. Ten years later, it is still true.

When *Setting Your Church Free* first came out, I was invited to teach a Doctor of Ministry class at a seminary on the subject. Normally, the limit on the class size is 25 people, but doctoral students kept trying to get in, and the class swelled to 40. Every pastor had a story to tell. One pastor had recently accepted a call and was told the previous pastor had resigned for personal reasons. The congregation honored him with many gifts of appreciation for his years of service. Not long after the new pastor arrived, members of the congregation discovered that the previous pastor was actually having an affair and that the board had asked for his resignation. The congregation felt totally betrayed when they learned the truth. The lay leadership was discredited for the cover-up and the new pastor's leadership was challenged.

Chuck and I believe that many churches are in bondage to sin and have many unresolved conflicts. Like individual Christians, churches need to resolve issues that are critical between themselves and the head of the Church—Jesus Christ. The Lord is praying that we be kept from the evil one. If your church is ready to walk in the light, speak the truth in love and face the issues for the purpose of resolving them, there is great hope for you. We close this chapter with a letter received from an evangelical pastor:

> I want to thank the Lord and you for the materials you have created. It is wonderful to use something that works with all sorts of people, with all sorts of problems. I stumbled onto your material a year ago and used it for Sunday School. God was also using it to work with a severely demonized man. In preparing for the Steps with him, the elders and I worked through the Steps first. I personally had the bondage to sin broken in my life. As a result of it, my wife found freedom from her family's occultic background.
>
> I'm in a new church and without advertising or promoting, God has sent over 12 people to me in January to go through the

Steps. There has been a great work of God in people's hearts. Two of our elders resigned to get their lives straightened out. One has been having an affair for the last two years. I'm taking him and his wife through the Steps next week.

I took the other elder and his wife through the Steps. He was in bondage to pornography and strip joints when he was on business trips. It was wonderful to see both find their freedom and renew their relationship. What a joy and privilege to encourage people as they go through the Steps.

One of our Sunday School teachers has been experiencing nighttime terror and demonic dreams. Through God's "chance events," she told my wife about her difficulties. I took her and her husband through the Steps. When we came to forgiveness, I had to teach, exhort and encourage her for over an hour. I had to physically put the pencil in her hand. It took another 30 minutes to write the first name. But eventually she made a decision and went for it. God is so good! The next Sunday there was so much joy, peace and freedom on the face of both her and her husband.

CHRIST-CENTERED MINISTRIES

My prayer is not for them alone. I pray also for those who will believe
in me through their message, that all of them may be one, Father,
just as you are in me and I am in you. May they also be in us so that
the world may believe that you have sent me. I have given them the glory
that you gave me, that they may be one as we are one: I in them and
you in me. May they be brought to complete unity to let the world know
that you sent me and have loved them even as you have loved me.

JOHN 17:20-23

Having requested our protection from the evil one, the next petition of our Lord is for unity amongst believers. The implication is that the world will know that the Father has sent the Son if we dwell together in unity. If that is the case, how are we doing? So pervasive is the problem of disunity that several Christian periodicals and organizations that minister and speak to the masses have consciously steered away from theological issues. Theology is perceived as being divisive. Such conclusions have prompted David F. Wells to write *No Place for Truth, or,*

Whatever Happened to Evangelical Theology? (W. B. Eerdmans Publishing Company, 1993). Wells argues that "modernity" has abandoned absolute truth for a "psychologized," pragmatic and subjective view of truth. "What is true" has been replaced by "what works." Is theology divisive? It can be if the truth is not proclaimed in love or if we allow doctrine to be an end in itself.

The purpose of good theology or right doctrine is summed up in the great commandment, " 'Love the Lord your God with all your heart and with all your soul and with all your mind.' This is the first and greatest commandment. And the second is like it: 'Love your neighbor as yourself.' All the Law and the Prophets hang on these two commandments" (Matt. 22:37-40). Knowledge of God's Word should govern our relationship with God and others in righteousness, and the proper preaching and teaching of God's Word should result in the Body of Christ falling in love with their heavenly Father and each other.

THE GOAL OF OUR INSTRUCTION

Having the right goal is essential for Christian education to be effective. According to Paul, "The goal of our instruction is love from a pure heart and a good conscience and a sincere faith" (1 Tim. 1:5, *NASB*). If we make doctrine an end in itself, we will distort the very purpose for which it was intended. Teaching truth should enhance the sanctification process, and the students should be able to say, "I am more loving, kind, patient, gentle and joyful than I was a year ago." If they can't say that, they are not growing. It is possible for students to graduate from a good seminary or Bible school solely on the basis that they answered most (not even all) of the questions right! You can do that and not even be a Christian.

In some settings, we have extolled the virtues of the theologian and the apologist at the expense of the soul winner and lover. However, Scripture teaches, "He who wins souls is wise" (Prov. 11:30) and "By this all men will know that you are my disciples, if you love one another" (John 13:35). Godly theologians and humble apologists utilize their

God-given abilities to bolster our confidence in God, set us free in Christ, and put us on the path of sanctification of knowing and becoming like Christ. Without godliness and humility, even the brightest and best get into trouble with God. Paul was a religious zealot and leading candidate for theologian of the year when Christ struck him down. Only then was Paul able to say, "I consider everything a loss compared to the surpassing greatness of knowing Christ Jesus my Lord" (Phil. 3:8).

Do not get me wrong. I am totally committed to the truth of God's Word, but God intended His Word to unite and liberate us, not to be intellectually discussed without personal appropriation. Humility and godly character are the primary requirements for spiritual leaders. Theology isn't divisive, but intellectual arrogance is. "Knowledge puffs up, but love builds up" (1 Cor. 8:1).

When academia is substituted for godliness, Christianity gets reduced to an intellectual exercise instead of a personal relationship with a living God. We can know all about God, but not know Him at all. We can develop our skills, exercise our gifts and learn better ways to become a professional Christian, yet be totally off base.

> If I speak in the tongues of men and of angels, but have not love, I am only a resounding gong or a clanging cymbal. If I have the gift of prophecy and can fathom all mysteries and all knowledge, and if I have a faith that can move mountains, but have not love, I am nothing (1 Cor. 13:1-2).

Let's take a closer look at the Lord's Prayer quoted at the beginning of this chapter: "That they may be one as we are one: I in them and you in me" (John 17:22-23). Unity is the result of Christ within us. The world will know that the Father has sent the Son because of His presence within us. Unity is the effect, not the cause. The model is the Godhead.

A parallel concept can be found by examining John 15:8, which says, "This is to my Father's glory, that you bear much fruit, showing yourselves to be my disciples." Does this verse and the preceding context require us to bear fruit? No, it does not; it requires us to abide in Christ!

If we abide in Christ, we will bear fruit. Trying to bear fruit without abiding in Christ is fruitless, because Jesus says, "Apart from me you can do nothing" (John 15:5).

MISPLACED LOYALTIES

Older generations were taught to be loyal to their country, denominations and institutions. I remember hearing, "Mine was not to reason why, mine was to do or die. My country right or wrong." That kind of blind loyalty probably set up the rebellious '60s. The younger generation may not appear to be as loyal or dedicated as we were, but I'm not sure that is the case. They won't commit themselves to institutions and organizations like we did, but they will commit themselves to the Lord. When properly challenged, they will sacrificially do Kingdom work.

Trying to establish unity by requiring adherence to denominational distinctions and doctrines will not work in the long run. If you get any two evangelicals together, you will have at least three opinions! I can't even get my wife to agree with me on all issues, and we have been living together in unity for nearly 40 years. Is there anyone more irritatingly arrogant than those who insist they are right and everyone else is wrong? Only God is right, and the rest of us are just starting to have one eye slightly open. "Now we see but a poor reflection as in a mirror; then we shall see face to face. Now I know in part; then I shall know fully, even as I am fully known" (1 Cor. 13:12).

When I pastored a church, I used to tell the new members' class that somewhere my theology was wrong. I paused for a moment to let that sink in. Then before any mass exodus could occur, I said, "If you think about it, how presumptuous to believe otherwise!" I then assured them of my commitment to preach the Word of God as honestly and accurately as I could. Theology is our attempt to systematize truth. I am less committed to my own theology now than I was when I first graduated from seminary, but I am more committed to truth than I have ever been. Over the years, my theology has changed. What has not changed is truth, but my understanding of truth has changed as I have grown in the Lord.

I have no commitment to any one systematic theology written by any one person or school. I am thankful for all their contributions, but I doubt if any one person or school has it perfectly right. We will never learn so much that we will no longer need to be dependent upon the Lord. A greater sense of dependency upon the Lord should be the result of continuing Christian education.

LABORING UNDER HALF A GOSPEL

The corporate unity the Lord is praying for cannot be accomplished without individual awareness of who we are as children of God. When we are established alive and free in Christ, "The Spirit himself testifies with our spirit that we are God's children" (Rom. 8:16). The greatest determinant of our success in ministry is conditioned by our own sense of identity and security in Christ. One pastor wrote:

> I am in the first steps of recovering from a church split. I have never known pain like this, Neil, but I am finding it to be a tremendous time of learning and growth in the Lord. Your *Victory Over the Darkness* book has been especially helpful in that I have tried to find too much of my identity in what I do as a pastor and not enough in who I am in Christ.

Let me further illustrate this truth by quoting a shortened version of a missionary's personal testimony he sent to his own mission:

> I grew up in a family of high achievers. I felt that I did not receive as much affirmation or affection as I needed to balance their expectations. I believed I had to be perfect the first time and every time in order to win their approval. I saw myself as a failure, a quitter and a loser.
>
> I got involved with a great Christian organization my first week in college. Their high standards made me feel comfortable with them. A lot of love, acceptance and affirmation came from

the guys who discipled me. They taught me by personal example how to meet the organizational standards (i.e., quiet times, Bible study, Scripture memorization, prayer, witnessing, etc.). They became, in a very real way, my family and my God.

Although I was learning good things about God and His Word, my security and identity were primarily being developed in the relationships I had within the organization, and not in God Himself. It was more important to be an integral part of this ministry than it was to be a Christian. Being associated with this group was the peak of my spiritual experience. Spiritual pride was setting me up for a fall. Had it been a cult that had met my needs for affirmation and acceptance, I would have swallowed it hook, line and sinker. In spite of the mistakes I made, the training I received was excellent, and there were many positive results in my life.

As I "matured" in my walk with God, and as my ministry responsibilities increased, I found myself getting fewer strokes from my relationship with people, especially the leadership. It was even more true when I served on my first tour of duty overseas. Although I struggled with this, I fully expected my lifetime career to be with them. During my first furlough, I was told that I would not be invited back. I thought God had rejected me. I felt I had been kicked out of my family where I had found my love, acceptance and identity for the past 10 years. Since I had not built my identity on my position in Christ, the only identity that I had to fall back on was that of a failure who was never good enough.

My wife and I joined another missionary organization, and the only reason we stayed with them for eight years was because of the love and acceptance we found with them. However, I have always been afraid that they would find out what I was really like, and they would kick me out, too. My wife said they did see what I was really like, and that is why they kept me. I never could accept other people's positive belief in me until I came across Dr. Anderson's materials.

I realized that I was living in bondage to perfectionism, fear and bitterness. I also learned that the first and most foundational step to freedom from living in bondage to the lies of the devil is to firmly establish my scriptural position and identity in Christ, which was something I had never done.

I was believing the lies of Satan. Events in the past were blown out of proportion, and they had become my judge and jury without being balanced by the truth of Scripture. It was almost impossible to meet with God, and there was no motivation for ministry (especially to the nationals whom I did not know or trust). My life on the mission field was characterized by guilt, depression, confusion and lack of desire to learn the language.

I have found immediate freedom and release from my bondage to perfectionism, fear and bitterness by these truth encounters as I verbally challenged the enemy's lies with the truth of God's Word.

Much of the Church in America is laboring under half a gospel. We have presented Jesus as the Messiah who died for our sins, and if we believe in Him, our sins will be forgiven and we will get to go to heaven when we die. What is wrong with this gospel presentation? Two things could be wrong. First, it gives us the impression that eternal life is something we get when we die. That is not true. "He who has the Son has life; he who does not have the Son of God does not have life" (1 John 5:12). Second, it is only half the gospel.

If you wanted to save a person who had died from an illness, what would you do? If you just gave him life, he would only die again. To save the dead person, you would have to first cure the disease that caused him to die. "The wages of sin is death" (Rom. 6:23). So Jesus went to the cross and died for our sins. Is that the whole gospel? No, finish the verse! "The gift of God is eternal life in Christ Jesus our Lord."

Jesus said, "I have come that they may have life, and have it to the full" (John 10:10). In reference to believers, the most repeated prepositional phrases in the New Testament are "in Christ," "in Him" and "in the beloved." There are 40 such references in the book of Ephesians alone. One pastor used his Bible software program to print out every text that included those phrases and similar ones. As he showed his congregation, the computer printout extended from the pulpit to the front row of the church. We were dead in our trespasses and sins, but now we are alive in Christ.

FINDING OUR IDENTITY IN CHRIST

Our new life in Christ is the basis for our true identity. "Yet to all who received him, to those who believed in his name, he gave the right to become *children of God*" (John 1:12, emphasis added). "You are all *sons of God* through faith in Christ Jesus" (Gal. 3:26, emphasis added). "How great is the love the Father has lavished on us, that we should be called *children of God!*" (1 John 3:1, emphasis added).

People cannot consistently behave in a way that is inconsistent with what they believe about themselves. So who are you? Are you a Baptist? Pentecostal? American? Republican? Elder? It is not what you do or where you live that determines who you are. Who you are determines what you do. So, according to the Bible, who are you?

People are prone to follow others and seek their identity from that association. "For when one says, 'I follow Paul,' and another, 'I follow Apollos,' are you not mere men? What, after all, is Apollos? And what is Paul? Only servants, through whom you came to believe" (1 Cor. 3:4-5). So what is a Baptist? What is a Presbyterian or a Pentecostal? Who is Billy Graham, Bill Bright or Dwight Moody? They are servants and organizations through whom we came to believe, for which we are thankful. But they are helpful only to the degree that they unite us with Christ and contribute to the kingdom of God. "For we are God's fellow workers; you are God's field, God's building" (1 Cor. 3:9).

Paul wrote, "My God will meet all your needs according to his glorious riches in Christ Jesus" (Phil. 4:19). The most critical needs in our lives are the *being* needs, and they are the ones most wonderfully met in

Christ. He met our greatest need of eternal life, but He also meets our need for identity, acceptance, security and significance. Let me encourage you to read aloud the following truths and personally appropriate them for yourself:

IN CHRIST

I Am Accepted

John 1:12	I am God's child
John 15:15	I am Christ's friend
Romans 5:1	I have been justified
1 Corinthians 6:17	I am united with the Lord and one with Him in spirit
1 Corinthians 6:20	I have been bought with a price; I belong to God
1 Corinthians 12:27	I am a member of Christ's Body
Ephesians 1:1	I am a saint
Ephesians 1:5	I have been adopted as God's child
Ephesians 2:18	I have direct access to God through the Holy Spirit
Colossians 1:14	I have been redeemed and forgiven of all my sins
Colossians 2:10	I am complete in Christ

I Am Secure

Romans 8:1-2	I am free from condemnation
Romans 8:28	I am assured that all things work together for good
Romans 8:31	I am free from any condemning charges against me
Romans 8:35	I cannot be separated from the love of God
2 Corinthians 1:21	I have been established, anointed and sealed by God
Colossians 3:3	I am hidden with Christ in God
Philippians 1:6	I am confident that the good work God has begun in me will be perfected
Philippians 3:20	I am a citizen of heaven
2 Timothy 1:7	I have not been given a spirit of fear, but of power, love and a sound mind
Hebrews 4:16	I can find grace and mercy in time of need

| 1 John 5:18 | I am born of God and the evil one cannot touch me |

I Am Significant

Matthew 5:13,14	I am the salt and light of the earth
John 15:1,5	I am a branch of the true vine, a channel of His life
John 15:16	I have been chosen and appointed to bear fruit
Acts 1:8	I am a personal witness of Christ's
1 Corinthians 3:16	I am God's temple
2 Corinthians 5:18	I am a minister of reconciliation
2 Corinthians 6:1	I am God's coworker
Ephesians 2:6	I am seated with Christ in the heavenly realm
Ephesians 2:10	I am God's workmanship
Ephesians 3:12	I may approach God with freedom and confidence
Philippians 4:13	I can do all things through Christ who strengthens me

Sanctification is based on our relationship with God. In Colossians 2:6-7 (*NASB*), Paul says, "Therefore as you have received Christ Jesus the Lord, so walk in Him, having been firmly rooted and now being built up in Him." We have to be firmly rooted *in Him* before we can be built up *in Him*. We can't expect to live (walk) *in Him* as mature Christians if we have not first been built up *in Him*. We would be like cars without gas. We may look good, but we can't go anywhere. If the root issues are not faced and resolved, growth will be stymied.

According to Luke 2:52, "Jesus grew in wisdom and stature, and in favor with God and men." In other words, Jesus matured spiritually, mentally, physically and socially (see Diagram 2.A). Desiring to do the same, many of us have consulted our concordances to discover what God has to say about marriage, parenting, rest, prayer, meditation and other relevant topics. Over the years, I have either taught, preached or given seminars on almost every one of these topics, as have most pastors if they have been in ministry long enough. So why aren't our people growing? Considering all the available resources, why aren't Christians bearing more fruit?

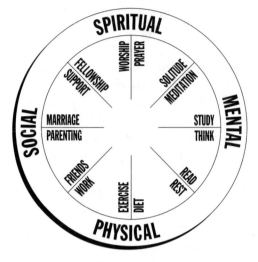

Diagram 2.A

INDIVIDUAL DISCIPLINES

Each of the spiritual disciplines is like the spoke in a large Christian wheel. The problem is that the spokes may not be connected to the Hub (Christ), resulting in a subtle form of Christian behaviorism, which will likely lead to burnout. *You're not trying hard enough. If only you would try harder maybe your Christianity would work!* Guilt! Condemnation! Defeat! Not wanting to be Pharisees, we have shifted from negative legalism (you *shouldn't* be doing that) to positive legalism (you *should* be doing this). Instead of being called, we are driven. The further we are from the Hub, the harder we try and the less we accomplish.

Those closest to the Hub are sweet-spirited and gentle. They bear fruit with little effort. They are living testimonies of the Beatitudes (see Matt. 5:3-12). Those furthest from the Hub tend to be judgmental and legalistic. They believe they are scripturally right, and they may be in a legalistic and moralistic sense. They have captured the letter of the law, which kills, but not the Spirit, which gives life (see 2 Cor. 3:6). They are living under the law and missing the joy of the Lord.

While writing the book *Breaking the Bondage of Legalism* (Harvest House Publishers, 2003), Rich Miller, Paul Travis and I asked George Barna to conduct some research for us. Respondents were given three statements and asked to what degree they agreed or disagreed with each one. For the first statement, "The Christian life is well summed-up as 'trying hard to do what God commands,'" it was reported that 82 percent agreed (57 percent strongly and 25 percent somewhat strongly). The second statement read: "I feel like I don't measure up to God's expectations of me." Of those responding, 58 percent said they agreed (28 percent strongly and 30 percent somewhat strongly). For the third statement, "Rigid rules and strict standards are an important part of the life and teaching of my church," we intentionally used words that people normally shy away from—"rigid" and "strict"—in order to give the congregations the benefit of the doubt. Despite that effort, 39 percent of those who responded said they strongly agreed with the statement and 27 percent said they somewhat agreed. Legalism is alive and well in many of our churches.

Many of these people living under the bondage of legalism have never had any bonding relationships, and they are not experiencing their freedom in Christ. I hurt for these people, but I hurt even more for the families and congregations who have to live with them. Most of these individuals are the victims of dysfunctional families (home and church). Unless they are established alive and free in Christ, they will continue the cycle of abuse.

I recall statements made in the early '60s that claimed if families had devotions and prayed together, only 1 in 1,000 would separate. Such statements cannot be made today. The rebellious '60s wreaked havoc with the family. This started a movement to save our marriages and families. Seminaries developed programs and offered degrees in marriage, child and family counseling. Clinical psychologists replaced ministerial faculty in pastoral care. Most were educated in secular schools, because in those days Christian schools did not offer doctoral degrees in psychology. Evangelism and discipleship were deemphasized, because the other needs were so overwhelming.

Some of the largest parachurch ministries and radio programs are geared toward the family. More Christian books are sold to this market than any other by far because it is the number-one felt need in America. Never in the history of the Christian faith has such a concerted effort been made to save the family. How are we doing? Have our families become any stronger? Are our children doing any better? What is wrong?

New Testament theologians have correctly pointed out that the first half of Paul's Epistles is "theological" and the second half is "practical." Many people, wanting to know their role in relationships and personal responsibilities, consult their concordances and are directed to some Old Testament passages and the second half of Paul's Epistles, which addresses the application of our faith. The problem with this approach is that it is the first half of Paul's Epistles that establishes us in Christ.

If we can help people understand and appropriate the first half of Paul's Epistles, they will *supernaturally* do the second half. Living out what God has born into us is the natural thing for children of God to do. Trying to get people to act like children of God when they have little or no clue as to who they really are in Christ is fruitless. We must help them get connected to God in a living and liberated way so that they can live like children of God.

I have told many struggling couples, "Forget your marriage. You are both so torn up on the inside that you couldn't get along with your dog much less each other!" Nobody is keeping them from being the people God created them to be, and when they get right with God, they can carry out their respective roles in life as children of God. According to Jesus, it is not what goes into people that defiles them, but what comes out of them (see Matt. 15:11). The problem is not primarily external and resolved by learning to behave better. The problem is internal and resolved by repentance and faith in God. Marital conflicts can be resolved when each person decides to become the person God created him or her to be, but they won't be resolved if all we are doing is suggesting behavioral changes to them. We are spending too much time trying to monitor and change behavior and not enough time trying to establish God's children alive and free in Christ.

Proverbs 23:7 (*NKJV*) reads, "For as he thinks in his heart, so is he." What do we see? The "so is he." What do we try to change? The "so is he"! We should be trying to find out what is going on inside. If someone's belief is wrong, his or her behavior will be wrong. That is why the battle for the mind is so critical. If we do not "take captive every thought to make it obedient to Christ" (2 Cor. 10:5), we will not behave in a way that is Christian. If we first establish people free in Christ (connect them to the Hub) so they know who they are as children of God, then all those good how-to books will be effective. All those studies on family systems and role relationships will work. The individual disciplines diagram should look like this:

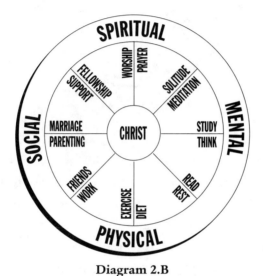

Diagram 2.B

CHURCH DISCIPLINES

The same problem exists corporately in our churches as we have seen with individuals (see Diagram 2.C on church disciplines). Many excellent books teach on evangelism, discipleship, leadership and worship. Having taught practical theology for 10 years, I can't think of one spoke in the wheel that I have not taught, as have most seminary professors who teach pastoral ministry.

Body life was the big issue in the '70s, popularized by Ray Stedman's book by the same title. The Church is more than an organization; it is a living organism in which every member has a part. This rekindled interest led to the spiritual gifts movement. People were encouraged to discover their spiritual gifts and be rightly fitted into their local living organism. The church growth movement followed.

Diagram 2.C

Reports will vary, but overall I would say that the Church as a whole declined in America during the '80s and '90s, both in number and influence. Much of the numerical loss can be attributed to the decline of attendance in liberal churches. The contribution and focus of the church growth movement probably kept the decline from being far worse. I am thankful for the focus on the Great Commission and for the biblical principles of church growth. However, as with individual disciplines, church disciplines must be centered in Christ as well (see Diagram 2.D).

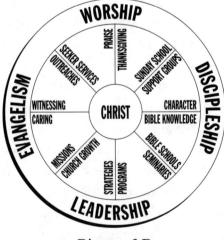

Diagram 2.D

Nothing is wrong with the programs and strategies developed by the church growth movement if Christ is at the center. The problem is so subtle because the programs and strategies can be so biblical. The life begins to drain when our confidence and dependence upon God shifts to confidence and dependence upon programs and strategies. We search for a better program or model and try to duplicate what others are doing. The church growth movement created a lot of guilt in some pastors who were not able to see measurable growth. Some transferred their guilt to the congregation and berated them for not sharing their faith and doing their part. Some burned themselves out trying to produce fruit. God, however, has not called us to *produce* fruit, only to *bear* it as we abide in Christ.

The churches that did profit greatly from the church growth movement were dynamically connected to the life of God, and they were motivated to share Christ because they genuinely cared for the lost. Churches in third world countries have grown significantly during this time, although their situations are hardly perfect. Three factors that make their situations different from ours stand out in my mind. First, the Church in Africa, South America, Indonesia and China is not as sectarian as it is in America. They have a greater sense of unity because Christ is more preeminent. Second, they have a greater understanding of the spiritual world. Third, they are less materialistic and self-centered than the Western world.

Many people have been blessed with the Restoration videos that George Otis, Jr. produced. He has documented tremendous cultural changes in which revival has broken out. All the examples were in third world countries where the social degradation was so great that annihilation was possible if God didn't intervene. People were desperate and had nowhere to turn other than to God. I asked George if he knew of any similar situations in Western Europe, Canada or the United States. He didn't, and we both agreed that it is not likely, either, since our situation is not desperate enough. However, I do know of some churches that are so apostate and immoral that closing the doors would be a merciful act.

When I taught evangelism at Talbot School of Theology, I heard a pastor share in chapel his strategy for reaching his city for Christ. Being the chairman of the chapel committee, I invited him to come back to give a series of lectures on church growth. On the first day of the lectures, he made it abundantly clear that the key to effective church growth was "brokenness" (i.e., a growing recognition of the need for total dependence on God). He then went on to share his strategy, which I thought was excellent. My evangelism class was meeting every day after his lecture. On the last day, I asked the class what they thought the key was to his success. They all brought out various aspects of the visiting pastor's strategy. Not one person, however, said brokenness, even when I pushed them to think again.

David had a whole heart for God. He knew it was not he who slew the giant. What marked his early years was his complete confidence and reliance upon God. Then one day, "Satan rose up against Israel and incited David to take a census of Israel" (1 Chron. 21:1). So what is wrong with taking a census? After all, David was the commanding officer; he should know what his military strength is, right? Joab, however, knew it was wrong and asked David why he was bringing guilt upon Israel (see 1 Chron. 21:3). David had been successful before because he knew that "the king is not saved by a mighty army; a warrior is not delivered by great strength. A horse is a false hope for victory; nor does it deliver anyone by its great strength" (Ps. 33:16-17, *NASB*). David did take the census, and many died as a result.

Satan knew that he could not sit down face-to-face with David and get him to serve anything other than the Lord his God. So the devil subtly worked at shifting David's confidence off the resources of God and onto his own resources. Is that happening today? When our hope and confidence is in God, we will be able to say with Paul, "For it is we who are the circumcision, we who worship by the Spirit of God, who glory in Christ Jesus, and who put no confidence in the flesh" (Phil. 3:3).

CHRIST-CENTERED OR PROGRAM-CENTERED?

Few churches have contributed more to church growth than First Baptist Church of Modesto, California. Thousands flocked to their

"Institute of Church Imperatives." I attended twice when I was a pastor. I also got the chairman of our church board to go and see how a church should function according to the New Testament principles of evangelism and discipleship. It became a model church for some consulting groups who taught First Baptist's principles to other churches. As a seminary professor, I offered credit to students who attended the conference. Tremendous church growth took place, and most of it by conversion. Few churches had as many good spokes in their church disciplines' wheel as this church did. Most of their present staff is homegrown.

After several years of growth, the ministry reached a plateau. Their dynamic pastor, Bill Yaeger, retired, and Wade Estes was handed the mantle. I had the privilege of conducting a conference in this fine church. Here is Wade's story as he shared it with me:

> Pastor Bill Yaeger is a man for whom I have great affection. In a very real sense, he has been a father in ministry to me, much as Paul was to Timothy. I cannot imagine having a finer or greater ministry legacy than that which I have received from him.
>
> During the 1970s, when Bill and the pastoral staff were putting their ministry plan together, the Church in America was struggling to understand its mission and its methods to get the gospel out. In 1972, First Baptist Church in Modesto undertook a survey of churches around the country and found that small-group discipleship was almost unheard of. Laymen did not know how to express their faith. Campus Crusade for Christ and Evangelism Explosion took the lead and came through with some great tools. As Bill told me, "There was much to be done just in the basics of 'how do we fly this thing?'" That was the challenge of the day.
>
> The Lord led in a powerful way as revival broke out. Hundreds of people came to Christ and became a part of small-group Bible studies. In the 24 years that Bill was senior pastor, the church grew tenfold. In the early 1970s, a vision for training men and women for professional ministry was born. Today, the

pastoral staff is almost entirely a second-generation team, trained in our church. More than 200 men and women from our internship training ministry have been sent out over the past 24 years.

The ministry skill training that was imparted to our young pastoral staff (while they were involved in our internship program) was superb in content, modeling and supervision. However, for many of the younger staff, our confidence slowly came to rest in our ability to duplicate and fine-tune the ministry programs that were entrusted to our leadership.

As with many second-generation ministries, a "program mind-set" (institutionalization) can subtly take over and replace a conscious and intentional dependence upon Christ, without whom we can do nothing (see John 15:5).

Teaching other pastors and leaders through the "Institute of Church Imperatives" only added to our youthful deception, heightening our sense of self-sufficiency. We would teach the need to seek God's wisdom through prayer, but unconsciously, that was really secondary to hard work and the execution of biblical principles. We slowly became aware that our hard work was no longer bearing the fruit it once had.

A growing sense of discontent began to characterize our staff. We were fine-tuning, tweaking and renovating every program we had, but the fruit neither increased nor remained (see John 15:16). We were stymied. We began to realize that program motivation was not the answer. But what was? We found ourselves in the same position that Bill was in 24 years earlier. We had to seek the Lord's will and leading for the work to which He had called us.

When we finally saw our helplessness, the Lord began revealing the need to fully rely upon Him and not our ability to work for Him. The Lord powerfully led us to spend increasing amounts of time in prayer. We devoted two pastoral staff retreats to prayer and fasting, seeking the Lord's direction and blessing. It became clear that the Lord was calling us to lead the church into a life of dependence upon Him, expressed through prayer.

I preached on prayer for four months in morning worship services. We worked with the leaders of the church to equip them to lead their groups in prayer. I must emphasize that this call to prayer was not a program. It was seeking forgiveness and looking for the blessing and leading of God in our church. It was a resignation to His perfect will, whatever it might be. It was a recognition that without His strength empowering us, without His leading and guiding us, and without the manifestation of His presence in our midst, we were doomed to mediocre ministry.

During this time, a church in our town hosted a Freedom in Christ conference. We sent a few pastoral staff members and some laypeople. They returned with such a glowing report that a few of us began to read *Victory Over the Darkness* and *The Bondage Breaker*. Later, at a pastoral staff retreat, the Lord totally disrupted our schedule following a time of prayer. We shifted gears and viewed a video of a counseling session conducted by Dr. Anderson. I told our staff, "We're not going to just watch this; we need to go through it." As he led the counselee through the Steps to Freedom in Christ, we would listen, turn off the VCR, and go through the Steps ourselves. Later in the week, the Lord led us to contact Freedom in Christ Ministries regarding a conference for our church. We agreed to hold a community-wide conference.

To prepare for the conference, the entire pastoral staff, board of deacons and other leaders, along with our spouses, blocked out a week and went through the entire conference on video. By the time the conference arrived, about 200 leaders had worked through the process and the Steps to Freedom. Two hundred key leaders walking in spiritual freedom is quite an army with which to begin a conference!

On Saturday evening before the event began, Dr. Anderson and I talked about the conference and what the Lord had been doing in our congregation. As we talked, I was overpowered with a renewed assurance that the Lord had been guiding us through the changes we were experiencing. Dr. Anderson explained the trap we had fallen into and the need to be Christ-centered in our ministry as opposed to being program-centered. He made the same presentation to our entire staff later in the week. It crystallized in our hearts and minds the deception we had fallen into and the new path we were on.

When the conference began, the attendance and level of participation were incredible! More than 2,200 people from our church and community were involved. God was working so powerfully in people's lives that we changed our plans for the Sunday morning worship services. We invited people to share with the congregation what God had done in their lives that week. The degree of transparency and love that was openly shared was amazing. It was apparent that people were truly free in Christ!

We are continuing to strive to be a ministry that depends upon Christ and not ourselves or the programs we are able to create and maintain. The patterns of the flesh don't change easily, but we are seeing remarkable progress in our thinking and actions. We still work hard, but we realize that if we only receive the fruit that comes from our hard work, we are missing God's blessing upon our lives and ministry.

The Body of Christ is like a big ocean. When the spiritual tide is in, all the fish swim together. Effortlessly they glide through the water and each movement is synchronized as though something or someone is guiding them. The storms are only on the surface where the big waves create all the turbulence. But when the spiritual tide is out, every little fish wants his or her own little tide pool to swim in. There is unity in the Body of Christ because the Holy Spirit has made us one, and we can learn to swim together if we are united to the One who synchronizes us. Then we can swim in truth, in unity and in love, and the high priestly prayer will be personally answered in our lives.

BALANCE OF POWER

Chapter   3

Then they said, "Come, let us build ourselves a city, with a tower that
reaches to the heavens, so that we may make a name for ourselves and
not be scattered over the face of the whole earth." The LORD said,
"If as one people speaking the same language they have begun to do this,
then nothing they plan to do will be impossible for them."

GENESIS 11:4,6

What did these people have going for them that God would say,
"Nothing they plan [*NASB* reads "purpose"] to do will be impossible." I
first saw this pointed out in *Management: A Biblical Approach* by Myron
Rush (Victor Books, 1983). He identified four essential ingredients for
the success of any Christian ministry. They are, in my words, purpose,
unity, effective communication and a desire to do the will of God.
Because the people in Genesis did not possess the desire to do the will of
God, the tower was not built. Looking at these four prerequisites for
effective ministry from a practical perspective, let's see if we can inte-
grate them into a balanced organizational structure in our churches.

Author Burt Nanus says, "There is no more powerful engine driving an organization toward excellence and long-range success than an attractive, worthwhile, and achievable vision of the future, *widely shared*."[1] I emphasized "widely shared" because that is a major key to unity. Although the book by Nanus, *Visionary Leadership*, is secular, it is helpful for those who want to understand how a clear purpose (mission) statement is essential to keep a ministry moving cohesively in a meaningful direction. *Vision-Driven Leadership* by Merrill Oster (Thomas Nelson Publishers, 1991) and *The Power of Vision* by George Barna (Regal Books, 1992) are also helpful.

DEFINING YOUR PURPOSE

A purpose statement is the basis for all future planning. It asks the question, "Why are we here?" Having Scripture in mind, how do you specifically determine God's unique purpose for your church? Some pastors may be tempted to climb into the clouds like Moses, descend with the final answer and announce it to the people. In rare occasions that may work when the followers are immature and the situation calls for immediate action, as we shall see in chapter 4. However, if the purpose is to make a name for yourself, the Lord will thwart those plans. He will build His Kingdom, but not help us build our Towers of Babel. Keep in mind that people may help you, but if you want God's blessing, He must be the architect of the vision. If the purpose is to do God's will, even the gates of hell will not be able to overcome it. The Lord initially may impress His vision for the church upon the pastor, but others will also sense God's leading.

A responsible pastor will honestly and openly share with the rest of the leadership team what the Lord is doing in his life. If God is leading the church in a new direction, all the leadership and eventually the entire church family must be incorporated into the process. Let me suggest a workable plan to bring this about. Divide the church Body into relatively small groups and invite each cluster to an evening of sharing hosted by one of the board members or staff. Invite them to talk openly about their perceptions of the church. Ask questions such as:

- What are the strengths of our church?
- What are the weaknesses?
- What are we doing right?
- What are we doing wrong?
- What kind of church would you like to see us become?
- What needs are being overlooked?

Although needs don't constitute a call, they certainly do contribute to establishing a purpose statement. You may want to consider this evening of sharing before you have your leadership go through the Steps to Setting Your Church Free, described in appendix A of this book.

Once the congregation has been heard, the leadership needs to evaluate its contribution and collectively establish a purpose or mission statement. Messages from the pastor to the church Body may be necessary, because you cannot move any faster than you can educate. When there is unanimity on the board and the staff, share the results with the congregation in a service of celebration. If the process is done right, the congregation will be united around a common purpose. They will be committed because they have been heard and have actually contributed to the process. (In chapter 6, Chuck will share a model for drafting the purpose statement itself.)

In working toward consensus, understand that not everyone will agree with everything that is said or done, nor is it realistic to expect that the final decision will be everybody's first choice. The fact that everyone had an equal opportunity to express his or her views while working toward a group decision is what is important. Lethargy is evident in churches *when* the people have no sense of ownership.

Consensus implies conflict—it thrives on conflict in a constructive sense. Not everybody will perceive the present condition of the church the same way, nor perfectly agree with what it should be. The best picture will emerge when all perspectives are heard and appreciated. By entertaining diverse ideas and perspectives, the group has the potential to unearth more alternatives from which to choose. If not handled right, the process can lead to stalemates rather than decisions and cause major interpersonal hostilities. Whether the process is constructive or destructive will be determined as follows:

Destructive When:	Constructive When:
Members do not understand the value of conflict that naturally comes when other opinions and perspectives are shared.	Members understand the need to allow everyone to share so that group consensus can be achieved.
There is a competitive climate that implies a win-lose situation; "Getting my own way" is all-important.	There is high team spirit, commitment to the group and mutually agreed upon goals; doing it God's way is all-important.
Members employ all kinds of defense mechanisms, including projection suppression, blame, withdrawal and aggression.	Members are not defensive and assume that disagreements evolve from another person's sincere concern for his or her church.
Members are locked into their own viewpoints, unwilling to consider the value of other ideas and perspectives.	Members believe that they will come to an agreement eventually that is better than any one individual's initial suggestion.
Members resort to personal attacks instead of focusing on the issues.	Disagreements are confined to issues rather than personalities.
Personal ideas and opinions are valued over relationships.	Relationships are valued higher than the need to win or be right.

In destructive situations, cliques form, subgrouping emerges, deadlocks occur, stalemates are common and tension is high. In these settings, a lot of unresolved personal conflicts become evident, which need to be resolved first before anything constructive can take place. In constructive situations, there is unity and trust. Sharing between members is open and honest.

THE POWER OF WORDS

Good communication is the key to successful operations. All the Lord had to do to totally stop the Tower of Babel building program was to destroy the people's ability to communicate with one another. "Come, let us go down and confuse their language so they will not understand each other" (Gen. 11:7). That is about all the devil has to do to stop the progress in your church. Find some disgruntled member, whisper a lie in his ear and he will wreak havoc in your church. The father of lies is very effective at creating havoc and confusion in the Church.

A pastor friend of mine shared how a board member in his church started to rant and rave uncontrollably at a business meeting, making incredible accusations. The pastor had little knowledge of spiritual warfare, but somehow he knew he had to pray out loud. The man stopped as abruptly as he started. Everyone knew what the problem was, but nobody knew what to do about it.

An exceptionally sharp seminary student once stopped by my office to make sure that what he had done to resolve a disciplinary problem with his son was enough. He had three wonderful children, but his most loving and pious child had started to lie and steal things around the house. Being responsible parents, they lovingly disciplined him. The problems continued until one day the father asked his son if he had thoughts in his head telling him to lie and steal. The eight-year-old boy blurted out, "Daddy, I had to, the devil said he would kill you if I didn't." The father told me that if he had not heard me talk about the battle for our minds, he would not have responded properly, and the real problem would have gone unresolved.

Instead of saying, "How dare you blame it on the devil," the father asked his son if he was hearing voices that were threatening him. The boy said he was, and then the father explained that the devil was trying to destroy their family and future ministry. Once the boy understood that he was paying attention to a deceiving spirit, he stopped lying and stealing. I wish I could say that this was an isolated case, but similar situations are occurring all over the world, especially with the children of spiritual leaders. If that is happening in our Christian families, is it happening in our churches?

I recall an experience several years ago when I was on an early morning walk with my wife. By the time we finished the walk, I knew I had to preach a certain message. Ten minutes into the sermon the next Sunday, a young man, who was something less than a spiritual giant, suddenly fell out of his chair and had a "seizure." Two doctors in the church immediately attended to him. When the nature of the problem was made known to me, I stopped and prayed. I knew it was a spiritual attack designed to distract the people from the message. I publicly asked for God's protection and commanded Satan to release the young man. He did. After the service, the chairman of the board said he did not like the way I prayed, because it implied that the young man had a spiritual problem. I told him that I didn't imply it; I clearly said it. Then I asked him to inquire about what happened to the young man after I prayed. He never brought up the subject again. Consider the words of James:

> The tongue also is a fire, a world of evil among the parts of the body. It corrupts the whole person, sets the whole course of his life on fire, and is itself set on fire by *hell*. Out of the same mouth come praise and cursing. My brothers, this should not be (Jas. 3:6,10, emphasis added).

Could you say it any stronger than that? What is the origin of the problem?

> If you harbor bitter envy and selfish ambition in your hearts, do not boast about it or deny the truth. Such "wisdom" does not come down from heaven but is earthly, unspiritual, of the *devil*. For where you have envy and selfish ambition, there you find disorder and every *evil practice* (Jas. 3:14-16, emphasis added).

How essential it is that we learn to personally "take captive every thought to make it obedient to Christ" (2 Cor. 10:5).

> Therefore each of you must put off falsehood and speak truthfully to his neighbor, for we are all members of one body. Do not let any unwholesome talk come out of your mouths, but only

what is helpful for building others up according to their needs, that it may benefit those who listen (Eph. 4:25,29).

But if we walk in the light, as he is in the light, we have fellowship with one another, and the blood of Jesus, his Son, purifies us from all sin (1 John 1:7).

God does everything in the light; the devil operates in the dark. The Lord can speak only the truth; the devil is the father of lies. Do you have secret meetings going on in your church? You are in trouble with God!

I made a point of telling the seminary students I taught that their loyalty to their senior pastor would be tested. Should anyone come to them for the purpose of talking about the pastor, they should immediately stop the conversation, because they are talking to the wrong person. They should go first to the pastor in private. If you are around church members who are talking negatively about the pastor (or anybody for that matter), do all you can to stop the ungodly chatter. Instead of gossiping, these people should be praying. If someone points out to you some minor little character defect in another person, you cannot help but notice it the next time you see that person. With a pastor, it gets amplified. The next time you sit under his teaching, that little defect that went unnoticed before will now stand out like a sore thumb. No pastor will survive disloyalty.

Chuck served at Rose Drive Friends Church for years. All the staff followed a simple rule. When someone criticized another pastor, they would ask, "Have you talked with him (or her) about it?" If they said, "I can't talk to him," the staff would respond, "I'll be seeing him soon, and I'll let him know that he should talk to you." Usually they would respond, "No, don't do that." Some would then talk personally to the pastoral staff member in question, and usually there was a satisfactory resolution.

Our churches are being destroyed by gossip. What is it about us that wants to hear all the garbage? If you think you are innocent because you only listen, consider Proverbs 17:4: "A wicked man listens to evil lips; a liar pays attention to a malicious tongue." You cannot hear it without it contaminating you.

I played golf one day with the music director of the church I was attending. I had just left the engineering field to attend seminary. I was impressed with the pastor of the church until I asked the music director what he thought of the pastor and what it was like to work with him.

"Frankly, I can't stand the man" was his response.

For the next 18 holes, I heard about every little defect the pastor had. I never noticed them before, but he was right. This man was definitely not qualified to be a member of the Trinity! Within a matter of months, I actually hated that pastor. I finally made an appointment to see him and ask his forgiveness for not loving him. The pastor continued to have a great ministry, but the music director ran off with another woman.

I recall that Bill Gothard suggested that we ask the following questions before we listen to gossip:

1. What is your reason for telling me this?
2. Where did you get your information?
3. Have you gone directly to the source?
4. Have you personally checked out all the facts?
5. Can I quote you if I check this out?[2]

It is Satan's strategy to discredit spiritual leaders or destroy them through relentless accusation and temptation. I am sure Paul had this in mind when he wrote, "Do not entertain an accusation against an elder unless it is brought by two or three witnesses" (1 Tim. 5:19). Hearsay does not count; two or three people must witness it. The accusations must be based on observed behavior, not on the judgment of character. You can't bring an accusation against a pastor simply because you do not like him. If in fact you do not like the pastor, find another church or keep your judgments to yourself, and start praying for God to bless the pastor's life.

Obey your leaders and submit to their authority. They keep

watch over you as men who must give an account. Obey them so that their work will be joy, not a burden, for that would be of no advantage to you (Heb. 13:17).

One time, as we entered a city to conduct a conference, my wife and I couldn't help but sense the spiritual opposition. This was not passive resistance; it was active opposition. Without saying a word, we knelt by our hotel bed to pray before we did anything else. The pastor of the church where we were conducting the conference had resigned to keep the church from splitting. He had a tremendous ministry for more than 20 years before an associate pastor undermined his authority. Both were now gone and out of ministry. The staff, board and church were split down the middle.

At the same conference, a denominational leader asked for my help. One of his pastors was accused of being a satanist. The accusation came from a Christian counselor. Her client, who had since committed suicide, made the charges. We were able to clear the pastor and his wife of all charges, but why was that necessary? We had no witnesses, only "testimony" from the grave of a deceived girl.

This does not mean that we should be blindly loyal to spiritual leaders. Being submissive does not mean that we don't give honest feedback. The secure leaders gladly accept it, because it helps them become better leaders. If they are guilty of immorality, they need to be confronted personally like any other member of the Church. In addition, spiritual leaders will give an account for watching over the souls of others, and those who teach will incur a stricter judgment.

DEVELOPMENT OF LEADERSHIP ROLES AND RESPONSIBILITIES

Given the heavy responsibility, how can leaders be effective? To answer that question, let's explore the development of leadership roles and responsibilities starting with the Old Testament.

In Deuteronomy 17:14–18:21, the Lord set forth the roles and responsibilities of the prophet, priest and king. The concept of checks and balances in our government, as well as the idea of executive, judicial and legislative branches, originated from these passages. The king is roughly parallel to our president or the executive branch of government. The Lord never told the Israelites to have a king, but He anticipated that they would ask for one in order to be like other nations (see Deut. 17:14-15). Notice the restrictions the Lord put upon the king in Deuteronomy 17:16-17:

> The king, moreover, must not acquire great numbers of horses for himself or make the people return to Egypt to get more of them, for the LORD has told you, "You are not to go back that way again." He must not take many wives, or his heart will be led astray. He must not accumulate large amounts of silver and gold.

As a united nation, Israel only had three kings: Saul, David and Solomon. Saul sinned and lost his crown. The prophet Samuel brought the Word of the Lord to him and said, "To obey is better than sacrifice, and to heed is better than the fat of rams. For rebellion is like the sin of divination, and arrogance like the evil of idolatry" (1 Sam. 15:22-23). Why did Saul sin? Because he feared the people and listened to their voices (see 1 Sam. 15:24). David slew Goliath (see 1 Sam. 17) and drove the evil spirit away from Saul by playing his harp (see 1 Sam. 16:23), but David also sinned and lost his son (see 2 Sam. 18). Solomon violated every restriction God had placed on the king and lost it all. Listen to the sad summary of Solomon:

> All King Solomon's goblets were gold, and all the household articles in the Palace of the Forest of Lebanon were pure gold. Nothing was made of silver, because silver was considered of little value in Solomon's days. Solomon accumulated chariots and horses; he had fourteen hundred chariots and twelve thousand horses. Solomon's horses were imported from Egypt. He had seven hundred wives of royal birth and three hundred concubines, and his wives led him astray (1 Kings 10:21,26,28; 11:3).

One other restriction was placed on the king: "When he takes the throne of his kingdom, he is to write for himself on a scroll a copy of this law, taken from that of the priests, who are Levites" (Deut. 17:18). The king was not to interpret the law; he was to execute it as it was interpreted by the priests, whose function roughly parallels the judicial branch of government. The priests were not lawmakers; they ensured that the law was correctly carried out. They had one major restriction: "They shall have no inheritance among their brothers; the LORD is their inheritance, as he promised them" (Deut. 18:2). In other words, they were to have no conflict of interest.

One of the biggest breakdowns of the checks and balances system in the United States is in the judiciary branch of government. Judges are not to create law; they are only to interpret it. However, it is estimated that the courts generate 60 percent of the laws of our country. Furthermore, once a court precedent is established, it becomes law unless a higher court overturns it. Most of our judges are not elected, so they neither speak for nor represent the people. For instance, *Roe v. Wade* was not a legislative decision. The people did not vote on this issue. If the people had voted at that time, they would have defeated abortion on demand. To overturn the Supreme Court by the legislative branch requires a two-thirds majority.

A prophet is a lawgiver and represents the legislative branch of government. The prophet had one major restriction: "But a prophet who presumes to speak in my name anything I have not commanded him to say, or a prophet who speaks in the name of other gods, must be put to death" (Deut. 18:20). The prophet was not to speak presumptuously. Prophets were to announce only God's words. Our legislative lawmakers are supposed to represent those who elected them, not just themselves.

God gave the law through the prophets, the priests interpreted it, and the king ruled the people by it. Sounds good, but false prophets started to spring up. The priests lost their commitment and the kings were mostly corrupt. Not one godly king ruled the Northern kingdom of Israel after the nation divided. Jeroboam led the rebellion against Solomon (see 1 Kings 11:26). In monotonous repetition, Scripture records for every king that followed, "He did evil in the eyes of the LORD, walking in the ways of Jeroboam and in his sin, which he had caused Israel to commit" (1 Kings 15:34). Instead of worshiping God in Jerusalem, the Israelites built high places and worshiped Baal. Israel's official calf idol was set up by Jeroboam. Prophets were sent to Israel, but repentance never came. Eventually God raised up Assyria as a rod of His anger to bring down the Northern kingdom of Israel in 722 B.C. (see Isa. 10:5-6).

Obviously the sins of previous generations can affect following generations unless they are dealt with specifically. The Ten Commandments clearly reveal this:

> You shall not make for yourself an idol in the form of anything in heaven above or on the earth beneath or in the waters below. You shall not bow down to them or worship them; for I, the LORD your God, am a jealous God, punishing the children for the sin of the fathers to the third and fourth generation of those who hate me, but showing love to a thousand generations of those who love me and keep my commandments (Exod. 20:4-6).

One reason for the demise of the theocratic government in the Old Testament was the Israelites' failure to carry out the command given in Deuteronomy 18:9-13:

> When you enter the land the LORD your God is giving you, do not learn to imitate the detestable ways of the nations there. Let no one be found among you who sacrifices his son or daughter in the fire, who practices divination or sorcery, interprets omens, engages in witchcraft, or casts spells, or who is a medium or spiritist or who consults the dead. Anyone who does these things is detestable to the LORD, and because of these detestable practices the LORD your God will drive out those nations before you. You must be blameless before the LORD your God.

REQUIREMENTS OF LEADERSHIP

"But when they [Israel] said, 'Give us a king to lead us,' this displeased Samuel; so he prayed to the LORD. And the LORD told him: 'Listen to all that the people are saying to you; it is not you they have rejected, but they have rejected me as their king'" (1 Sam. 8:6-7). The Israelites were no longer connected to the Lord (the Hub). The Southern nation of Judah faired only slightly better, having 7 godly kings out of 20. They did experience periods of revival; the one recorded in 2 Chronicles 29 reveals what must happen if we desire to see true freedom and renewal in the Church.

It started with Hezekiah: "He did what was right in the eyes of the LORD, just as his father David had done" (2 Chron. 29:2). Similarly, renewal in the Church has to begin with ourselves. God has done all He has to do for us to have a right relationship with Him. Choose now to do what is right in the eyes of the Lord. Pastor, do not wait for others; it begins with you. The Church cannot be renewed without you leading the way. Nor can it be done without the church staff and board. As Hezekiah said, "Listen to me, Levites! Consecrate yourselves now and consecrate the temple of the LORD, the God of your fathers. Remove all defilement from the sanctuary" (2 Chron. 29:5).

Just getting the spiritual leaders consecrated was not enough. They had to make right what was wrong in their worship setting. The priests had to be cleaned up before the Temple could be cleaned up. Once that was done, Hezekiah "ordered the burnt offering and the sin offering for all Israel" (2 Chron. 29:24). True worship followed and the revival spread.

I leave the details and thrilling results of this revival up to you for further study. One aspect of this revival, however, has especially caught my attention. The sin offering came first. In the Old Testament, only the blood was sacrificed in the sin offering. The carcass was taken outside the city gate and disposed of. Jesus was our sin offering. After the crucifixion, His body was taken outside the gate and buried. The burnt offering came next. Unlike the sin offering, the entire animal was sacrificed. Who is the burnt offering in the New Testament? We are! "Therefore, I urge you, brothers, in view of God's mercy, to offer your bodies as *living sacrifices*, holy and pleasing to God—this is your spiritual act of worship" (Rom. 12:1, emphasis added).

Revival will not come simply because our sins are forgiven. All Christians have their sins forgiven, but in most cases they are not experiencing revival. Notice what happened when the burnt offering was given: "Hezekiah gave the order to sacrifice the burnt offering on the altar. As the offering began, singing to the LORD began also" (2 Chron. 29:27).

"Burnt" literally means "that which ascends." We must consciously yield ourselves to God as living sacrifices. Notice what happens when we offer ourselves to the Lord and He fills us with His Holy Spirit:

> Do not get drunk on wine, which leads to debauchery. Instead, be filled with the Spirit. Speak to one another with psalms, hymns and spiritual songs. Sing and make music in your heart to the Lord, always giving thanks to God the Father for everything, in the name of our Lord Jesus Christ (Eph. 5:18-20).

What happens? The music begins! People start speaking and singing to one another (communicating). Hearts are made right. People connect to Christ (the Hub). Unity returns, because the Lord is King of their lives. How can we bring about this kind of New Testament revival? Like the revival under Hezekiah, it must start with those who are responsible. This prerequisite for the spiritual renewal of our churches is the intended purpose for the Steps to Setting Your Church Free. Our churches are not governed by kings, prophets and priests, as was the Old Testament kingdom. But we do have pastors (*poimen*), elders (*presbuteros*) and overseers (*episkopos*). Let's examine these roles.

Let's consider the role of the elder first. The root word *presbus* is often used to represent age (see John 8:9). An elder cannot be a new convert (see 1 Tim. 3:6). In reference to church leadership, the term "elder" emphasizes the maturity and dignity of the office. An elder is to be spiritually mature and above reproach (see Titus 1:5-9). With the exception of passages that refer to a specific elder, Scripture always refers to elders in the plural sense.

The word "overseer" is derived from two root words: *epi* meaning "over," and *skopeo* meaning "to look or watch." Hence, an overseer (or bishop) provides oversight or administration. In reference to church leadership, the overseer emphasizes the duty or function of the office. The spiritual requirements are the same for the overseer as they are for the elder. Similar to elders, Scripture refers to bishops in the plural sense except in those passages that describe what a bishop should be (see 1 Tim. 3:2; Titus 1:7).

Poimen, or pastor, is one who tends herds or flocks, and can be used metaphorically to describe Christian pastors. The pastor guides as well as feeds the flock. In the Bible, all three titles—elder, overseer and pastor—represent the same office. Elder and overseer are interchanged in Titus 1:5-9, pastor and overseer in Acts 20:28 and 1 Peter 2:25, and pastor and elder in 1 Peter 5:1-2. No special gifts or talents are required. The first requirement is to have a desire (see 1 Tim. 3:1) combined with the right motive (see 1 Tim. 6:6-9) and then meet the character requirements as set forth in 1 Timothy 3:1-7 and Titus 1:5-9.

MOVEMENT TO MINISTRY

Why then does the Church make a distinction between a pastor and elders or deacons? First Timothy 5:17-18 indicates that double honor was due those who did well in teaching and preaching. It also allows for a possible distinction between a ruling elder and a teaching elder, although all elders should be able to teach (i.e., know and apply the Word of God). Financial support was needed so that some could be free to give their full attention to spiritual things (see Acts 6:2).

The elders appear to be responsible for and to the church. Within this plurality of elders, some are pastor-teachers who are to equip the Body so that they may do the work of the ministry (see Eph. 4:12). It would seem that during the Church Age, God has uniquely called evangelists and pastor-teachers to equip the Body of Christ.

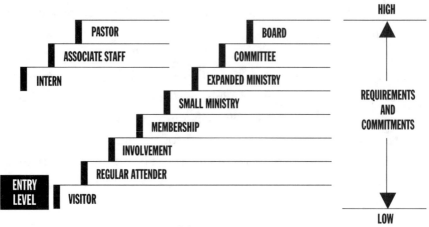

Diagram 3.A

As we seek to move people to maturity and ministry, consider Diagram 3.A. The full-time pastoral staff should see themselves as equippers. The pastor is on the same level of leadership organizationally as the board of the church. The associate staff is on the same level as the standing committees. Together, they comprise the major leadership of the church. They are to exercise oversight and watch over the souls of the saints. Some rather obvious differences exist between small, fruitless ministries and growing ministries.

A small church—and one destined to stay small—believes that the decisions should be made by all the membership and the work done by a few—usually the pastor. A growing church sees that the work of the ministry should be done by all (as equipped by the pastoral staff) and the decisions made by the few who are spiritually qualified and recognized by the church. This is only possible if the congregation holds the leadership in high regard and the leadership in turn seeks to represent and meet the needs of the people.

It is critical to make a distinction between form and function. I am describing the function of leadership, not the form. Scripture gives little instruction about the form church government should take, and denominations vary considerably. Church growth research indicates that small churches usually function with a congregational style of government, no matter what the official polity of the church or denomination. As the church grows, the government becomes more and more representative. In a larger organization, decisions cannot be made on a monthly basis; they have to be made on a daily basis by people who represent the Body. Churches that fail to make the transition stop growing.

Another important concept is the necessity to increase the commitment and requirements for leadership as the movement to ministry continues upward. Visitors should feel loved and accepted just as they are. A growing church makes the initial entry as easy as possible by encouraging only a commitment to Jesus Christ as Lord and Savior. On the other hand, the requirements and commitment level should increase for each level of ministry, holding the staff and board to the character requirements defined in 1 Timothy 3:1-13 and Titus 1:5-9. The unfruitful church will slide to the middle from both ends, increasing the requirements for membership and backing off from the requirements for board and staff members. In nominal churches, any volunteer can teach or serve on a committee. It can get so bad that some of these churches start looking for bodies to fill slots rather than spiritually alive saints to assume responsibility.

As members show themselves faithful in small things, be prepared to entrust them with greater things (see Luke 16:10; 19:17). Some will experience the call of God as they continue their movement to ministry. An expanded ministry should go beyond the boundaries of the local church. Ministry should be taking place in neighborhoods and places of employment. Ideally, people should not consider themselves eligible to be on an established committee until their witness has made itself known in the community. The church then becomes an equipping center for worldwide ministry.

Although the terms "pastor," "elder" and "overseer" refer to leadership, they do not describe the same function. Other than the pastoral staff, you can usually divide the board into two groups: those who are more gifted to do administrative work, and those who are more gifted to shepherd the flock. They roughly parallel the Old Testament roles of prophet (pastor), priest (elder) and king (overseer). Chuck will show later how the functions of cause, community and corporation relate to having a balanced ministry. Diagram 3.B is a simplistic model that enables all the people and ministries of the church to be represented by the elder board.

ELDER BOARD		
PASTOR *Poimen* (Pastor-Teacher)	SHEPHERD *Presbuteros* (Elder)	ADMINISTRATOR *Episkopos* (Overseer)
Pastoral Staff (Professional/Called)	Shepherding Ministries	Standing Committees
Equippers	Counseling	Missions
Associate	Visitation	Evangelism
Intern	Teaching	Finance
Enablers	S.S. Leader	Worship/Music
Secretary	Small Group	Christian Education
Custodian	Outreach	Building & Grounds

Diagram 3.B

BALANCED LEADERSHIP BREEDS UNITY

Regardless of a church's specific polity, unity on the highest leadership level will be present if all the leaders are free in Christ and qualified spiritually according to 1 Timothy 3:1-13 and Titus 1:5-9. If a balanced leadership team is functioning properly, an opportunity for effective communication should be possible, because every person and ministry is represented on the board. Purposeful planning will be possible if the people are being cared for and listened to as described earlier and if the leaders are committed to do the will of God. This balance of power and ministry is essential to working together in harmony.

One church I visited was deeply divided between the staff and the board. The pastor was a godly man, but he came to the church thinking that God had called him to give vision to the church. He saw himself as being in authority on the board, or at least that is how the board perceived their working relationship. Because the board was made up of highly successful people, they agreed that the pastor was not going to control them, so they informed him that he was indeed subordinate to them.

Neither arrangement will work. The pastor and board members are on the same organizational level of leadership and have the same degree of authority. No one person is mature enough to function as prophet, priest and king. Only Jesus can fulfill all functions. This delicate balance works when leaders know their place and faithfully serve in the capacity to which they have been called. If you are tempted to grab for more power by stepping beyond your borders, remember that absolute power corrupts absolutely. King Uzziah was rewarded with leprosy when he tried to enter the Temple and perform the functions of a priest (see 2 Chron. 26:16-23).

How can a church work with a plurality of leaders when no other organization does? For instance, countries have one president, states have one governor, cities have one mayor and corporations have one chairman of the board. The answer is Christ. He is the head of the Church. People are no different today than they were in the days of Moses. Rejecting God as King, the Israelites wanted their own king, as did the pagan nations. There are always a few sad souls who want to be king.

Servant leaders (which I will discuss in chapter 5) are dependent upon the Lord. They are accountable to one another and see the need for one another. Only these kinds of leaders will be able to lead their churches to freedom in Christ.

I have mentioned that 1 Timothy 3:1-13 and Titus 1:5-9 are the passages that present the character requirements of elders. Nobody perfectly measures up to these requirements, because perfection belongs only to Christ. However, disqualification can and should come to any elder for two reasons. First, if an elder willfully chooses not to accept these standards as God's credentials for leadership. This becomes evident when an elder makes an appeal to some other standard of qualification, such as talent or position, or if the elder willfully commits some act of immorality. Second, if an elder fails to deal with character defects, either by self-justification or by an unrealistic evaluation of himself or herself.

I recall telling my young seminary students that the best asset they will have in ministry is spiritually mature saints. They won't have a generation gap or a communication problem with these individuals, for they are sweet people who have grown through the trials and tribulations of life. There is a wisdom that only time can teach.

On the other hand, I told my students that the greatest liability they will have is old saints who never matured, for those individuals are no more loving now than they were 20 years ago. The fruit of the Spirit is not evident in their lives. All they do is censor and critique. Brothers and sisters in Christ, this ought not to be. The life of Christ should become more and more evident in our lives every year. Are the basic qualifications for leadership evident in your life? Use the following 20 questions, extrapolated from 1 Timothy 3:1-13 and Titus 1:5-9, to evaluate yourself:

1. Do you have a good reputation in your church as a mature Christian who speaks the truth in love?
2. Do you have an intimate and loving relationship with your spouse? How well do you handle sexual temptations?
3. Do you have a biblical philosophy of life? Does it reflect temperance? Are you living what you profess?
4. Are you prudent and humble, realizing that all gifts are from God and apart from Christ you can do nothing?
5. Are you respected because of your Christian character?
6. Are you hospitable (i.e., exhibiting a love for strangers)?
7. Are you able to teach (i.e., understand and apply the Word of God)?
8. Are you free from addictions to tobacco, alcohol, gossip and so on?
9. Are you self-willed? Do you always have to be right and have your own way?

10. Do you lose your temper easily or harbor feelings of resentment?

11. Are you pugnacious (i.e., do you use physical means to get even or to control others)?

12. Are you contentious? Do you purposely take the opposite point of view, stir up arguments and destroy unity, or are you a peacemaker?

13. Are you a gentle person, reflecting forbearance and kindness?

14. Are you free from the love of money?

15. Are you able to manage your household? Do your spouse and children love and respect you?

16. Do you have a good reputation with non-Christians?

17. Do you pursue that which is good and right? Do you desire to associate yourself with truth, honor and integrity?

18. Are you just and able to make objective decisions and openly honest in your relationships with other people?

19. Are you pursuing personal and practical holiness?

20. Are you in the process of continual growth in your Christian life, becoming more and more like Christ?

Note

1. Burt Nanus, *Visionary Leadership* (San Francisco: Jossey-Bass Publishers, 1992), n.p. Emphasis added.

2. Bill Gothard, "How to Guard Against the Defilement of Listening to an Evil Report," Institute in Basic Youth Conflicts publication, 1981.

SITUATIONAL LEADERSHIP

Chapter   4

Jim was an exceptional seminary student. He graduated with honors in Christian education and had several offers from churches because of a fine track record. He was happily married and excited about his first full-time position as minister of Christian education. He was challenged by his senior pastor to give leadership to their church's Sunday School ministry, which was bulging at the seams. Recent church growth had made the position both necessary and possible.

Mary, the Sunday School superintendent for the past 25 years, was looking forward to working with Jim. She had been a public school teacher for many years. Her love for the church and education was evident by her many years of loyal and sacrificial service. The ministry had grown too big, however, for a working layperson, no matter how dedicated. She was part of the search team that recommended Jim, so Mary felt relieved that help was on the way.

Jim was anxious to implement some of the wonderful ideas he had learned at seminary. What the church had been doing was okay, but he knew it could be done better. So he took charge and began to exercise his leadership to improve the Sunday School. He felt personally called to take the ministry of Christian education into the twenty-first century. Although the people initially received his energy and ideas well, opposition to his leadership soon began to arise, and his relationship with Mary began to deteriorate. Then he received a letter that read:

Dear Pastor Jim,

I have been praying about my involvement in the Christian education ministry at our church. I have been at it for a long time, too long, my husband says. So, effective immediately, I am resigning my position as Sunday School superintendent. I have been asked to do a number of things at my school, which I have not been able to do in the past because of my involvement in church work. I wish you God's best.

Sincerely,
Mary

Six months later, Mary was teaching Sunday School at another church. What went wrong? Was Mary being overly sensitive and resentful? Had she wrongly assumed ownership of the Sunday School? Was Jim "messing with her baby," or did he unwittingly drive her off?

Wasn't Jim called to oversee the Christian education ministry and give it new leadership and direction? Asking that question raises several others: First, what is leadership? Second, how does one give direction? Third, does the church need leadership? (Does it ever! But what kind of leadership?) Fourth, will the wrong leadership create conflicts in the church, no matter how good people's intentions are?

COMMONLY ACCEPTED DEFINITIONS OF LEADERSHIP

To answer these questions, let's examine several definitions of leadership. First, a leader is a charismatic person who has the ability to inspire people to follow him or her. Such a leader gathers a following because of personality and/or power. Power is the ability to rule or influence through charm, persuasion or threats. The con artist wins followers by using charm and deception. The cult and occult leaders have a diabolical or spiritual hold over their subjects, usually maintained by fear and intimidation. Charismatic people who lead from this perspective usually develop a "ministry" around themselves that will fall apart when they leave. Some are authoritarian. Question their rule and you will be charged with not being submissive. (I will address abusive leadership in chapter 5.)

A leader is also the one who comes closest to realizing the norms that the group values highest. This conformity gives the leader the highest rank, which attracts people and implies the right to assume control. This definition best describes the unofficial leader or leaders that every church has. These leaders are quality people who have the ability to represent and unite the church. They may or may not be part of the staff or on the board. They have tremendous influence, whether or not they hold any leadership positions. Pastors must never be threatened by the popularity of these people. If a strong personal bond exists between the pastoral staff and these leaders, tremendous things can be accomplished in the church. If an adversarial relationship exists, a split or staff dismissal is imminent. A successful long-term pastor usually has this leadership trait.

Pulpit committees should look for a pastor who best "fits" their situation; i.e., someone who represents the norm in their church culturally, academically and spiritually. If the pastor does not represent the norm of the church in one of those dimensions, there will be only a partial acceptance of his of her leadership. For instance, the pastor can be a great fit theologically but not socially, or vice versa.

I knew a pastor who was having an exceptional ministry. His church had grown from 200 to 800 in a relatively short time. One evening during devotions, the pastor had an unusual encounter with the Lord. He wondered if he should share it with the congregation. He chose to do so, and that was the end of his ministry at that church. Because of his experience with the Lord, he no longer represented the norm of that church theologically, and he had to go. The church attendance dropped to 150 people in a matter of months.

A founding pastor who stays with a church for a number of years usually represents the norm of that church, because every person who joins the church has done so because he or she relates to the teaching, personality and style of leadership. The pastor is the center of a bell-shaped curve, and people on either side identify with him. The numbers drop off rapidly as you move further from the center. Every church has a norm that is often more related to culture than theology. If you are far from the center of that norm, you will feel a little out of place if you attend that church. It is unlikely that anyone could be chosen from the Body to a leadership position if that person does not come close to representing the norm.

Unless they are clones, new pastors will not represent the norm to the degree that the first pastor did. If they are far from the center, they will probably never feel like "one of them," nor will they be accepted as such. If they are fairly close to the center, people on the extreme other side of the bell-shaped curve will probably drift away, and the center of the curve will shift in the direction of the new leadership, attracting new people who identify with the pastor.

A FUNCTIONAL DEFINITION OF LEADERSHIP

A third definition of leadership is the ability to gain consensus and commitment to common objectives, beyond organizational requirements, which are attained with the experience of contribution and satisfaction on the part of the whole church. Although awkward, this is the best *functional* definition of leadership, because it includes five elements critical to good leadership.

The first element critical to good leadership is the "ability to gain." Whenever a group is in a stalemate, natural-born leaders have the ability to pull the group together and get them moving in the right direction. This aspect of leadership is why some believe leaders are born, not made.

I'm not sure this ability can be taught. Some people just seem to have it.

The second element, consensus and commitment, is the result of the leader's "ability to gain." Without this, there will be no substantial movement forward. Tragic is the pastor who thinks he has won a great battle because the board finally gave in and voted with a narrow majority to do what he wants. He got his way, but he will probably do it all by himself. He has neither consensus nor commitment.

The consensus and commitment is to common objectives, which is the third element. If I had to determine the spiritual health of a church on only one issue, I would find out if the governing board of the church consisted of people coming together to persuade each other of their own independent will or spiritually mature children of God coming together to collectively discern the will of God. What a group holds in common is the strongest link in the organizational chain by which objectives are determined. If we are collectively bonded to Christ and are committed to building His Kingdom, we can collectively and easily come up with meaningful objectives.

In this setting, the center of the bell-shaped curve is Christ. In spiritually dead churches, the common bond can be similar occupations (we are all blue-collar or white-collar), social interests (we are all hunters or golfers) or politics (we are all conservative or liberal). The common norm of a church becomes more and more influenced by culture as it drifts further and further from Christ (the Hub). Healthy churches do not primarily establish programs around social norms because, in most churches, very few people hold everything in common socially. Having a little fairway fellowship is fine for those who play golf, but not for the whole church.

Please don't get me wrong. Some churches may have wonderful social events. Friendships are usually established because of common social interest, but Christian fellowship, which by definition is spiritual union, can only be established around the One we all have in common. "Here there is no Greek or Jew, circumcised or uncircumcised, barbarian, Scythian, slave or free, but Christ is all, and is in all" (Col. 3:11).

The fact that what was mutually agreed upon was also attained constitutes the fourth element in this functional definition of leadership. I have seen visionary leaders who possess the first three elements but lack the crucial follow-through. They get people excited and in agreement to do something, but the goal is never achieved. Good ideas that never get off the ground will torpedo any leader over time, because people will become disillusioned.

I once heard Bob Biehl give the following definition: "Leadership is knowing what to do next, why it is important, and what resources are needed to make it happen." The leader who lacks this fourth element of obtaining his or her objective needs to know why his or her direction is important and what resources the people need to make it happen. If the leader is successful, the whole church will experience a sense of accomplishment. Jesus said:

> For which one of you, when he wants to build a tower, does not first sit down and calculate the cost to see if he has enough to complete it? Otherwise, when he has laid a foundation and is not able to finish, all who observe it begin to ridicule him, saying, "This man began to build and was not able to finish" (Luke 14:28-30, *NASB*).

A manager will see that the work conforms to plan, but a leader will accomplish something beyond organizational requirements. When it is accomplished, the whole church will enter into the experience of contribution and satisfaction of a ministry well done, which is the fifth element in the definition. They will be satisfied because they had a part in it and because it was carried through. In such settings, the Body is functioning as a whole, and Christ is at the center.

HISTORICAL DEVELOPMENT OF LEADERSHIP THEORY

So far we have looked at what leadership is, but what do leaders do? I will start by tracing the historical development of leadership theory. Prior to the industrial revolution, the "great man" theory was the most prominent. The idea behind this theory was to study the leadership characteristics of great leaders such as Moses, Nehemiah, David, Paul and, most of all, Jesus, to observe their character and study their ways. For instance, I will draw some critical spiritual principles from Moses in the next chapter. Until the '60s, this approach was by far the most common among Christians. It is still quite prominent and does have value, but there are limitations, as we will mention later.

The industrial revolution brought forth the "traitist" theory, which asked the question, What traits do successful leaders possess? Those who ascribed to this theory studied the mannerisms of successful leaders, compared their physical statures and observed their personalities, as well as personal grooming, to see what traits produced the greatest results. The concept of "dress for success" was a product of this kind of thinking. All other things being equal, the taller man got the nod over the shorter man, the quicker thinker over the contemplative thinker, and so on. Every conceivable feature, characteristic, personality and intellect was studied, compared and evaluated. But the theory left many questions unanswered. Why was Napoleon such a great leader? He, along with many others, seemed to defy the odds.

In the early '50s, the focus changed from leadership traits to leadership behavior. Studies were conducted to find out what successful leaders do and should do. The studies were narrowed down to two primary activities: consideration of people and initiating structure. In other words, relationships and tasks. The tool most used by researchers was the "Leader Behavior Description Questionnaire."[1] In 1964, Robert Blake and Jane Mouton wrote *The Managerial Grid* (Gulf Publishing House, 1964), which included the grid shown in Diagram 4.A.

Blake and Mouton concluded that the best leaders were proficient both at initiating structure and at showing consideration toward people. According to Diagram 4.A, they were 9-9 leaders. A 9-1 leader was task oriented (i.e., high in structure but low in consideration). A 1-9 leader was high in consideration but low in initiating structure.[2]

Does this have any application to Christianity? When I was finishing my doctorate in institutional management at Pepperdine University, I wanted to find out, so I conducted my research on church leaders and

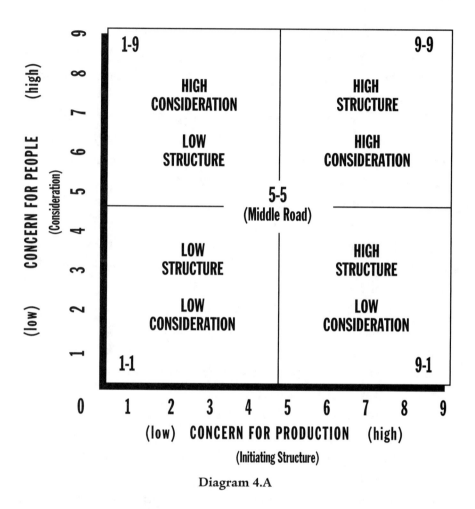

CONCERN FOR PEOPLE
(Consideration)
(high) (low)

9 8 7 6 5 4 3 2 1

1-9

HIGH
CONSIDERATION

LOW
STRUCTURE

9-9

HIGH
STRUCTURE

HIGH
CONSIDERATION

5-5
(Middle Road)

LOW
STRUCTURE

LOW
CONSIDERATION

HIGH
STRUCTURE

LOW
CONSIDERATION

1-1

9-1

0   1   2   3   4   5   6   7   8   9

(low)   CONCERN FOR PRODUCTION   (high)

(Initiating Structure)

Diagram 4.A

wrote my dissertation on the results. My theory was that the administrative duties of pastors and their desire to bear fruit roughly paralleled task behaviors (initiating structure). Showing consideration should also be a high need for pastors known for their love. In *Strategy for Leadership*, authors Edward Dayton and Ted Engstrom wrote, "Christian leaders are continually faced with the irresolvable tension between moving the work forward and caring for those doing the work."[3]

In doing research for my dissertation, 94 associate ministerial staff were contacted and asked to complete two Leader Behavior Description Questionnaires (LBDQ), a morale test, and a demographic sheet. They were asked to take the LBDQ as they perceived the leadership behavior of their senior pastor, and then take the test a second time as they perceived an "ideal" pastor. The demographic sheet was used to determine their age, sex, length of paid ministerial service and whether or not they were seminary graduates.

The results showed a positive correlation of .62 (range is from 0 to 1, with 0 showing no correlation) between staff morale and the perceived leadership behavior of the pastor.[4] Correlation does not establish causation, but by squaring the derived correlation (.38), one can arrive at a coefficient of determination. Thus, 38 percent of the variance in staff morale can be accounted for by its correlation with the pastor's perceived leadership behavior. More revealing were the comparative results with other studies. The mean score of the pastor's leadership behavior was lower in both initiating structure (task) and consideration (relationships) than of air force commanders and public education administrators. One would hope that pastors would have tested higher in consideration, but such was not the case. Let me point out that the LBDQ was an objective questionnaire. The participants answered questions purely on the basis of observed behavior.

When the associate staff was asked to take the LBDQ-Ideal, they were asked to answer the questions based on how they perceived an ideal pastor would behave as a leader. Every participant in the study perceived the ideal pastor as being high in both initiating structure and consideration. There was no correlation between the perception of an ideal pastor and age, sex or length of ministerial service, or whether the participant in the study had graduated from seminary. In other words, there was a uniform perception of the ideal pastor being 9-9 on the managerial grid. It would seem that the pastor who really loves people but has no ability to initiate structure would struggle in bearing fruit. On the other hand, the task-oriented leader who does not know how to lovingly relate to others would also fall short of the ideal.

In 1969, Kenneth Blanchard and Paul Hersey, authors of *Management of Organizational Behavior*, added another important dimension.[5] They suggested a curvilinear relationship between leadership style and the maturity of the follower, as indicated in Diagram 4.B.

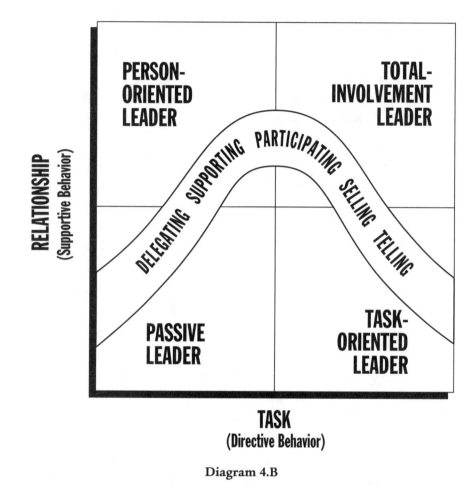

Diagram 4.B

According to Blanchard and Hersey, if the group is immature, the leadership style should be predominantly task-oriented. Leaders should provide specific instructions and closely supervise performance. As the group matures, the leader should direct less. This style is much like that of a coach, who works toward team unity by fostering good relationships, welcomes the feedback of the members and encourages them to share their opinions in the decision-making process.

As the group continues to mature, the leader becomes more people-oriented and less task-oriented. The group assumes a greater responsibility and sense of ownership. They become less dependent upon the leader and more confident in their own abilities. The leader shifts from directive behavior to supportive behavior. When the group is mature enough, the leader shifts to a passive style of leadership. The leader has helped the group to mature to the point that he or she can delegate with confidence. The leader then turns over to the group the responsibility for decisions and implementation.

CHOOSING AND TRAINING LEADERSHIP

Choosing the right style of leadership is very much determined by who the followers are. Every leader must determine the followers' readiness and adapt a leadership style that best relates to the followers' ability and maturity. Those who are unable to do a task must be shown how. Only a task-oriented leader will be effective when the maturity and ability level of the follower is low.

Suppose there is a pastor in your church who has been doing it all when it comes to weddings at your church. He senses the need to recruit a wedding hostess to relieve him of this task, and after prayerful consideration, he asks a woman named Nancy if she would consider such a responsibility. "It is just what I have been praying for," she responds. So the pastor says, "That's wonderful, Nancy. Let me show you where all the stuff is, and you can begin by leading the rehearsal for the Smith and Olsen wedding this Friday night. By the way, I won't be able to make it!"

Is that a good leadership move? It is disastrous! The pastor has adopted a passive style of leadership when the situation requires a more task-oriented style. The pastor who understands leadership will have Nancy observe at the first wedding rehearsal as he walks her and the wedding party through the whole process. At each successive wedding rehearsal, Nancy will then assume more and more responsibility. The pastor moves away from the role of a task-oriented leader to the total-involvement leadership style.

Nancy has progressed from inability to capability. At first, she felt insecure at the prospect of being the wedding hostess because she did not fully know how to do it. Many people are unwilling to commit themselves to accept an assignment or volunteer to a ministry because of the insecurity they feel of being inadequate. The only way to get them over that hurdle is to let them learn by example, with a lot of instruction and close supervision.

Now suppose that Nancy feels pretty secure in working with the pastor until he informs her that she will be in charge at the next rehearsal; he will be there to provide moral support only. The pastor is in the process of shifting his leadership style to one of personal orientation. Taking on a greater responsibility has caused Nancy to feel a little insecure; however, the pastor's presence at the rehearsal will help her become more secure as her confidence and ability increases. Nancy will eventually be ready, willing and able to be the wedding hostess of the church, at which time the pastor will fully delegate the responsibility to her.

It is important to note that a good leader never stops being a loving, relational person, regardless of the followers' maturity. Immature and unqualified people need instruction and supervision. As they mature, they should have more involvement in the decision-making process. As they start to assume more responsibility, they need their leader's emotional support. Once they have been fully delegated the responsibility, they may resent the constant interference and intrusion of the one who entrusted the ministry to them. Ask yourself a question: If your immediate supervisor delegates a responsibility to you because you are competent enough to do it, will you appreciate his or her looking over your shoulder and evaluating your every move? On the other hand, if you are new in your ministry, do you appreciate it if your senior pastor is unavailable to you, leaving you alone to sink or swim?

Let's apply this to evangelism. Have you ever tried to teach evangelism from the pulpit or in a classroom? It will probably not be very effective. The majority of the congregation will go home feeling guilty and intimidated. They will feel insecure and, in some cases, unable to witness. Recognizing this discrepancy in leadership was the wisdom behind Evangelism Explosion developed by Dr. James Kennedy. Rather than telling people to witness, Evangelism Explosion shows them how to witness.

I conducted a school of evangelism in my early years of ministry. I had the privilege in a large multistaff church to see a nonproductive visitation program grow from 20 coerced volunteers to 100 selected and trained people who were winning an average of 10 people a week to Christ. How did we get there? I started with myself. I followed up on enough visitors until I felt competent to train others. I carefully selected a few members whom I personally taught in a classroom until they felt they were ready to give it a shot. I teamed up the more experienced with the less experienced until they all felt comfortable doing visitations on their own.

Then we selected another visitation group, which doubled our numbers. The first few times, these new recruits went on visits with their trainer and were instructed only to observe. As they felt comfortable, they were invited to participate with their trainer. They felt more secure as they continued making visits with their trainer, and eventually the night came when they were asked to take the lead. The trainer would be with them only for support. The trainer had just shifted from a total-involvement style of leadership to a person-oriented style. The process is complete when the trainee is ready to train others.

That is the kind of leadership the Lord modeled for us. He began His public ministry by Himself. Many started to follow Him. After a year of public ministry, He prayerfully selected the twelve apostles. They walked together for the next two years before the Lord sent them out (see Luke 9:1-2). Then Jesus appointed 70 others (see 10:1). He gave them authority and power over demons and charged them to proclaim the kingdom of God. Finally, they were delegated the responsibility to go into all the world (see Mark 16:15). You could summarize Jesus' leadership strategy as follows:

1. I'll do it; you watch.
2. We'll do it together.
3. You do it; I'll watch.
4. You do it!

CAN LEADERSHIP STYLE BE CHANGED?

Keeping this in mind, let's return to the story of Pastor Jim and Mary at the beginning of this chapter. Mary was a mature and responsible person, but Jim came in with a task-oriented leadership style. Mary was not used to being told what to do at the church, and she should not have had to suffer under it. What should Jim have done? I suggest that he should have sat down with Mary and said something like this:

> Mary, I am so impressed with what you have been able to do in this church for so many years while being a mother and a teacher. You probably know more about education and teaching than I will be able to absorb in the next 10 years. I'm going to spend the first few months getting to know our teachers and the Christian education staff. I need to know where we have been, what we are presently doing and who we are as a ministry team. This is my first full-time ministry position, so I'm likely to make a few mistakes. Naturally, I have a lot of ideas that I would like to see implemented, as well as a sense of direction for this ministry. I need someone of your experience with whom to discuss my ideas and to give me some feedback on how they might fit this church. I can't abdicate the position and responsibility that God has called me to, but I can't do it alone either. Would you help me?

In my early years of ministry, I was asked to oversee a thriving high school group while having other responsibilities in a large multistaff church. I recruited five mature people to serve with me on the youth committee. Between them, they had more than 75 years of combined experience working with young people. I recruited a gifted and talented youth pastor to take my place as I shifted to adult ministries. He was one of the most effective youth pastors I have ever known when it came to working with kids. However, working with the committee he inherited was another story.

After every committee meeting, this youth pastor was in my office showing me his bullet holes from the shots he had taken the night before. "They're all loyal to you," he complained, which may have been somewhat true, but that was not the primary problem. Coming from a small church, he had run a solo ministry. He never learned how to work with mature people. He would attend the youth committee meetings with a lot of wonderful plans, looking for a rubber stamp. When he was not trying to tell them what to do, he was trying to sell them on what he wanted to do. Their response was, "No, you're not!" Eventually, two of the committee members resigned and one left the church.

After teaching a Doctor of Ministry class on church administration, I asked the pastors what they were going to do when they got back to their churches. One young pastor said, "I'm going home to beg the forgiveness of my elders!" His church was an affluent body with a strong board of capable people. You guessed it; he was a task-oriented leader and was experiencing a lot of opposition.

Can a leader easily change from one orientation to another? Yes, within limits. Some pastors who are called into ministry are more gifted at initiating structure. These task-oriented leaders should search for ministries that can best utilize their skills. Church planting would be one. They have the drive to organize, motivate and accomplish a lot when the church is immature and struggling to get on its feet. They are capable of growing a church up to 200 people, but it will plateau if they continue to exercise that task-oriented style of leadership. If they can't adjust their leadership style to allow others to participate, they should move on to another task that is in better alignment with their calling.

Some task-oriented leaders have an overbearing authoritarian style of leadership, yet they continue to add numbers to their membership. Although the numbers are growing, the people probably aren't. These types of leaders attract people who are willing to let others think and do for them. I knew of one such leader who attracted over 3,000 people. When he left for another church, the attendance dropped to 1,200 in six months, but they didn't lose one worker, and the giving dropped only slightly.

Passive or laissez-faire leaders can also be effective when mature people surround them. They may be capable of giving direction, but they prefer to work with and relate better to those who do not need a lot of affirmation and direction. If you are a capable person who likes a lot of freedom to work within broad parameters, this kind of leader is who you are looking for.

Everybody has a predominant leadership style. If you are about as equally adept at initiating structure as you are at relating to people, you will be more capable of adjusting your leadership style. If you would like to know what your leadership style is, I recommend that you read Norman Shawchuck's *How to Be a More Effective Church Leader* (Spiritual Growth Resources, 1990), which includes a test followed by examples and explanations.

SITUATIONAL LEADERSHIP

Another vital component of leadership introduced in the '70s is that leadership is not just a function of the leader and the follower but is also a function of the situation. In other words, situations greatly determine what kind of leader will be most effective. Let's say a missionary group decided to have a major leadership conference in Indonesia. They chartered a plane and invited top executives and experts to fly to Indonesia. A newly converted tribesman was also on the plane, which crash-landed in the middle of a vast jungle. Assuming they all survived, who would arise as the one who would most likely be able to lead them out of that situation?

Ken Peters was a faithful member of a church I pastored. Other than finances, I knew of no other contribution he made to our church. His name was never mentioned for any leadership position. He was a relatively successful civil engineer. When our church decided to relocate and build new facilities, guess who came to the forefront? The leadership he provided as chairman of the building committee was incredible. He was the right man in that situation. Such leadership is often referred to as "expert power." People rise to the top, or to the occasion, because they possess a certain expertise.

Various situations call for certain leadership styles. If there are time limitations, someone needs to take charge. The relational leader does not function as well under time pressure as does the task-oriented leader, and the group will be more cohesive when somebody takes charge and gives much-needed direction. There is not enough time to seek group consensus. When the group is under a lot of time pressure the consensus is, "Somebody do something!" If the designated leader doesn't act, probably someone else will, saving the day. When there is no time pressure, however, the group is more cohesive with a relational leader. Moses never called for a committee when the Egyptians were breathing down his neck. He held up his staff and said to the Red Sea, "Part!"

If the pastor's support base is strong, he or she can initiate a lot more structure than if it isn't. When the support base is moderate, a relational style of leadership is more effective. Research reveals that if the support base is weak, task orientation seems to be more effective. I suspect this is so because critics are more likely to respond positively if something constructive is getting done, or at least being attempted.

IN SUMMARY

Leadership is a function of the leader, the follower and the situation. Just because a pastor does well in one situation does not guarantee he or she will do well in another. A pastor may be effective with one congregation, but not another. The history of World War II reveals that Winston Churchill was a task-oriented leader who was the right man for that situation. When the war ended, however, his leadership skills were no longer in demand.

We are spending a lot of time on leadership and corporate structure because dysfunctional leadership and organizational pathology cause many of our church problems. The first and foremost factor in church health and growth is the pastor's Christ-centered leadership ability. The second most important factor is the Christ-centered leadership of influential lay leaders. When the pastor and representative leaders are spiritually mature, competent, committed and united in Christ, the church moves forward in both spiritual health and numerical growth.

When I was sharing with a group of missionaries who were struggling to overcome their experiences on the mission field, one young lady insisted she would never return. As we met privately, she related that her relationship with the nationals was great. She loved that part; it was her own missionary organization and fellow team members that caused all the pain. The conflict between the missionaries traced to an administrative nightmare; a problem that has since been corrected.

Leadership conflicts happen to the best of us. A sharp division arose between Paul and Barnabas about who should go on the second missionary trip. "Barnabas wanted to take John, also called Mark, with them, but Paul did not think it wise to take him, because he had deserted them in Pamphylia and had not continued with them in the work. They had such a sharp disagreement that they parted company" (Acts 15:37-39).

Who was right is a matter of conjecture. Barnabas was certainly more relational in his leadership style. Possibly under the pressure of the moment, he did not act wisely in wanting Mark to go. Mark apparently had not yet proven that he was mature enough, at least not to Paul. The fact that Paul knew how to reconcile and move people to maturity and ministry is demonstrated in his last letter: "Get Mark and bring him with you, because he is helpful to me in my ministry" (2 Tim. 4:11).

The important thing to keep in mind is that you can correctly choose the right style of leadership and behave admirably, yet still not be connected to Christ. If God is not in it, no leadership style or organizational structure will work. If God is in it, any style will work, but it will be far more effective if it is done right. Dedicated incompetence is still, unfortunately, incompetence. "Brothers, choose seven men from among you who are known to be full of the Spirit and wisdom. We will turn this responsibility over to them" (Acts 6:3).

Notes

1. Andrew W. Halpin, *Manual for the Leader Behavior Description Questionnaire* (Columbus, OH: Bureau of Business Research, College of Commerce and Administration, Ohio State University, 1957).

2. Robert R. Blake and Jane S. Mouton, *The Managerial Grid* (Houston, TX: Gulf Publishing House, 1964), n.p.

3. Edward Dayton and Ted Engstrom, *Strategy for Leadership* (Grand Rapids, MI: Fleming H. Revell, 1979), n.p.

4. Neil Anderson, "The Perception of Pastoral Leader Behavior and Its Correlation with the Morale of the Associate Staff in the Southwest Baptist General Conference" (EdD diss., Pepperdine University, 1982).

5. Kenneth Blanchard and Paul Hersey, *Management of Organizational Behavior* (Englewood Cliffs, NJ: Prentice-Hall, 1969), n.p.

SERVANT LEADERSHIP

Moses said to the LORD, "You have been telling me, 'Lead these people,'
but you have not let me know whom you will send with me. You have said,
'I know you by name and you have found favor with me.' If you are pleased
with me, teach me your ways so I may know you and continue to find favor
with you. Remember that this nation is your people." The LORD replied,
"My Presence will go with you, and I will give you rest."

EXODUS 33:12-14

Have you ever considered the responsibility Moses was saddled with?
When Pharaoh would not voluntarily let God's people go, the Lord
orchestrated a few object lessons—10, to be exact. Finally, with a little arm-
twisting, Pharaoh capitulated. Even then, Pharaoh changed his mind and
chased the Israelites half way across the Red Sea. Safely on the other side,
however, the Israelites had to find a way to survive in the wilderness.
Moses was charged by God to lead them to the Promised Land.

I remember taking 125 high schoolers to a Christian camp. Somebody prepared our meals for us, we had clean bunks to sleep in and the

scenery was spectacular. After one week, my wife was so exhausted that camping was no longer a family option. Moses embarked on a 40-year camping experience in a wilderness so awful that modern-day Israel gave it back to Egypt after winning it in a war. They had no showers, no commodes, and little food, and Moses' assignment was to lead a multitude of ex-slaves to only God knew where! No wonder Moses reminded the Lord that these were His people!

Overwhelmed by the task, Moses petitioned God: Who are you going to send with me? Teach me your ways (see Exod. 33:12-13). If I had a lifetime to come up with the two most critical issues for effective spiritual leadership, I could do no better. The Lord answered, "My Presence will go with you, and I will give you rest" (Exod. 33:14). Rest? Forty years of wandering in a wilderness is not my idea of rest. Did the Lord give Moses rest? The only way to evaluate whether an event is restful is to ask how you feel when it is over. Have you ever taken a "restful" vacation, only to come home more tired than before you left?

Forty years later, Moses stood on Mount Nebo to view the Promised Land, which he could not enter. He had successfully led God's people. Deuteronomy 34:7 records, "Moses was a hundred and twenty years old when he died, yet his eyes were not weak nor his strength gone." God gave him rest.

THE PRINCIPLE OF BIBLICAL REST

Biblical rest is not a cessation of labor, nor is it an abdication of responsibility. Biblical rest is relying on the power and presence of God and living responsibly according to His ways. Moses actually experienced biblical rest. In his youth, Moses had tried to do God's work his way, relying on his own strength and resources. He pulled out his sword and spent the next 40 years tending his father-in-law's sheep on the back side of the desert. Then one day he turned aside to see a marvelous sight— although a bush was burning, it was not being consumed. If it had been burning because of the substance it was made of, it would've burned up immediately. It continued to burn, yet not be consumed, because God was in the bush. Moses could not set the people free; only God could do that, and it was not going to be done Moses' way. It was going to be done God's way or not at all. The same is true today. We can't set any person or group of people free; only God can do that, and He will do it His way.

"Off-Center" Leadership

Leaders suffer burnout not because the burden is too heavy or the task too difficult. They burn out when they try to serve God by their own strength and resources in their own way. Think of the local church as an industrial factory regulated by a sophisticated set of gears. Suppose one of the gears suddenly becomes eccentric. It is slightly off center or lacks the same center as all the others. What happens to production? It creates havoc with all the other gears connected to it. Imagine what happens if many of the gears are eccentric. If Christ is not the center of people's lives, it will affect every person connected to them. If the leadership is eccentric, it will affect the whole church.

The Need for a Wilderness Experience

If we are serious about our walk with God, He will bring us to the end of our resources so that we may discover His. Paul wrote, "For we who are alive are always being given over to death for Jesus' sake, so that his life may be revealed in our mortal body" (2 Cor. 4:11). The Lord will guide us through a wilderness experience in order to break us free from our self-sufficiency. It took 40 years to re-educate Moses after the training he received in Egypt. The Lord would not allow him to rely upon the privileged position he occupied in Pharaoh's court. Our service for God is based on our position in Christ. Chuck Colson was of no use to God in the White House, but God mightily used him in prison, and now even more.

This is one reason why new converts cannot be elders. They will attempt to serve God in their own strength and in their own way until they are broken and learn His ways. Paul said of an elder, "He must not be a recent convert, or he may become conceited and fall under the same judgment as the devil. He must also have a good reputation with outsiders, so that he will not fall into disgrace and into the devil's trap" (1 Tim. 3:6-7). Woe to any church if one of the elders has fallen into the devil's snare. If left unresolved, the whole church factory may grind to a halt because of that one gear. The elder's personal problem will become a corporate problem.

Falling Prey to Deception

When Satan incited David to take a census, it brought judgment upon the whole nation. "So the LORD sent a plague on Israel, and seventy thousand men of Israel fell dead. And God sent an angel to destroy Jerusalem" (1 Chron. 21:14-15). Satan deceived David. Nevertheless, David was responsible for giving the order to number the troops. His elders also were guilty because they went along with it. God will not let anyone off the hook because they are deceived. The devil did not make David do it. David chose to believe a lie and ordered a census that Scripture forbids (see 1 Chron. 21:1-7). It is our responsibility not to sin, and it is our responsibility not to be deceived. Because David's personal problem became a corporate problem, it had to be dealt with as such.

> David looked up and saw the angel of the LORD standing between heaven and earth, with a drawn sword in his hand extended over Jerusalem. Then David *and the elders,* clothed in sackcloth, fell facedown. David said to God, "Was it not I who ordered the fighting men to be counted?" (1 Chron. 21:16-17, emphasis added).

Properly Fitted Together

Jesus said, "Come to me, all you who are weary and burdened, and I will give you rest. Take my yoke upon you and learn from me, for I am gentle and humble in heart, and you will find rest for your souls. For my yoke is easy and my burden is light" (Matt. 11:28-30). Jesus invites us into His presence, not into a program or organization. Only then can we truly learn from Him and be able to carry out His program in the organization He calls us to.

"Take my yoke," Jesus says. You may feel as though so many yokes are already hanging around your neck that one more would only be a noose! What kind of yoke is Jesus talking about? Yoke is a metaphorical reference to the heavy wooden beam that fits over the shoulder of two oxen. Look at the picture He is painting. Would the yoke work if only one ox had it on? Only when both oxen are properly fitted together can the work be done easily.

Those who still use oxen for labor will take a young ox and yoke it together with an old seasoned ox. The old ox knows he has a whole day's work ahead of him, so he no longer falls into the temptation of running on ahead and burning out by 10:00 A.M. If he strays off to the left or the right, he knows he will get a sore neck. In other words, the old ox "learned obedience from what he suffered" (Heb. 5:8). Young oxen often want to run on ahead because the pace is too slow, but all they get from their efforts is a sore neck. "Even youths grow tired and weary, and young men stumble and fall; but those who hope in the LORD will renew their strength. They will soar on wings like eagles; they will run and not grow weary, they will walk and not be faint" (Isa. 40:30-31). Some are tempted to sit down or drop out, but life goes on, dragging the irresponsible with them.

Walking with Jesus

I owned a neurotic dog named Buster. When Buster was young, I sent him off to dog obedience training with my son. After two weeks, the dog had thoroughly trained my son! Before I finally gave up trying to train that dumb dog, I gave it one more shot. I put the choke chain around his neck and took the dog for a walk. (Notice I did not say, "run.") Buster nearly choked himself to death! He wanted to run, but I did not. After all, I was the master, and I knew the way. When he stopped to sniff a flower (or some gross thing), I kept walking. Whenever he strayed to the right or the left, I kept on walking. Did Buster ever learn to walk by his master? No! He never did, and I have met a lot of Christians who haven't either. Some want to run on ahead. Others stray off to the left or the right, while others drop out.

The master is still saying to all of us, "Come to Me."

What will you learn if you walk with the Lord? You will learn to take one day at a time. You will learn the priority of relationships. You will learn to be compassionate. You will learn to be like Jesus. You will learn to be dependent upon Him because He is the lead ox. How do you put on this yoke that fits all sizes? He made it just for you, but you can't put it on unless you throw off the yoke of legalism and all the other man-made crutches that enable you to limp along.

Do you find yourself huffing and puffing your way through life? "There remains, then, a Sabbath-rest for the people of God; for anyone who enters God's rest also *rests from his own work*, just as God did from his. Let us, therefore, make every effort to enter that rest, so that no one will fall by following their example of disobedience" (Heb. 4:9-11, emphasis added). In summation, when the task seems overwhelming, learn the principle of biblical rest.

THE PRINCIPLE OF SHARED LEADERSHIP

Some will see Moses as an authoritarian leader, the lawgiver who lorded it over God's people. I see another Moses, a servant leader who was burdened for the needs of those he was called to lead. Scripture records that the Israelites began to grumble:

> If only we had meat to eat! We remember the fish we ate in Egypt at no cost—also the cucumbers, melons, leeks, onions and garlic. But now we have lost our appetite; we never see anything but this manna! (Num. 11:4-6).

Here is how Moses responded:

> The LORD became exceedingly angry, and Moses was troubled. He asked the LORD, "Why have you brought this trouble on your servant? What have I done to displease you that you put the burden of all these people on me? Did I conceive all these people?

Did I give them birth? Why do you tell me to carry them in my arms, as a nurse carries an infant, to the land you promised on oath to their forefathers? Where can I get meat for all these people? They keep wailing to me, 'Give us meat to eat!' I cannot carry all these people by myself; the burden is too heavy for me. If this is how you are going to treat me, put me to death right now—if I have found favor in your eyes—and do not let me face my own ruin" (Num. 11:10-15).

Burdened by People's Needs

Have you ever been so burdened by the needs of your people yet felt so inadequate for the task that you would rather die or resign than stick around for your own demise? No matter how good you are at preaching and teaching, someone will say, "I'm not getting fed around here." Where are you going to get meat to feed your people? Can a pastor or teacher feed everyone in the congregation or class? Should they even try? Sometimes it is older saints who say that. The Lord would likely respond, "You have been a Christian for many years and you are still expecting someone to spoon-feed you? No pastor or teacher in the world can give you enough food on Sunday to live on, much less grow. Why aren't you feeding yourself every morning in your devotions that you are supposed to be having with Me? You should be mature enough by now to start feeding others who are not yet able to feed themselves."

When you become burdened by the ministry, it may help you to know that the two most powerful Kingdom figures in the Old Testament, Moses and Elijah, both cried out to God that they wanted to die (see Num. 11:5; 1 Kings 19:4). Even Jesus wept over Jerusalem (see Luke 19:41). Consider the incredible physical hardship that Paul endured: "I face daily the pressure of my concern for all the churches. Who is weak, and I do not feel weak? Who is led into sin, and I do not inwardly burn?" (2 Cor. 11:28-29). If you care, it hurts to see people living in bondage when they can be free in Christ. I struggle saying no to these people; I am sure you do as well.

Distributing the Burden

The Lord told Moses to tell the people that He was going to give them meat to eat every day until it came out of their nostrils, and they loathed it because they had rejected the Lord (see Num. 11:18-20). To Moses the Lord said:

> Bring me seventy of Israel's elders who are known to you as leaders and officials among the people. Have them come to the Tent of Meeting, that they may stand there with you. I will come down and speak with you there, and I will take of the Spirit that is on you and put the Spirit on them. They will help you carry the burden of the people so that you will not have to carry it alone (Num 11:16-17).

This was similar to the advice given to Moses by his father-in-law, Jethro, in Exodus 18:17-23:

> What you are doing is not good. You and these people who come to you will only wear yourselves out. The work is too heavy for you; you cannot handle it alone. Listen now to me and I will give you some advice, and may God be with you. You must be the people's representative before God and bring their disputes to him. Teach them the decrees and laws, and show them the way to live and the duties they are to perform. But select capable men from all the people—men who fear God, trustworthy men who hate dishonest gain—and appoint them as officials over thousands, hundreds, fifties and tens. Have them serve as judges for the people at all times, but have them bring every difficult case to you; the simple cases they can decide themselves. That will make your load lighter, because they will share it with you. If you do this and God so commands, you will be able to stand the strain, and all these people will go home satisfied.

Don't be tempted to look at this passage as support for authoritarian or hierarchical rule over others. The purpose for appointing others was to relieve Moses' burden; he was trying to do it all by himself. The organizational hierarchy was just a means to accomplish effectively the task of meeting needs, not to lord it over others. The needs were far too great for any one person to meet. Although Jethro suggested a hierarchy to Moses, God did not. The Lord simply said to him, "They will help you carry the burden of the people."

Choosing Helpers

Moses was told to select elders who were known to him as leaders. If they were already available, why hadn't Moses turned to them himself? Why don't we? The reason is because some of us are codependent and need to be needed. Others are overly conscientious. *I've been called to do this, so I better do it.* For some, it just never crosses their minds to enlist the help of others. Others have a messianic concept of themselves. They reason, *I alone can help this person.* This is the danger of professionalism, which assumes that only professionals (pastors, counselors and so on) can really help these people. There are not enough "professionals" in the United States to meet the spiritual needs of our people. If we do not equip and mobilize the church laity, it won't be done. Paul admonishes us to "Carry each other's burdens, and in this way you will fulfill the law of Christ" (Gal. 6:2). The text in Numbers that we are looking at, however, reveals an even more insidious reason.

Fear of Competition

When the Spirit rested on the 70 elders, they prophesied but did not do so again (see Num. 11:25). "However, two men, whose names were Eldad and Medad, had remained in the camp. They were listed among the elders, but did not go out to the Tent. Yet the Spirit also rested on them, and they prophesied in the camp" (Num. 11:26). Joshua, Moses' aide, said, " 'Moses, my lord, stop them!' But Moses replied, 'Are you jealous for my sake? I wish that all the LORD's people were prophets and that the LORD would put his Spirit on them!' " (Num. 11:28-29).

I pray that every Christian leader will say what Moses said. Do we really want God's Spirit to rest upon others to the same degree that He rests upon us? Do we desire the Lord's anointing to be as obvious on others as we desire it for ourselves? Do we get as much delight when others have the spotlight in the Kingdom as we do when it is our turn? Do we earnestly seek to help every person in our church reach his or her highest potential, even if it is higher than our own? Does it threaten us to share the pulpit with a gifted layperson who the congregation requests to speak? Does it bother the youth pastor when he or she invites a sharp college student to speak to the kids and they respond better to the guest speaker than they do when the youth pastor talks?

Probably every Christian leader has experienced some twinge of envy or jealousy. I know of several former students who were run off by the senior pastor in their first ministry, not because they were doing a bad job, but because they were too popular. I know of several insecure pastors who keep a thumb on every ministry and protect the pulpit as if it were their own. Some even refer to it as "my pulpit." In too many cases, the number one hindrance to every member reaching his or her fullest potential is the pastor. What a tragedy! A pastor's greatest desire should be to see every member reach his or her highest potential. This is another reason why a Christian leader's personal identity and security in Christ are what will determine his or her success in ministry. If the burden is too heavy, learn the principle of shared leadership.

THE PRINCIPLE OF HUMBLE INTERCESSION

Have you ever had a staff member rebel against you? How about the whole congregation? The elder or deacon board? How did you handle it? Moses had all three rise up against him. First it was his staff:

Miriam and Aaron began to talk against Moses because of his Cushite wife, for he had married a Cushite. "Has the LORD spoken only through Moses?" they asked. "Hasn't he also spoken through us?" And the LORD heard this (Num. 12:1-2).

The attack by Moses' staff on his marriage was a pretext. The real issue was the prophetic gift of Moses and his special relationship with the Lord. Their rebellious attitude angered the Lord, and He ordered them out to the Tent of Meeting to speak to them:

> When a prophet of the LORD is among you, I reveal myself to him in visions, I speak to him in dreams. But this is not true of my servant Moses; he is faithful in all my house. With him I speak face to face, clearly and not in riddles; he sees the form of the LORD. Why then were you not afraid to speak against my servant Moses? (Num. 12:6-8).

Moses Pleads for Miriam

When the Lord departed, Miriam was leprous. God judged her, and she deserved it. How about Aaron, Lord? Nothing for him? I think he deserves at least a cold sore or maybe a boil. Wouldn't the best of us have a little tendency to think that way? After all, they both attacked Moses' character, and God judged Miriam. If God did it, it must be right. Aaron, however, upon seeing Miriam's leprosy, suddenly realized that they had sinned and was ready to confess it. How did Moses respond? "Moses cried out to the LORD, 'O God, please heal her!'" (Num. 12:13). The Lord relented, but not totally. Miriam had to remain outside the camp for seven days with her leprosy. The whole camp had to wait for seven days until she healed. As we evaluate how Moses responded to his critics, keep in mind Numbers 12:3: "Now Moses was a very humble man, more humble than anyone else on the face of the earth."

Moses Considers the Needs of the People

The next thing this humble man had to face was the rebellion of his whole congregation. One member of each tribe had been sent to spy out the Promised Land. Ten came back with a negative report, saying there were giants in the land. The whole community rose up against Moses and Aaron. Moses and Aaron immediately fell on their faces before the assembly. Joshua and Caleb begged them not to rebel against the Lord, but the congregation wanted to stone Moses and Aaron. The glory of the Lord again appeared at the Tent of Meeting. The Lord said to Moses, "How long will these people treat me with contempt? How long will they refuse to believe in me, in spite of all the miraculous signs I have performed among them? I will strike them down with a plague and destroy them, but I will make you into a nation greater and stronger than they" (Num. 14:11-12).

Who could blame Moses for saying, "Thank You, Lord, they were about to stone me to death. I've gotten a little tired of these folks myself. By the way, great choice in choosing me to start this new nation!" Instead, Moses asked the Lord to withhold judgment because he was concerned about God's reputation. Moses did not consider himself; he considered the people's needs and God's reputation. The Lord forgave the people, but all those who witnessed His miraculous works could not go into the Promised Land.

Moses Asks God to Withhold Judgment

Finally, Moses had to face the rebellion of his board, as recorded in Numbers 16. Korah, Dathan and Abiram led the rebellion, but 250 Israelite men who were well-known community leaders and chosen members of the council also joined them.

> They came as a group to oppose Moses and Aaron and said to them, "You have gone too far! The whole community is holy, every one of them, and the LORD is with them. Why then do you set yourselves above the LORD's assembly?" (Num. 16:3).

Again, Moses fell on his face. Then he told Korah:

> "You and all your followers are to appear before the LORD tomorrow—you and they and Aaron. Each man is to take his censer and put incense in it—250 censers in all—and present it before the LORD. You and Aaron are to present your censers also." So each man took his censer, put fire and incense in it, and

stood with Moses and Aaron at the entrance to the Tent of Meeting. When Korah had gathered all his followers in opposition to them at the entrance to the Tent of Meeting, the glory of the LORD appeared to the entire assembly. The LORD said to Moses and Aaron, "Separate yourselves from this assembly so I can put an end to them at once" (Num. 16:16-21).

"Thank You, Lord, for vindicating me, and how far should I separate myself from them?" Was that how Moses responded? Hardly! "Moses and Aaron fell facedown and cried out, 'O God, God of the spirits of all mankind, will you be angry with the entire assembly when only one man sins?'" (Num. 16:22). God relented and spared the assembly, but the ground swallowed alive the entire families and possessions of Korah, Dathan and Abiram. In addition, fire came down and consumed the 250 leaders who had participated in the rebellion. It is important to note that judgment not only affected those who instigated the rebellion, but also those who participated in it, although the judgment was less severe. God spared their families.

How many times have we been tempted to pray that God would bring judgment upon those who oppose us? Moses demonstrated his humility by praying that God would withhold His judgment. Moses was a servant leader. Rest assured that God will bring judgment upon those who reject Him, but what He is looking for is someone who will intercede on behalf of the people:

I looked for a man among them who would build up the wall and stand before me in the gap on behalf of the land so I would not have to destroy it, but I found none. So I will pour out my wrath on them and consume them with my fiery anger, bringing down on their own heads all they have done, declares the Sovereign LORD (Ezek. 22:30-31).

In this instance, there was no Moses to intercede for the people. For us there is Jesus. "He is able to save completely those who come to God through him, because he always lives to intercede for them" (Heb. 7:25). Would our churches profit more if they had pastors who prayed for God's judgment upon their churches or for God's mercy? Do we have a ministry of condemnation or a ministry of reconciliation?

Repenting of Individualism

In my first role as a senior pastor, I found myself embroiled in a power struggle with a board member. He was a charter member, and it was rumored that he was the biggest contributor in the church. I went to see him personally in his home to see if we could work out our differences. It was not going to happen, so I asked if he would have breakfast with me once a week. I invited him to share any problems that he had with my ministry or me. I wanted this to be an issue between us, rather than a board issue. It was a sparring match for six months. I can honestly say that I was not trying to change him; all I wanted to do was establish some kind of meaningful relationship. I thought I could get along with anybody. Realizing that I could not develop a relationship if the other person did not want it was a hard lesson for me to learn.

When I asked permission from the board to use my vacation to conduct a tour of the Holy Land, that board member opposed it. "I know how that works," he said. "If he gets enough people to go, he can go for nothing, and that is like giving him a bonus!" So I used my vacation and went by myself. It was a tremendous time of spiritual renewal. The Garden of Gethsemane was especially meaningful. I spent an afternoon in the Church of All Nations, which enshrines the rock believed to be where Jesus surrendered His will to the Father. It was there that He decided to take upon Himself the sins of the world. I left that place knowing that I had to take the sin of that elder upon myself if I was going to forgive him as Jesus had forgiven me. I made that decision.

The storm seemed to pass until that elder decided to go after my youth pastor. That did it. I made a stand against the man and told the board that if they did not do something about him, the entire staff was going to resign. They arranged a time for us to meet, and we were to ask each other for forgiveness. I thought, "Great, sweep it under the carpet, and we can trip over it later." I did ask for his forgiveness for not loving him, because I did not, and I did not feel good about that. The meeting ended in a stalemate. I realized the board was not going to do anything, so I decided to resign.

I wrote my resignation letter one morning from home. By that evening, my temperature was 103.5 degrees and I had totally lost my voice. It does not take a genius to recognize that God was not pleased with my decision. My original plan was to read my resignation the following Sunday, but I was too sick to do that. Flat on my back and with no way to look but up, I came across a passage of Scripture in Mark 8:22-26. Jesus had touched the eyes of a blind man who was brought to Him, with the result that the man saw men walking around like trees. The Lord touched him a second time, and now he saw everything clearly. I got the message.

I saw this elder as a tree; he was blocking my goal. But he wasn't. I was! I wanted the man out of the way; I wanted justice. God wanted me to love the man. I cried out to God, "I don't love that man, Lord, and I know You do. There is nothing within me that is able to do that, so if You want me to love him, You are going to have to touch me." God did! The next Sunday I preached from Mark 8:22-26 with a husky voice. Although it has been years since this happened, I can still remember the message and the results. I confessed my individualism and shared my desire to love people and not see any of them as trees. I gave an invitation for those who needed God to touch their lives in order to love people.

I could never have anticipated what happened next. People came forward by the droves. Some went across the aisle to ask forgiveness of others. The front of the church could not handle the numbers, so the doors swung open and the people spilled out onto the lawn. It was a revival! But it came only after I got my heart right.

If I had got my way years ago, I would not be writing this book. I am forever thankful that God struck me down. Nobody on planet Earth can keep me from being the person God created me to be. Actually, God used that man to help me become the pastor I am today. When people question your leadership, learn the principle of humble intercession.

To this you were called, because Christ suffered for you, leaving you an example, that you should follow in his steps. "He committed no sin, and no deceit was found in his mouth." When they hurled their insults at him, he did not retaliate; when he suffered, he made no threats. Instead, he entrusted himself to him who judges justly (1 Pet. 2:21-23).

THE PRINCIPLE OF SERVANT LEADERSHIP

Some leaders who are not secure in Christ try to establish their worth by seeking prominent positions. Parents even desire it for their children. Such was the case when the mother of Zebedee's sons approached Jesus to ask a favor. She wanted one of her sons to sit at the right of Jesus and the other to sit at His left in His Kingdom. The Lord said it was not His to offer and asked her sons if they were prepared to drink the cup He was about to drink. They said they were. When the other 10 disciples heard about this, they became indignant (see Matt. 20:20-28).

When people clamor for position in any organization, it creates problems in relationships between the staff. What are secure people supposed to do when one or two try to climb over the backs of others? They don't want those kinds of people in position over them, and they don't want to succumb to the same self-serving, competitive tactics. In Matthew 20:25-28, the Lord used this occasion to teach about spiritual leadership:

You know that the rulers of the Gentiles lord it over them, and their high officials exercise authority over them. Not so with you. Instead, whoever wants to become great among you must be your servant, and whoever wants to be first must be your slave—just as the Son of Man did not come to be served, but to serve, and to give his life as a ransom for many.

Following that instruction, Luke records, "A dispute arose among them as to which of them was considered to be greatest" (Luke 22:24).

Jesus came to Peter and said, "Simon, Simon, Satan has asked to sift you as wheat. But I have prayed for you, Simon, that your faith may not fail. And when you have turned back, strengthen your brothers" (Luke 22:31-32). Peter then said he was ready to die or go to prison with Jesus, but the Lord answered, "I tell you, Peter, before the rooster crows today, you will deny three times that you know me" (Luke 22:34). This passage shows the opportunity available to Satan to have access to the Church when leaders succumb to pride. You can see the same connection in James 4:6-7 and 1 Peter 5:6-10.

Leaders Must Serve Their Followers

Nobody has a lower position than a servant or a slave. How does this apply to a leader in a prominent position? Who or what is every leader subject to, and who or what are they the servant of? I believe they are subject to the needs of those they are called to lead. As a father, I am subject to the needs of my wife and my children. Should something happen to my wife that requires my attention, I am not free to ignore that need and do as I please. I am charged to love my wife as Christ loved the Church. My children have no such commandment. When corporate America isn't functioning properly, they do not initially call the blue-collar workers. They call the leader who is ultimately responsible. That is why leadership can be lonely and burdensome. Nobody should strive to be a pastor or elder in a church in order to inflate his or her ego, or because he or she desires the power that comes from position. The same teaching can be found in 1 Peter 5:1-4:

> To the elders among you, I appeal as a fellow elder, a witness of Christ's sufferings and one who also will share in the glory to be revealed: Be shepherds of God's flock that is under your care, serving as overseers—not because you must, but because you are willing, as God wants you to be; not greedy for money, but eager to serve; not lording it over those entrusted to you, but being examples to the flock. And when the Chief Shepherd appears, you will receive the crown of glory that will never fade away.

Lines of Authority

Does this mean that there are no lines of authority? Of course there are. We are all under authority, but the instruction and basis for authority is different for those in leadership than it is for those who are under authority. Authority is the right to rule, which is based on position. God requires those who are under authority to be submissive to those people who are in positional authority over them. Scripture does allow for times when people must obey God rather than man, namely when authority figures operate outside the scope of their authority or when they tell people to do something that is a clear violation of Scripture. These positions of authority can be summarized as follows:

- Civil government (see Rom. 13:1-5; 1 Tim. 2:1-3; 1 Pet. 2:13-16)
- Parents (see Eph. 6:1-3; Col. 3:18-21)
- Husbands (see Titus 2:5; 1 Pet. 3:1-3)
- Employers (see 1 Pet. 2:18-21)
- Church leaders (see Heb. 13:17)

In position-based authority, people actually obey God by respecting the person's position, even though they may not necessarily respect the person. You may or may not like police officers, but it is best to obey them when they pull you over for speeding. Part of our spiritual protection is being under authority. We are never excused from being submissive because we don't like or respect a person in authority. Civilizations will experience chaos if there is not submission to governing authorities.

Basis of Authority

The instruction differs for those who are in a position of authority. After preaching the Sermon on the Mount, "The crowds were amazed at his teaching, because he taught as one who had authority, and not as their teachers of the law" (Matt. 7:28-29). Jesus, of course, was God, but His listeners did not know it at that time, and He had no earthly position of authority. He was not a representative of the Roman government, nor a member of the Sanhedrin. He was not even a Levite. So what was the basis of His authority?

Jesus' authority was based in the quality, conduct and character of His life, and in His intimate oneness with the Father. That should be the case for all spiritual leaders. Moses never defended his position as a prophet of God when people rebelled against him. The Bible records no passages of Jesus saying, in essence, "Listen, people, shape up and do what I tell you to do because I am God!" He certainly could have, because He is God.

Men, what happens to the quality of your relationship with your wife if you say to her, "You have to obey me because I am your husband and the head of our home"? Obeying you is her responsibility; loving her as Christ loved the Church is your responsibility. Submission is the *voluntary* responsibility of those under authority, which seldom works if those in authority demand it.

Being in a submissive position is like riding "shotgun" in a car. The rider will feel secure and have no problem letting the other person drive, provided two conditions are met. First, the driver must know where he or she is going. If the driver is lost and the rider knows the way, who can blame the rider for wanting to drive? Second, the driver must obey the rules of the road. If the driver starts speeding and running red lights, the rider will become very insecure. Faulty leadership often fosters a rebellious spirit. Leaders should know where they are going and obey all the laws as they go, rather than demanding that the rider be submissive.

Serving by Example

Scripture instructs those who are under authority to be submissive to those who are in a biblical position of authority over them. Authority is based on position. Those who are in authority are not to rule over others based on their position, but rather are to serve by example. This is a character-based authority. Spiritual leaders should strive to be such an example that others will want to follow, not be forced to follow. What qualifies a person to be an elder is godly character and knowledge of God's Word. Biblical gifts and talents, as well as secular positions of power and influence, do not qualify a person for leadership in the Church. Notice Paul's words in 1 Thessalonians 2:5-8:

> For we never came with flattering speech, as you know, nor with a pretext for greed—God is witness—nor did we seek glory from men, either from you or from others, *even though as apostles of Christ we might have asserted our authority.* But we proved to be gentle among you, as a nursing mother tenderly cares for her own children. Having so fond an affection for you, we were well-pleased to impart to you not only the gospel of God but also our own lives, because you had become very dear to us (*NASB*, emphasis added).

There is a need for accountability, but what are the conditions that make it possible? Consider the following four words:

- Authority
- Accountability
- Affirmation
- Acceptance

Ask yourself an important question: From which end of the list did God initially come to you?

Whose Servants Are We?
How you answer that question will say more about how you understand parenting and ministry than any other question I could ask. There is no doubt in my mind that my relationship with God began with acceptance. "But God demonstrates his own love for us in this: While we were still sinners, Christ died for us" (Rom. 5:8). Affirmation came after I decided to trust Him. "How great is the love the Father has lavished on us, that we should be called children of God! And that is what we are!" (1 John 3:1). People who know that they are accepted and affirmed will voluntarily be accountable to authority figures who graciously accept

and affirm those whom they lead. However, when authority figures demand accountability without acceptance and affirmation, they will never get it. Under duress, those who have an authoritarian leader will fill out a report form and provide some superficial answers, but they will never share what is going on inside. They will be vulnerable only to those they trust. Christian leaders need to be accepted and affirmed as well.

The same principle applies to parenting. If an angry parent asks a delinquent child, "Where were you?" the child will likely say, "Out." If the parent then asks, "And what were you doing?" the child will probably say, "Nothing!" The communication gap has more to do with the character of the leader than it does about culture or age.

Ultimately, whom are we trying to please? In Galatians 1:10, Paul responds, "Am I now trying to win the approval of men, or of God? Or am I trying to please men? If I were still trying to please men, I would not be a servant of Christ." If Paul were trying to please men, whose servant would he be? Every Christian should learn to play for the coach and not for the grandstand. Trying to please everyone has ruined many potentially good leaders. Paul writes in 2 Corinthians 5:9 that we are to "make it our goal to please him [God]."

Every believer has the spiritual authority in Christ to do His will and to overcome the kingdom of darkness through his or her position in Christ. We are seated with Christ in the heavenlies (see Eph. 2:5-7). At the same time, we are all called to "submit to one another out of reverence for Christ" (Eph. 5:21), because we are all called to love one another. You are not being codependent if you legitimately submit to the needs of others. You are being codependent if you let other people control your life and dictate how you are supposed to meet their needs. Make it your goal to be the kind of leader who will enable your people to live free in Christ. Remember, when people question your right to lead, you should learn the principle of servant leadership that is based in character.

THE CHURCH IN COMMUNION

In an insightful article in *Leadership Journal*, Jim Dethmer describes the Church as three interlocking circles or functions: "cause," "community" and "corporation."[1] The cause of the Church is its mission. The biblical image is an army, and the key person in the army is the one most highly committed. An army succeeds when it advances, capturing people or territory for its commander. Recruits enter the army by being enlisted or drafted. If battles are raging, they can leave the army only when the war ends or when they become casualties. The paybacks are glory and special honors. The "cause people" in the Church spread the gospel, win people to Christ, plant churches, launch mission efforts and take new ground for Christ. The role of communicator (prophet) would fit in the cause circle.

The community is the fellowship of believers who take care of one another. The biblical image is the family, the household of faith. The focus is on the person who is the weakest or the one with the greatest need. A new baby or the family member who undergoes surgery receives the greatest care. A family succeeds when it nourishes and provides for all its members according to their needs. Members are born or adopted into the family, and they never really leave it. They may divorce, disown or change names, but the social and psychological imprint always remains. Family members have a sense of belonging and feel secure and loved. "Community people" put their arms around the hurting and the needy. The role of caregiver (priest) would fit in the community circle.

The corporation of the Church is its organization. Finances and facilities, boards and procedures, and progress and expansion are its interests. The image is similar to that of a business. Although the Bible does not compare the Church to a business, it does speak of gifted leaders and administrators who organize God's people for their progress and well-being. They ensure that everything is done decently and orderly. The key person in a business is the one who most effectively leads the people. "Corporation people" motivate and organize the people to reach mutually shared goals and provide for the proper stewardship of facilities, finances and services. The role of leader (king) would fit in the corporation circle.

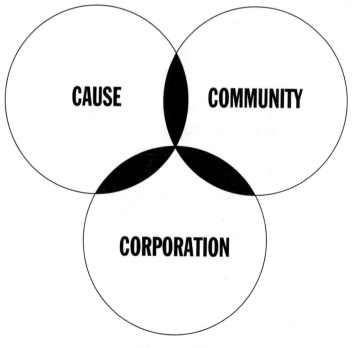

Diagram 6.A

IMPROVED COMMUNICATION

Combining the roles of cause, community and corporation identifies which "hat" leaders are wearing and why they are all needed for a balanced ministry. For example, consider this conversation between a pastor and a part-time youth leader who also is attending seminary.

"Joe," says the pastor, "I need to have a talk with you, in private. Let me put my corporate hat on for a moment. It seems that things are not going as well as we expected. Some of the high schoolers are unhappy, and the parents are complaining. It seems that many of the activities lack organization, and some kids find out too late about special events. If we do not see some changes for the better in the next six months, some changes will have to be made.

"Now, Joe, let me take off my corporate hat and put on my community hat. It seems to me that you are living under too much stress. Your wife gave me permission to let you know that she has been in to talk with me. She feels abandoned at home, alone with the preschoolers while you are always at church or school or busy studying.

"Joe, here's what we're going to do. We're going to cut back your time requirements here at church by five hours per week, but we are not going to cut your pay. In addition, I've arranged for the church to pay for some counseling for you and your wife over the next six to eight weeks. I'll make some personal appeals for volunteers to help your youth staff. We'll look for individuals with good organizational and promotional skills. You have a lot to offer, Joe, and I'm for you. I'm convinced you have a wonderful ministry ahead of you and that God's call and gifts are evident in your life."

Such a paradigm helps identify what kind of communication is going on and the motivation of the pastor. It is a contemporary way of showing how the functional roles of prophet, priest and king work in a practical way. However, such a model can apply to any social organization. I suggest that there is a fourth circle, which makes the Church unique from any other organization. This circle represents our communion with our heavenly Father. Without Christ as head of the Body, no social organization is really a church. The true Church is first and foremost an organism, a spiritual Body united together by the Holy

Spirit. It is organized for effective service. The fourth circle encompasses the other three functions of ministry (see Diagram 6.B).

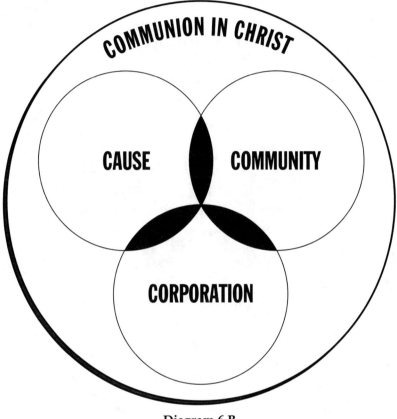

Diagram 6.B

THE MISSING CIRCLE

Let's call this fourth circle "communion in Christ." It represents the Church in fellowship with its Head. It means living in union, intimacy and harmony with Christ and practicing His presence. The biblical image is the body. The most important part of a human body is the head. In a similar way, the most important part of the Church Body is our head, the Lord Jesus Christ. The formation of a human body begins with conception. The only way a member is severed from the Body is by death or by being cut off. Those closely connected with the head live righteous lives, bear fruit and are guided by His Holy Spirit.

"Communion people" pray, worship and practice the presence of God. The role of every saint fits in the communion circle, as indicated in the Ministry Model (Diagram 6.C).

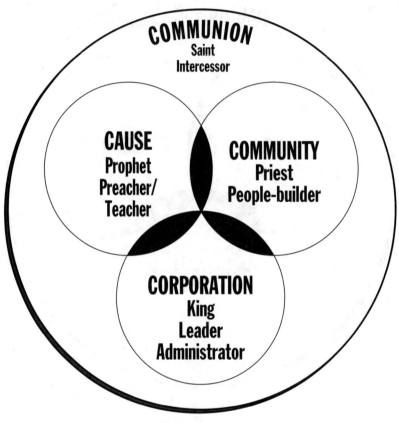

Diagram 6.C

In the ideal church, the communion circle is primary. Our Lord Jesus Christ is both the circumference and the center of the Church. He is alive, present, active and guiding the decision-making process. He encompasses every other circle:

- For the cause, Jesus is the message and the messenger—the prophet.
- For the community, Jesus is the counselor, helper and healer— the priest.

• For the corporation, Jesus is the CEO, president and commander—the king.

THE DYSFUNCTIONAL CHURCH

No church is perfect, and few seem close to ideal. Like people, all churches have strengths and weaknesses, good memories and painful ones. Most tolerate or participate in corporate sins. Members and attendees are imperfect people and vulnerable, at least to some degree, to the world, the flesh and the devil, who tempts, accuses and deceives.

It is possible to "do church" without the big circle of communion in Christ. An organized church can teach the Bible (cause), look after its own (community), and keep its organization and finances in order (corporation) without being connected to the Head. Somebody once said that if the Holy Spirit were removed, 95 percent of our church programs would go on as scheduled. The point is that we can preach, offer counsel and administrate in the flesh. At times, we have all done it.

A church can proclaim its cause, socialize in its community and direct its corporation without constant communion in Christ. Any or all of these three functions can bypass His presence, direction and counsel. In reality, some people in the Church do maintain constant communion in Christ, but others do not. Some are keenly aware of Christ's presence and power while carrying out their functions of cause, community and corporation, but others are not (see Diagram 6.D).

Thank God for those among us who are always conscious of Christ's presence and praying without ceasing. Unfortunately, however, many committed Christians fit Diagram 6.D, at least part of the time. Sometimes we feel in tune with Christ; at other times, our hearts are far from Him. Some cause-functions—teaching, evangelizing, serving—are done in union with Christ; others are not. Some community functions—counseling, caring, helping—are offered with Christ's love; others are offered with human effort. Some corporation functions—raising funds, making decisions, hiring or firing—are guided by the Spirit; others aren't. The point is that we can walk by the flesh or we can walk by the

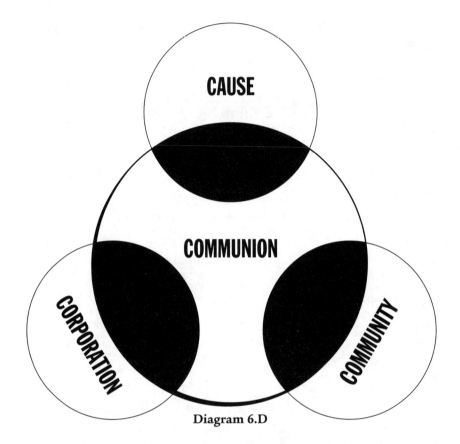

Diagram 6.D

Spirit, and the deeds of the flesh are evident (see Gal. 5:19).

The subtle danger in any church Body is to miss the communion, inspiration and direction from its Head. What a deception to assume that Christ is central while at the same time ignoring Him! Where is Christ—really, not theoretically—in relationship to your church? When visitors come to your church, do they sense His presence? Is He the unseen chairman of your committees? Is He the unseen teacher in your classrooms? Is He the unseen counselor as you seek to help people? Or are you trying to serve Him by your own strength and resources?

A BALANCED PURPOSE

Suppose your people in your church understand the four basic functions of communion, cause, community and corporation and that they execute each function reasonably well, but would like to improve. The first step to help them improve might be to write a balanced purpose statement. The Ministry Model given in Diagram 6.C can help to balance the process if all four functions are considered.

In a Doctor of Ministry class, Neil and I asked the students to write a purpose statement that fit their own church. One of the pastors in the class submitted the following:

> As people of faith, we seek to center our lives on Christ as we take the good news to people in our local and worldwide community and celebrate our relationship as God's children while carefully administering the resources God has bestowed on us.

Notice how the above purpose statement fits the Ministry Model:

Communion:	As people of faith, we seek to center our lives on Christ
Cause:	as we take the good news to people in our local and worldwide community
Community:	and celebrate our relationship as God's children
Corporation:	while carefully administering the resources God has bestowed on us.

The following is a more generic model:

Communion:	As (church name) in living communion with Christ we exist to fulfill
Cause:	the Great Commission and
Community:	the Great Commandment
Corporation:	as biblical stewards of our resources
All four:	to the glory of God.

Some churches may want to write a more specific mission or vision statement just for the cause function. When I was general superintendent of the Evangelical Friends Church Southwest, we adopted the following statement (remember, this is only for the cause and not for any of the other functions):

> We exist to make more friends, and deeper, better friends of our Lord Jesus Christ. Our passion is for everyone in every culture to know Jesus and to know Him better. Our intent is to penetrate the cultures around us, whether at home or abroad, with the life-changing gospel and loving acts of service in the name of our Lord Jesus Christ.

For those who prefer 15 words or fewer, the first 15 words could stand alone!

CRUCIAL PROBLEMS

Having a comprehensive purpose and specific mission in mind, let's apply the Ministry Model even further. Each ministry function—communion, cause, community and corporation—may have unique problems for the local church. Resolution of these problems propels the congregation to greater health and growth. If neglected, these problems result in painful pitfalls.

Conflict

The crucial problem in the communion function is unresolved personal and spiritual conflicts. Genuine repentance and faith in God enables people to live free in Christ. Liberated children of God know who they are "in Christ." What if all the members could say, "In Christ I am a child of God" (see John 1:12)? Clinton E. Arnold, associate professor of New Testament at Talbot School of Theology, wrote the following observation about the Christian's identity:

> We cannot forget that our new identity as Christians is not only individual but also corporate. We have been joined to fellow Christians in the solidarity of a corporate body. Christ has cre-

ated the church as the primary vehicle for his grace to resist and overcome the powers of darkness.[2]

Knowing one's identity and position in Christ, both personally and corporately, is a key foundation for winning the battle for the mind. The personal Steps to Freedom in Christ are helping thousands to win these battles. Neil and I believe the Steps are so important that we require everyone to process them personally before attempting the Steps to Setting Your Church Free (see appendix A), described in the remainder of this book.

Leadership

Moving from the communion function to the cause function of your church, the greatest need will be for godly competent leadership. You will be disappointed if you wait until your church reaches a certain number before you start looking for additional leaders to help you. It won't happen. You train and equip leaders in order to grow and bear fruit. If your church has reached a plateau, you need to improve your leadership so that they can inspire, plan, motivate, enlist and mobilize others for ministry. If your church is declining, your leadership needs to return to their first love. If your church Body is living in "first love" and still declining, you need God-given leadership and outside help.

Stewardship

When people are bearing fruit, the community expands and the quality of community life becomes crucial. People are satisfied when the quality of their relationships and ministry are high. People will be more satisfied if they do a few things well rather than if they do a lot of mediocre things. This is the plight of small struggling churches. Everybody is stretched thin because there aren't enough workers to fill all the slots. The same holds true for relationships. Proverbs 18:24 reads, "A man of too many friends comes to ruin, but there is a friend who sticks closer than a brother" (NASB). Nobody needs a lot of superficial relationships, but we all need a few good ones.

People may be dissatisfied with many things, but solving their dis-satisfactions seldom leaves them satisfied. Responding to their complaints will not guarantee satisfaction, because what they complain about usually is unrelated to what it takes to satisfy them. Jesus said, "Blessed are those who hunger and thirst for righteousness, for they shall be satisfied" (Matt. 5:6, *NASB*). They will be satisfied only when they have resolved their personal and spiritual conflicts and start living in a righteous relationship with God and others.

Christians are more committed when they are satisfied, and they give more because they are getting more return for their investment. Why do people continue to give to dying ministries that aren't bearing any fruit? That is poor stewardship. Grace-giving is an investment in the kingdom of God that results in eternal rewards. A church that is faithful in its stewardship and wise in its money management will have stability and longevity. The church that neglects its finances will severely limit its potential for ministry. The right staff will always pay for themselves if they are bearing fruit. Money invested in righteous people has the best return.

Great Opportunities

People tend to value and relate to one or two of the ministry functions more than the others. Community people meet together while corporation people meet in committees and cause people are busy doing things. Communion people pray that God will bless all of them. A balanced ministry offers opportunities for every gifted person, as shown in Diagram 6.E. Different ministries require different gifts and talents. When all are working in balance, you learn to appreciate one another more and "look not only to your own interests, but also to the interests of others" (Phil. 2:4).

Most churches have enough programs and opportunities for ministry. What is most often lacking is communion. How can you become more intentional about making communion with Christ your first priority? Here are a few suggestions that you may want to consider:

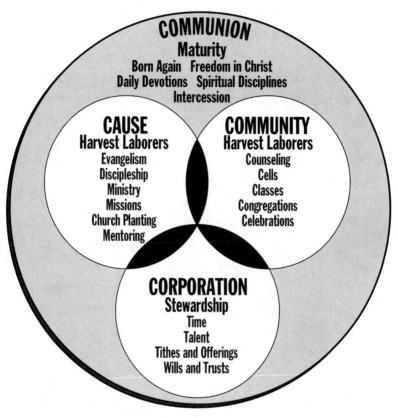

Diagram 6.E

1. Have worship services that focus on the person and finished work of Christ more than the performance of the musicians and preacher. God is the audience, not the congregation. The New Testament is balanced perfectly between the indicative (what Christ has already accomplished) and the imperative (how we should respond). Worship should celebrate the finished work of Christ, communicate who we already are in Him so we can rest in the finished work of Christ, and then instruct us how to live out our salvation as children of God.

2. Preach and teach the whole gospel, including who we are in Christ. Knowing who we are in Christ is the basis for a proper sense of worth (see *Overcoming a Negative Self-Image* by Neil Anderson, Regal Books, 2003). No person can consistently

behave in a way that is inconsistent with what he or she believes about himself or herself.

3. Guide the people in your church to personal freedom in Christ. Faith without repentance leads to stagnation of personal growth and ministry. Christians who have not resolved their personal and spiritual conflicts do not grow, and they bear no fruit.

4. Appoint a prayer coordinator for every board, committee and member of the ministry staff. The task is to stimulate prayer before, during and after meetings or ministry events. We should never plan and then ask God to bless our plans. We should always start with prayer and seek together what His plan is for our church.

5. Help marriage partners become one in Christ. A divided marriage is a divided home and a hindrance to community (see *The Christ Centered Marriage* by Neil Anderson and Charles Mylander, Regal Books, 1996).

6. Free your corporate Body from its past. Choose a wise, godly Christian leader who will lead your pastors, elders and governing board through the Steps to Setting Your Church Free.

7. Follow through with diligence on the last two steps of the Setting Your Church Free event. Pray the Prayer Action Plan (see chapter 11) consistently and faithfully, and carry it out!

AN ILLUSTRATION

Some churches have pursued putting the communion function first. They have taken steps to set their people, their marriages and their ministries free in Christ. Consider Pastor Brent, who understands the four functions of communion, cause, community and corporation, and the corresponding functions of saint, prophet, priest and king. He uses the Ministry Model for strengthening his ministry and for building up the Body of Christ as follows:

- He models what he has learned (saint) and demonstrates it in the church's communion.
- He preaches and teaches it as a communicator (prophet) and makes it the church's cause.
- He coaches and encourages it as a caregiver (priest) and builds it into the church's community.
- He motivates and organizes it as a leader (king) and develops it in the church's corporation.

Pastor Brent first modeled freedom in Christ in his own life. Along with a fellow pastor, Pastor Brent worked through The Steps to Freedom in Christ and found the process soul-searching, uplifting and helpful. With a fresh sense of freedom in his own soul, he wanted to share these truths with his congregation. He fervently longed for personal freedom for his people and corporate freedom for the church. He became an example of the believer for the communion function of the church.

Pastor Brent preached through the book of Ephesians, helping the congregation understand their identity and position in Christ and the spiritual battle that threatens to divide them. At the same time, the adult Sunday Schools and home groups were going through the "Beta, the Next Step in Discipleship" study, which is based on Neil's books *Victory Over the Darkness* (Regal Books, 2000) and *The Bondage Breaker* (Harvest House, 2000). Beta teaches who we are in Christ, how to walk by faith, and how our mind, emotions and will function together as we walk by the Spirit. The course also gives people the opportunity to go through The Steps to Freedom in Christ.

At the same time, the youth leaders in Pastor Brent's church were teaching material from *Stomping Out the Darkness* (Regal Books, 1999, the youth version of *Victory Over the Darkness*) and *The Bondage Breaker: Youth Edition* (Harvest House, 2001). Many of the young people discovered for the first time who they are in Christ and how to resolve their personal and spiritual conflicts.

Pastor Brent began to lead others through The Steps to Freedom in Christ. Those who sincerely wanted help found amazing breakthroughs.

In time, he began to notice a pattern. People who saw the Steps as a shortcut or a pat-answer formula received little lasting help, but those who saw it as a way to seek God with all their hearts moved rapidly toward a renewed mind and a transformed heart. Pastor Brent also began to realize that there were too many people who needed help and that he couldn't do it alone. So he prayerfully selected 12 mature Christians who were inclined to help others and trained them to do discipleship counseling.

Pastor Brent asked these participants for a commitment of 16 weeks. In the first four weeks, he had them read *Victory Over the Darkness* and its corresponding study guide. During weekly meetings, the participants watched the video series *Resolving Personal Conflicts*. In the next four weeks, they read *The Bondage Breaker* and its corresponding study guide, and watched the video series *Resolving Spiritual Conflicts*. In the final eight weeks, they read *Discipleship Counseling* (Regal Books, 2003) and *Released from Bondage* (Nelson Books, 2002), and watched the video series *Discipleship Counseling*. This training constitutes Freedom in Christ Ministries' basic training for discipleship counseling.

Seeing the transformation in people's lives, Pastor Brent began to use *Beta: The Next Step in Discipleship* in both the membership class and the new believers' class. The community function of the church took on a refreshing spiritual depth in Christ.

Pastor Brent sensed new life in the congregation, but he also was aware that many corporate issues had not been addressed. His district superintendent knew some of the difficulties the church had faced in the past and suggested that they consider going through the Steps to Setting Your Church Free. He talked to his board and they liked the idea, so they found a mutually satisfactory date when they could all attend. Just before the date, however, one board member had to go out of town. The seminar leader suggested they shouldn't proceed without everyone present, so they rescheduled.

On the designated weekend, they were all present and each one of them had personally worked through The Steps to Freedom in Christ. Working through the corporate steps took about seven hours. The leaders experienced some difficult moments as they recalled painful memories from the past, but they worked through it and collectively forgave those who had caused the pain. The interaction, prayers and insights were eye-opening. With the Holy Spirit's guidance, the group identified their strengths, weaknesses and corporate sins.

They were all amazed at the accuracy of insight into the spiritual condition of the church. Pastor Brent knew that some of these problems were around, but now they were out in the open. The group experienced a sense of unity about what the problems were and what to do about them. It was almost as if Jesus had written something similar to the seven letters in Revelation (see Rev. 2—3) exclusively for their church. It was what they needed to know if they were going to turn the ministry around.

WHAT'S NEXT?

The remaining chapters explain the Steps to Setting Your Church Free process. They provide the theological basis for corporate conflict resolution and how that conflict can be resolved. Just like going through the individual Steps to Freedom in Christ, there is nothing to lose by going through the corporate process—but you may have a lot to gain. Processing the Steps to Setting Your Church Free is only part of a larger whole. You may simply find your church cleaner and healthier for a while. Repentance is only a beginning, but it makes possible the growth that can and should follow. All the programs and ministries will be far more effective if repentance is genuine and complete. Take the time to read Revelation chapters 2 and 3 before you read the rest of this book.

Notes
1. Jim Dethmer, "Moving in the Right Circles," *Leadership Journal: A Practical Journal for Church Leaders* (Fall Quarter, 1992), pp. 86-91.
2. Clinton E. Arnold, *Powers of Darkness: Principalities and Powers in Paul's Letters* (Downers Grove, IL: InterVarsity Press, 1992), p. 213.

LOOKING AT YOUR CHURCH'S STRENGTHS AND WEAKNESSES

Chapter 7

(Steps 1 and 2 in the Setting Your Church Free Event)

What if Jesus wrote a letter to your church like He did to the seven churches in Asia (see Rev. 1–3)? What would He commend or compliment you for? What would He describe as your greatest strengths? What weaknesses would He point out with the intention of giving you the grace to correct them? What discipline could you expect if you failed to obey? Do you want Him to write your church a letter? Would you read it?

Each letter written to the seven churches in Asia ends with the same statement: "He who has an ear, let him hear what the Spirit says to the churches." We can know with certainty that God is speaking to His churches. But are we listening? Unless all the leaders are perfectly hearing from the Lord, no church will have a letter from Jesus with the same Scriptural authority, but they should be able to discern His will if they are rightly related to Him.

JESUS KNOWS

Our Lord Jesus Christ was and is present in every local church. He perfectly knows everything—all the strengths and all the weaknesses. He usually began His letters to the seven churches by mentioning their strengths, unless they were prideful. In such cases, He begins with their weaknesses. To every one of the seven churches He said, "I know."

I know your deeds, your hard work and your perseverance. I know that you cannot tolerate wicked men (to Ephesus, Rev. 2:2).

I know your afflictions and your poverty—yet you are rich! I know the slander (to Smyrna, Rev. 2:9).

I know where you live—where Satan has his throne. Yet you remain true to my name (to Pergamum, Rev. 2:13).

I know your deeds, your love and faith, your service and perseverance, and that you are now doing more than you did at first (to Thyatira, Rev. 2:19).

I know your deeds; you have a reputation of being alive, but you are dead (to Sardis, Rev. 3:1).

I know your deeds. . . . I know that you have little strength, yet you have kept my word and have not denied my name (to Philadelphia, Rev. 3:8).

I know your deeds, that you are neither cold nor hot (to Laodicea, Rev. 3:14).

The personal pronoun "I" is present at least 50 times in these seven short letters to the churches. "I" refers to Jesus. Concerning His Church, we know that:

Jesus feels:	"I hold this against you: You have forsaken your first love" (Rev. 2:4; see also 3:15).
Jesus threatens:	"If you do not repent, I will come to you and remove your lampstand from its place" (Rev. 2:5; see also 2:21-22; 3:3).
Jesus promises:	"To him who overcomes, I will give" (Rev. 2:7; also see each of the letters).
Jesus predicts:	"I tell you, the devil will put some of you in prison" (Rev. 2:10).
Jesus rebukes:	"I have a few things against you: You have people there who hold to the teaching of Balaam" (Rev. 2:14).
Jesus judges:	"I am he who searches hearts and minds, and I will repay each of you according to your deeds" (Rev. 2:23).
Jesus acts:	"I have placed before you an open door that no one can shut. . . . I will make them come and fall down at your feet and acknowledge" (Rev. 3:8-9).
Jesus prophesies:	"I am coming soon" (Rev. 3:11).
Jesus counsels:	"I counsel you to buy from me gold refined in the fire, so you can become rich" (Rev. 3:18).
Jesus loves:	"Those whom I love" (Rev. 3:19).
Jesus disciplines:	"I rebuke and discipline" (Rev. 3:19).
Jesus is here:	"Here I am! I stand at the door and knock. If anyone hears my voice and opens the door, I will come in and eat with him, and he with me" (Rev. 3:20).

When you go to church next Sunday, when you meet with your Christian friends during the week, when you talk with another believer, when you think no one notices, when God seems far away—Jesus is there. When you meet for the Setting Your Church Free event, the risen Lord Jesus will be in you and among you. Jesus is present. By His written Word and by the leading of His Holy Spirit, He will enable you to discern His message to your church.

During the Setting Your Church Free event, each person needs to be sensitive to God's leading. We are to hear with the full intention of obeying. If He allows the leaders in your church to agree on their discernment of what Jesus is saying, will you treat it as a letter from Him?

A CLEAR VISION

Before we consider the process of setting your church free, we need to examine the biblical basis. The seven letters from Jesus in Revelation are built upon the insights and truths from a vivid vision given to the apostle John on the island of Patmos. John was in exile on this rock quarry island "because of the word of God and the testimony of Jesus" (Rev. 1:9). As the *Contemporary English Version* puts it, "We suffer because Jesus is our king, but he gives us the strength to endure. I was sent to Patmos Island, because I had preached God's message and had told about Jesus."

In Revelation 1:9-20, John received a vision from an angel (see v. 1) of the resurrected and ruling Christ. The symbolism seems strange to us, but the overall meaning is clear to careful Bible scholars who compare this vision with earlier ones given in the Old Testament. Bible expositor, Earl F. Palmer, writes:

John's vision brings to mind many Old Testament messianic phrases and images: *"Son of Man"* is a messianic phrase from Daniel (7:13); the white wool is found in Daniel 7:9 and the flame of fire in Daniel 10:6; the sound of water is from Ezekiel 43:2 and the sword from Isaiah 49:2. Though the name of our Lord does not appear in this description, it is clear that Jesus is the One whom John has seen. " . . . I died, and behold I am alive for evermore . . ." (Rev. 1:18, *RSV*). In the vision, John is assured of the reign of Jesus Christ, even over death and the place of death (Hades).[1]

In simple terms, the vision tells us that Jesus is alive and exalted to the highest place of authority. He has conquered His enemies, including the evil powers of darkness. The goddess *Hekate*, according to the pagans, was said to hold "the keys to Hades."[2] Because Jesus now holds them in His hand, He is the conqueror of the evil powers.

Jesus is pure, powerful and full of radiant glory. He possesses all the attributes of God. Yet He is present with His people and closely attentive to His churches. Bible teacher G. Campbell Morgan gives us a colorful word picture of what the vision teaches about the risen Lord Jesus:

> Take this picture and look at it again and again until the vision holds you in its marvelous power. His head and His hair white like wool, His purity and His eternity; His eyes like a flame of fire, His intimate knowledge, penetrating and piercing; His feet like burnished brass, signifying the procedure of strength and purity; His voice like the voice of many waters, a concord of perfect tones; in His hand seven stars, His administrative right, power and protection; from His mouth a sharp two-edged sword, keen and accurate verdicts concerning His people; His whole countenance as the sun, creating day, flashing light, bathing all the landscape with beauty.[3]

THE SEVEN LAMPSTANDS

The vision of the glorified Christ, once crucified but now resurrected and reigning full of purity and power, includes two more symbols that the Lord Himself singles out for special attention. John's first glimpse in his vision was of the "seven golden lampstands, and *among* the lampstands was someone 'like a son of man'" (Rev. 1:12-13, emphasis added).

At the end of the vision the meaning is given: "The seven lampstands are the seven churches" (Rev. 1:20). Jesus, the Son of man, "*walks* among the seven golden lampstands" (Rev. 2:1, emphasis added).

The same Jesus who is revealed in the vision as awesome in power and the conqueror of death and Hades is carefully inspecting His churches. The all-powerful, glorious Jesus is walking up and down the aisles of your church. He is observing, encouraging, rebuking, asking for change, motivating, promising rewards and warning of judgments.

When churches die or lapse into ineffectiveness, we tend to think the problem lies in poor attendance and financial problems, lack of leadership or dysfunctional patterns of infighting. We seldom consider the biblical truth that the living Christ may be carrying out His judgments: "If you do not repent, I will come to you and remove your lampstand from its place" (Rev. 2:5). When churches flourish, launch effective ministries that bring many to Christ, build up their people in Christ and serve the needy in Christ's name, we tend to praise the pastor for outstanding leadership and good preaching. We look to committed lay leaders in these churches with respect and admiration. They are planting and watering, but Jesus is the One who is causing the growth. In the seven letters to the churches in Revelation, Jesus promises a reward "to him who overcomes."

THE SEVEN STARS

Another symbol that Jesus Christ singles out for special attention is the seven stars. Jesus explains it like this: "The seven stars are the angels of the seven churches" (Rev. 1:20). Note here that the angels are just as literal as the churches. In others words, just as the lampstands represent churches, the stars represent angels. The angels are not the symbols, but rather the explanation of the symbols. It is our belief that they are real angels, not symbols for human messengers.

Angels Are Really There
Many Christians believe in guardian angels for children based on Jesus' statement in Matthew 18:10. Every Christmas we read about the angel

Gabriel appearing to Mary, and every Easter we read about the angels that appeared at the empty tomb. Jesus spoke often about angels, and the New Testament often refers to angels. Angels appear 51 times in the Synoptic Gospels, 21 times in Acts and 67 times in Revelation. Combined with other New Testament references to angels, the total is 175. Combined with the Old Testament, the total is almost 300! The Son of God always stands above the angels (see Mark 13:27; Phil. 2:9-11; Heb. 1:4-14).

New Age practitioners encourage contact with angels as spiritual mentors. Undoubtedly these are the fallen kind of angels the Bible warns against. A book such as *Ask Your Angels* promoted by Ballantine Books, one of New York's biggest publishers, is immersed in the occult and New Age.

> The authors present the channeled wisdom of Abigrael, a genderless being they claim was sent to instruct them. They also lead New Age-flavored workshops on getting in touch with "celestials" and aligning with "angelic energy fields." Conversing with angels, they write, is another "divination tool." Knowing that many readers face major decisions, the authors give instructions on making a deck of "Angel Oracle" cards.[4]

The apostle Paul warned the Corinthians about "a different spirit from the one you received" and stated flatly that "Satan himself masquerades as an angel of light" (2 Cor. 11:4,14). As mentioned earlier, the Bible also warns about demons who teach: "The Spirit clearly says that in later times some will abandon the faith and follow deceiving spirits and things taught by demons" (1 Tim. 4:1). The part about abandoning the faith ought to cause sober reflection on the part of every Christian and every church. This is a clear and present danger! It is all the more so in an age that actively promotes New Age and occultic themes in medicine, education, business and children's entertainment.

Deception is the adversary's primary strategy. In the book of Revelation, words such as "deceive," "deceives" and "deceived" occur often in relationship to Satan's activity (see Rev. 12:9; 13:14; 19:20;

20:3,8,10). Sometimes the *New International Version* translates the original Greek word into "led astray" or "deluded," but the meaning is the same. Twice in the book of Revelation, holy angels insist that John should not worship them; he should worship only God (see Rev. 19:10; 22:9). Paul also goes so far as to say that anyone who delights in the worship of angels is disqualified from God's prize and loses connection with the head—namely, Christ (see Col. 2:18-19).

How can we know whether we are following the Holy Spirit or paying attention to a deceiving spirit? We regularly come across people in counseling who are being deceived, and when they are led astray, they blame God! Spiritual counterfeits abound in churches that lack spiritual discernment and sound doctrine. (For more information, see Neil's book *Finding God's Will in Spiritually Deceptive Times,* Harvest House Publishers, 2003).

The Angels of the Churches

What is the ministry of holy angels? Andrew J. Bandstra, professor emeritus of New Testament at Calvin Theological Seminary in Grand Rapids, Michigan, summarizes five ways the Bible describes the work of angels:

1. Angels are God's messengers;
2. Angels praise God;
3. Angels exercise God's providential care;
4. Angels encourage Christian obedience;
5. Angels carry out God's justice.[5]

All of the letters from Jesus to the churches in Revelation (and to us) are addressed to the angels of the churches. For example, the first letter begins, "To the angel of the church in Ephesus" (Rev. 2:1), and all the other letters have similar headings. The angels are not mentioned in any other way in the seven letters. Further, it is clear that the letters are written to the churches from the risen Christ who is identified with the Holy Spirit. So why do we believe that the angels mentioned in Revelation 2 and 3 are real angels assigned to the churches—supernatural beings of the same nature as the holy angels that have appeared throughout Scripture?

In the original Greek language of the New Testament, the word "angel" can be translated either "messenger" or "angel." Some have thought that each letter was addressed to an overseer, the human messenger of the Church. This is a possible interpretation, but it does not fit the context of the book of Revelation. Throughout Revelation, angels are always real angels and never symbols for human messengers.

The best test of a text is its context. The use of the word "angel" in these passages should be consistent with how the word is used in the rest of the book of Revelation. "Probably 'the angels of the churches' (Rev. 1:20; 2:1, etc.) are really angels and not pastors," writes Hans Bietenhard in the scholarly *New International Dictionary of New Testament Theology*.[6]

Another theory is that "angel" means the personification of the prevailing spirit of the church people.[7] This interpretation fits neither the context nor the statement in Revelation 1:16 that Jesus holds the stars (angels) in His right hand. In the imagery of Scripture, the right hand is the sign of authority and power. God uses it to take action. When Jesus holds the angels in His right hand, it indicates that they are His executive agents or heavenly soldiers, ready to carry out His orders.

The risen and reigning Lord Jesus has already issued orders to His heavenly hosts (His angels) concerning His churches, including yours. His angels are poised, ready to carry out the orders of their commander in chief. They will administer rewards or judgments in light of His Word. The United States and United Nations have peacekeeping forces in many third world countries. Picture your church's angel as a huge United States soldier. The soldier is armed with weaponry capable of destroying any opposition and already has orders to shoot, even to kill, under certain conditions spelled out by the commander. Yet the soldier is escorting a truck loaded with food, clothes and the essentials of life. The soldier comes to bring life, not death. The soldier's mission is to save lives, not to destroy lives.

So it is with the angels of the churches. No angel takes the place of the commander, Jesus. The Lord Himself moves among His churches.

He initiates. He is at work in your church. He knows everything that is happening, all that is tolerated and every attitude that is displayed. He encourages and warns His churches. When a church obeys Him, angels hand out Christ's rewards. When a church disobeys Him, angels mete out Christ's judgments. We dare not play church. Jesus will not put up with continued indulgence in either personal or corporate sins. Jesus is far more concerned about church purity than church growth, because He knows that church purity is a prerequisite for church growth. He can't do His best work through a dirty vessel.

From the right hand of Christ, angels are ready to be released upon your church with rewards or punishments. It all depends on your church's response to Christ's Word. His Word is a two-edged sword, bringing blessing or judgment. He will bring conviction, grant repentance and guide us into all truth that will liberate His people and His church. Jesus expects church leaders to deal with false prophets and teachers, resist the infiltration of the adversary and obey Him, no matter the cost.

The risen Christ is still moving among His churches and He still holds their angels in His right hand. What was true for the seven churches of Revelation is true for all of Christ's churches for all time. Based on Revelation 1–3, your church might well have an angel assigned to it by our sovereign Lord Jesus. That is encouraging!

The angels of the churches are only one means by which the Lord Jesus Christ and the Holy Spirit work within your congregation. God never contradicts or bypasses His Word. He indwells every believer. In light of Jesus' close involvement in your church, it is imperative that your church seeks God's specific will for its local Body of believers and responds in faith. The grave danger is to ignore or to not even be aware of His presence. If you neglect and disobey, you can expect judgment to come.

PREPARING FOR THE PROCESS

We will return to the study of Revelation 2–3 and other passages as they give biblical background for the various steps. At this point, we will focus on the process for discerning your "letter from Jesus." The goal of this process will be to discern your church's strengths, weaknesses, memories that bless or bind, corporate sins and attacks from the evil one. A Prayer Action Plan (see chapter 11) can then be used to give direction for the church leadership.

Who should participate in the Setting Your Church Free event? This process is for the representative leaders of the church, not all of the people. We recommend participation by all of the pastoral staff and the members of the governing board or its equivalent. It helps in follow-through if the group has the primary role of leadership and already meets together on a regular basis. One or two key decision makers who do not presently hold office should be included as well. Sometimes it is helpful to invite past leaders who have a longer history with the church and are respected by the congregation.

You should strive for 100 percent participation by the governing body and all the ordained pastoral staff. You should consider postponing the event if key members cannot attend. The process works best when every member is present; it is greatly weakened if even one member is missing. When every leader participates, unity and ownership of the outcome builds. There is also less chance for misunderstandings and criticism if all are present. Confession and forgiveness take place in the process, and every church leader needs to experience this corporate cleansing.

Those who are opposed to this process usually have something to hide. Controllers and manipulators will be exposed if the rest are true shepherds. Nobody enjoys chasing off the spiritual wolves, but if you don't, you are just as wrong as they are. If you let a sick person control your church, the Lord Jesus is not controlling it, and you cannot let that happen. This is one reason why we recommend that an unbiased outside facilitator guide your church leadership through these steps. It might be a retired pastor, a denominational official or a capable leader from a nearby church. The senior pastor should be part of the process, but not be the facilitator. Qualifications for the facilitator include the biblical requirements for elders and deacons (see 1 Tim. 3:1-13; Titus 1:6-9).

The facilitator will want to process the personal Steps to Freedom in

Christ and be aware of the basics of resolving spiritual conflicts. If possible, find someone who understands group dynamics and has experience in working with church leaders. Although this is the ideal, it is important to note that the process almost carries itself and is not especially difficult to facilitate. The spiritual qualifications of the facilitator are the most vital to the process.

Prayer Power

Each participant must experience personal freedom in Christ before engaging in the corporate event. We also recommend a day of fasting and prayer by pastors, elders and anyone else who is willing to seek God's best before the event. Some may want to meet together the evening before the event for prayer. Consider asking prayer partners to intercede for this time together. Nearly every church has one or two faithful intercessors, so ask these prayer warriors to seek the Lord's face for this day together. The greater the prayer, the more lasting the benefits.

Scheduling

You cannot lead any faster than you can educate. It is important that pastors and teachers help prepare leaders and the congregation for spiritual renewal. As mentioned in the illustration in the last chapter, you should have the adult Sunday School and/or small groups go through the "Beta, the Next Step in Discipleship" study with the pastoral staff and lay leadership. Personal freedom is an essential prerequisite for corporate freedom. It helps greatly if the participants have already read this book (a video/audio series on Setting Your Church Free is also available from Freedom in Christ Ministries). A Friday evening and all-day Saturday format is the ideal schedule. Friday evening can be used for worship and prayer. If any of the leaders have not yet gone through The Steps to Freedom in Christ, Friday evening is the time to do so.

You should plan at least eight hours for the actual event. Many churches set aside two full days. Remind all the participants not to schedule anything immediately following the event on Saturday. The event sometimes goes longer than anticipated, and it is harmful to the process when the leaders have to leave early. Some groups enjoy a fellowship meal together at the close of this time.

Preparing the Room

Select a comfortable room with a lot of open wall space that has restrooms nearby. Check to make sure that heating or cooling keeps the room comfortable for the participants. The room will need to be large enough for tables and chairs. The ideal setting is for the participants to be seated on three sides of a large table, with the open side toward a blank wall. Use self-adhesive, large sized paper on the front wall. During breaks, some of the members can add more sheets as the process continues. You will probably need a total of 15 or 16 large sheets of paper. Bring a supply of fresh marker pens. Try them out to make sure they are not bleeding through the paper and onto the wall.

Poster or butcher paper is preferable to overhead projectors or chalkboards. Paper and marker pens leave a permanent record (in case the recorder missed something or abbreviated or paraphrased items that were discussed). The facilitator should write large enough for everyone to easily see. If enough wall space is not available up front, some of the sheets can be moved to another part of the room until they are needed at the close of the process.

Food for the Hungry

It is often wise to begin the actual Setting Your Church Free event after a simple but healthy breakfast on Saturday morning. Avoid taking too long with meals or making it a social event. Most groups will want to have light refreshments available for breaks, although some maintain a fast for the seven to nine hours of the process and then enjoy a meal together afterward. If a Saturday lunch is served, keep it light and as short as possible (some simply bring in sandwiches or salads). Trying to discern God's will after a big meal in the middle of the day is like fighting to stay awake during a less than inspiring sermon after a lousy night's sleep.

Day of the Event

When the group gathers for the event, it is wise to begin with prayer and Bible study. Follow the prayers and suggestions given in appendix A. During the initial prayer time, we find it helpful to begin with a renewal prayer. The participants pray it once silently and then out loud together:

Dear heavenly Father,

Open my eyes to see Your truth. Give me ears to hear and a compelling desire to respond in faith to what the Lord Jesus Christ has already done for me.

I confess Jesus Christ—crucified, risen, reigning and returning—as my one and only Lord and Savior. I renounce any past involvement with non-Christian religions or experiences. I announce that Christ died on the cross for me and for my sins and rose again bodily from the dead for my justification.

I confess that the Lord Jesus Christ rescued me from the dominion of darkness and transferred me into His Kingdom of light. I renounce Satan in all his works and all his ways. I announce that Jesus Christ is my Lord, Savior, teacher and friend. I give myself to obey everything that He commanded. I yield myself fully to Christ to do whatever He wants me to do, to be whatever He wants me to be, to give up whatever He wants me to give up, to give away whatever He wants me to give away, to become whatever He wants me to become.

I confess, reject, renounce and utterly disown every sin in which I have ever been involved. I announce that in Christ I have received redemption, the forgiveness of sins. I accept His reconciliation to the heavenly Father and welcome peace with God.

As an expression of my faith of Christ's forgiveness of me, I forgive every person who has ever hurt, abused or taken advantage of me. I let them off my hook and let God settle the score as the final judge who metes out perfect justice.

I open all the doors of my life to the Lord Jesus Christ and ask Him to take control of every part of my being. I gladly accept the filling of the Holy Spirit into every part of my life. I surrender myself to live in union with the Lord Jesus Christ from this moment until I stand before the judgment seat of Christ and hear my name read from the Lamb's Book of Life.

Thank You, heavenly Father, for uniting me with the Lord Jesus Christ and with all those who truly belong to You and live under Your gracious reign.

I pray in the powerful name of Jesus. Amen.

We find that this printed prayer is a simple yet powerful way to begin. It leads the participants to renew their commitment to Christ. It contains many of the essential elements of the personal Steps to Freedom in Christ. If church leaders have been well taught on these issues, they feel comfortable with this prayer. If they have not, it introduces them to some needed biblical concepts.

Processing the corporate steps to freedom is not business as usual. You cannot allow yourselves to settle into routine patterns of behavior. To move out of your comfort zone in a meaningful way, take the next step in prayer. Engage in a form of prayer that is not your church's usual custom. For instance, in many countries Christians pray out loud, all together, at the same time. If you have not done this before, stand in a circle holding hands, praying aloud at the same time. Ask the Lord to fill you personally with His Holy Spirit, to guide you and your church, and to protect you from the evil one. Claim Christ's resources against Satan and his evil forces. Conclude this time with the Lord's Prayer. If this is customary for your group, find a way to pray that is not your usual practice. If the facilitator is at ease in leading the group into another style of praying, the participants will find it interesting and faith stretching. Praying to God in a new style may well open your hearts and minds to look for new insights from God later on.

DISCERNING THE LORD'S PERSPECTIVE

The facilitator has the responsibility of explaining the process and making sure that each participant has a copy of the Steps to Setting Your Church Free (see appendix A). The facilitator must be sensitive to the group's dynamics and not let one or two individuals dominate the discussion. He or she should appoint someone to be a secretary who will record on notebook paper what is written on the poster sheets up front. This saves much time later on, as well as possible misunderstanding.

The facilitator writes on the sheets on the wall. A good tip in writing down the lists under each step is to use the actual words of the person who makes the suggestion. People feel heard when their thoughts are listed in their own words. If their description is too wordy to write out, the facilitator can simply request, "Can you say that again in fewer or different words so that I can jot it down?"

Every person should feel free to share without judgment or disagreement from others. The process will weed out what is not necessary or helpful. In the last four steps, however, the group needs to come to consensus.

PRAYING AND LISTENING

Each step begins with a group prayer, asking the Lord for guidance. For example, the following is the beginning prayer for step 1:

Dear heavenly Father,

Thank You for calling and choosing us as shepherds of the flock and servant leaders in Your Church. Thank You for this church and what You have done through it. Thank You for the people who worship and serve You here.

Show us what the living Lord Jesus commends in our church. Remind us of what we are doing right and the strengths You have given to our church. As we wait silently before You, show us our good works that glorify our Father in heaven [see Matt. 5:16].

After repeating this written prayer out loud together, spend a few moments in silent prayer. All the participants should ask the Lord to impress upon their minds the strengths of the church—those things the church is doing right. After two or three minutes of silence, the facilitator closes the time by praying audibly. In later steps, participation and variety are added so that two people are named to close the time in prayer. When both people have prayed, the group knows that it is time to begin listing what the Lord impressed on their minds and hearts. Each of the steps follows a similar process.

Listing Strengths

Step 1 has two parts. In the first part, the facilitator asks the group to list the church's strengths as the Holy Spirit brings them to their minds. No church is doing everything right nor everything well, yet every church that calls upon the name of the Lord is doing many things right. It is easier to face our weaknesses and corporate sins if we have already identified our strengths. Encourage all the participants to identify as many strengths of the church as possible.

For example, one small church came up with this short list of strengths:

- Pastor
- Worship
- Desire to do what's right
- Feeling of togetherness
- Adaptable, flexible
- Committed to having church
- Loving fellowship
- Truth
- Intolerance of false teaching
- Intolerance of sexual immorality
- Music
- Children's sermons
- Sense of family
- Dedicated core group
- Current leadership
- Denominational support
- Openness
- God's Spirit

LOOKING AT YOUR CHURCH'S STRENGTHS AND WEAKNESSES   151

Some churches will fill two or three poster sheets with strengths. When the group begins to fall silent because no more ideas are being given, the facilitator can say, "What else comes to mind? What other strengths has God given us? What are we doing right?" The additional questions often encourage the timid to speak and satisfy the whole group that most of the strengths are listed. The facilitator also can tell the group that it is fine to add other items to the strengths list if they come to mind later on during the day.

Listing Greatest Strengths
The second part of step 1 takes place after all of the strengths are listed. The facilitator asks the group to summarize the greatest strengths that God has given to the church. Good questions to ask here are, What are the things we always do best? What works for us every time? How has God uniquely gifted us as a church Body? Keep this list short and have only the greatest strengths identified. The list should be limited to five to seven items, unless the church is very large.

The facilitator then writes the greatest strengths on the poster board, beginning each one with "We thank God for . . . " These statements should be stated in complete sentences and saved for the final summary in the Prayer Action Plan (step 6). Here is a typical list that was drawn from several actual churches:

1. We thank God for a dedicated pastoral staff and other servant leaders.
2. We thank God for meaningful worship through fine music, the power of prayer and good preaching.
3. We thank God for a strong unity in Christ that creates a close family feeling and loving relationships.
4. We thank God for a strong and active children's ministry.
5. We thank God for a fine facility in a good location that gives us great potential.
6. We thank God for a core group of people who are faithful and dedicated to service.

7. We thank God that Christ is put first and the Bible is taught.

Each step concludes by praying a written prayer in unison. As an example, here is the group prayer for step 1:

Dear heavenly Father,

Thank You for the strengths You have given to us and to our church. Thank You for gracing us with Your presence and for working through the gifts, talents and service of Your people. We bow in gratitude for the ways that You have ministered through our church. We know that apart from Christ we can do nothing. We gladly acknowledge that every good and perfect gift is from above.

Continue to equip us to be good stewards of these strengths, as well as responsible managers of all the relationships and resources You have given us. In Jesus Christ our Lord we pray. Amen.

Listing Weaknesses

Step 2 begins the process of identifying the church's weaknesses. Patterns will emerge after looking at painful memories and corporate sins, so the goal for this step is not to determine the greatest weaknesses, as was done with the strengths. Instead, the objective is simply to let everyone state what they sense from the Lord—what they sense from their perspective.

The procedure for this step follows the same format as step 1. The group prays the printed prayer together, and then they spend a couple of minutes in silent prayer, asking the Lord to impress upon their hearts the weaknesses of the church. One or two of the participants, or the facilitator, can close this time with a spoken prayer.

The facilitator then encourages everyone to express an opinion. This is not a time for any objection or defensiveness from others. Absolute accuracy is not essential this early in the process. It is at this point that the first signs of discomfort begin within the group. The Setting Your Church Free process may be emotionally draining and spiritually taxing for some. If some of the contributions feel like criticisms, try not to be defensive. The facilitator, of course, will make sure that everyone focus-es on issues, not personalities. Some may experience ill feelings toward others who state weaknesses that seem to point a finger at them. Some may sense mental disturbances or a desire to leave. This type of interfer-ence is common in personal counseling, although it seems more rare among groups of leaders who have already experienced their own free-dom in Christ.

The facilitator can alert the group to the possibility of internal inter-ference and encourage them to share it. Usually, simply exposing such thoughts and feelings to the group will move them out of hiding and into the light of disclosure. Most often the honesty and openness will put a stop to the internal interference. If not, the facilitator may need to stop and pray against such opposition.

Few groups have a problem coming up with a list of weaknesses. In most groups, the list will be somewhat longer than the list of strengths. If some member of the group mentions this fact, which is not uncom-mon, the facilitator can simply ask, "Have we overlooked any strengths?" It is sometimes reassuring to tell the participants that most groups of church leaders see more weaknesses than strengths. The church is not abnormal for taking an honest look at its shortcomings, faults and flaws.

If the pace is normal, the group is now ready for its second break. The fellowship time is important for a relief in the concentration. When the strengths and weaknesses of the church are listed for all to see, the stage is set to dig deeper. We will focus more and more on Christ as the process continues. The next chapter deals with church memories, both good and bad.

Notes

1. Earl F. Palmer, "1, 2, 3 John, Revelation," Lloyd J. Ogilvie, ed., *The Communicator's Commentary* (Dallas: WORD Inc., 1982), p. 122.
2. Clinton E. Arnold, *Powers of Darkness: Principalities and Powers in Paul's Letters* (Downers Grove, IL: InterVarsity Press, 1992), p. 108; Craig Keener also cites the pagan gods of Hades, namely *Pluto* and *Anibus*, who hold these keys in Revelation, *The NIV Application Commentary* (Grand Rapids, MI: Zondervan Publishing House, 2000), p. 97.

3. G. Campbell Morgan, *The Letters of Our Lord: A First Century Message to Twentieth Century Christians* (London, England: Pickering and Inglis, n.d.), p. 18.

4. Timothy Jones, "Rumors of Angels," *Christianity Today* (April 5, 1993), p. 18.

5. Andrew J. Bandstra, "A Job Description for Angels," *Christianity Today* (April 5, 1993), p. 21.

6. Hans Bietenhard, *The New International Dictionary of New Testament Theology*, vol. 1 (Grand Rapids, MI: Zondervan Publishing House, 1975), p. 103.

7. Robert H. Mounce, *The Book of Revelation: The New International Commentary on the New Testament* (Grand Rapids, MI: Eerdmans Publishing Co., 1977), pp. 82, 85; for a full treatment of angels as impersonal entities that are the prevailing spirits of the churches, see the trilogy of books by Walter Wink: *Naming the Powers* (Fortress Press, 1984), *Unmasking the Powers* (Fortress Press, 1986) and *Engaging the Powers* (Fortress Press, 1992). For a scholarly answer to his major thesis, see Clinton E. Arnold's *Powers of Darkness* (InterVarsity Press, 1992).

DEALING WITH THE POWER OF MEMORIES

Chapter 8

(Step 3 in the Setting Your Church Free Event)

Memory is a powerful force for good or for evil—and sometimes for both. Good memories bring joy to the heart and delight to the mind. God often commands us to remember His mighty acts, His mercy and His compassion for our weaknesses. But painful memories nudge us toward regret and resentment—unless we forgive and find freedom in Christ.

My computer dictionary defines memory as "the mental capacity to retain and recall past experiences." Oscar Wilde called memories "the diary we all carry around with us."[1] It conditions our attitudes and our prejudices, our hopes and our dreams.

Appealing to the corporate memory of Israel, Ezra recounted in prayer God's powerful acts and loving forgiveness. The people turned back to God in great revival. The joy of the Lord became their strength (see Neh. 9). Stephen recalled a similar listing of good memories from God's mighty hand (see Acts 7). He proclaimed how God's sovereign action—memories engraved in Scripture—set the stage for the Lord's greatest gift of Jesus.

Sadly, Stephen was speaking to the Sanhedrin, the ruling council of men who sent Jesus to Pilate and the cross. They responded to Stephen's pricking their conscience by stoning him to death.

Memories of better days in times past can cause us to turn a corner. The prodigal son recalled the food and fare in his father's house and turned homeward in brokenness and humility. Jesus used the parable to teach how the heavenly Father receives each sinner who genuinely repents and turns his heart toward home (see Luke 15:11-32).

Recall some of your own good memories. Recall in your mind when you first received Christ Jesus as your Lord and Savior. Scroll back in your memory to the emotions, the humility, the relief, the joy and the relationship. If you do not remember, then think back to the first time Christ was meaningful to you. Remind yourself of some holy-ground experience with Christ, some time when He was really special to you. Then thank and praise Him.

Try another kind of warm memory. Recall one of the best experiences of your church. Reflect on a time when God moved among the people in a remarkable way. Think about the joy of Christ's people at Easter, Christmas or some other special occasion. Remember the achievement of a great goal accomplished by everyone working together. Think about the fun of a social time together as a church family. Thank God for the good memories from your church life.

Painful memories have their place too. Recall a painful memory from your church experience. Did someone you love and admire change churches or move away? Did someone criticize you, belittle you or oppose your ideas? Were you spiritually abused, taken advantage of or used for someone else's purpose? What is the most painful memory from your experience with the church?

CHURCH MEMORIES

Every church has memories. These memories are seldom neutral. They hold hidden power. They shape a church's sense of worth. They help build or destroy morale. They become foundations for more faith or reasons for more fear. They color how the leaders see the pastor, view church conflicts or approach fresh goals. These past events affect the present and the future of the church.

Memories are recalled in stories and rumors, buried in emotional joys and pain, and lived out in spiritual victory and deadening defeat. They are sources of pride and shame, happiness and sadness, health and disease. They provide us with opportunities or dangers. They serve as a shield against the enemy or as an open door for the adversary. They turn us toward God or away from Him.

The memories themselves are important, but not nearly as important as how well the church leaders respond to them. If a church's leaders rejoice in God and His goodness, recalling specific ways He intervened on their behalf, the church thrives. If the leaders recall their Lord and gladly obey Him in simple trust, the church prospers. If the leaders forgive those who hurt them and pray for God's blessing on them, the church flourishes. Such a church is on the way to health and freedom.

One pastor called the Setting Your Church Free event "a new window into the memories of the church." Another church completed most of the memories section (step 3) and then gave the participants a chance to pray in their own words. It was refreshing to hear the spontaneous prayers of forgiveness. The leaders named specific people as they prayed, knowing that everything would be kept in the strictest confidence. One woman began to weep. The others surrounded her, hugged her and stood by her as she released her resentment and regret. Just the day before she had gone through forgiveness in the personal Steps to Freedom in Christ, but this church-related problem had not come to mind. Like peeling another layer off of an onion, the Lord Jesus gently uncovered this painful memory and resolved it.

Resolving Differences

Memories, both those that bless and those that bind, can be abused as well as used positively. If church leaders take credit for what God does, they rob Him of glory and become preoccupied with themselves. If the leaders criticize former pastors, they build resentment into the congregation. If the leaders bury the painful past and refuse to discuss it, they cut themselves off from God's blessings for today and tomorrow. On the other hand, if they resolve differences, even among participants in the group, it can transform relationships within a church.

Those who do not understand forgiveness and the power of praying for past offenders sometimes refuse to face old painful memories. They delude themselves and fall into the devil's trap. Some of Satan's favorite deceptions are that darkness is safer than light, that hidden things are better not discussed, and that pain has no permanent resolution. Misguided leaders see painful church memories as something embarrassing that should be ignored, thus allowing the sores to fester instead of heal. Jesus warned us about covering up the past: "Be on your guard against the yeast of the Pharisees, which is hypocrisy. There is nothing concealed that will not be disclosed, or hidden that will not be made known" (Luke 12:1-2).

Wise church leaders walk in the light and are not afraid to embrace the truth. They recognize that the only thing they ever have to admit to is the truth, which is always a liberating friend. Such leaders know that neither they nor their churches are perfect. They claim God's grace to release them from the bondage of the past. They feel the pain, release it through forgiveness and bless those who curse them. The result is freedom and joy. Peace replaces pain. Wisdom grows from poor judgment. People, even people in their church, have permission to fail if they are attempting great things for Christ. Love, laughter and a sense of life mark these churches. High morale is their hallmark.

Good church memories will always bless if God receives the glory. Painful church memories will always bind unless leaders and people alike forgive as Christ forgave them. But painful memories can become good memories if they are redeemed by being released from the dark shadows of denial and used as teaching tools for the future. David Seamands shares some commonsense wisdom in his book *Healing of Memories*: "We cannot change the facts we remember, but we can change their meanings and the power they have over our present way of living."[2]

Turning away from the damage of sinful memories toward God

changes the meaning of our memories. Forgiving old offenders and doing good to those who hate us breaks the power that cripples. Courageous people forgive and bear the burdens of the offender's sins, but they don't tolerate sin. In one church, the leaders graciously forgave someone with a strong personality who tended to dominate people in their fellowship. But they also committed themselves in the Prayer Action Plan (step 6) to confront with love. Forgiveness prepares the way for tough love. If leaders sweep repeated offenses under the rug, they will soon trip over them.

There are a few instances of both good and painful memories listed in the letters to the seven churches in Revelation. Jesus commands the churches at Ephesus and Sardis to *remember*. He also reminds the church at Pergamum of a painful memory.

Lost Love

Let's start with the church at Ephesus (Rev. 2:1-7). After pointing out many of their strengths, Jesus said, "Yet I hold this against you: You have forsaken your first love. *Remember* the height from which you have fallen! Repent and do the things you did at first" (Rev. 2:4-5, emphasis added).

Jesus tells them to jog their memory, to recall the times when their love flowed back and forth from God and encouraged and built up one another. In spite of their hard work, doctrinal purity and perseverance, their love had grown cold.

The greatest danger in most evangelical churches is not that they will deny the deity of Christ or the authority of Scripture. The greatest danger lies in the warning of Jesus' prophecy in Matthew 24:12: "Because of the increase of wickedness, the love of most will grow cold." When evil spreads, people defend themselves or stick up for their rights. In the process, they stop loving each other and do not have as much love toward God as they used to.

It is painful for people to recall their first love and face up to the fact that they tumbled down the slippery slope. "*Remember* the height from which you have fallen!" (Rev. 2:5, emphasis added). Recalling the fact of their fall is not enough by itself. They must change their ways and do the loving things they used to do. This is what "repent" means.

Have you ever fallen out of love and then tried to will the old feelings back again? It does not work. Jesus does not tell you to feel love. He instructs you to start doing the loving things you did when you were in love. If it is your wife, start dating again. If it is God, start praising, thanking, believing, trusting, rejoicing and worshiping Him again. You can behave your way into feeling much faster than you can feel your way into behaving.

When it comes to recovering your first love, it always helps to remind yourself who you really are in Christ. Those who are in union with Christ can love, because God is love. The fruit of the Spirit is love, so if you are filled with the Spirit, you will begin doing loving things and feel again the joy of the Lord. Unresolved issues will keep you from being filled (controlled) by God's Spirit. Taking time for God, practicing spiritual disciplines and living up to your true identity in Christ are probably the things you did when you felt that first love. Climb back up the mountain you slid down. Perseverance pays. Each step brings you closer to the time when you, or your church, will regain the height of your first love.

Pain of Loss

To the church at Pergamum, Jesus reminded them of a bittersweet memory. He recalled "the days of Antipas, my faithful witness, who was put to death in your city" (Rev. 2:13). Antipas was a martyr, a soldier of Christ slain in spiritual combat. The church in Pergamum kept true to Christ's name and did not give up their faith in Him. But the loss of the faithful witness, Antipas, left an indelible mark on their corporate memory. It was the most traumatic event in the history of their church, and their troubles were not over.

The temples built to two of the Roman emperors and several false gods were outward evidence of a spiritual reality. Pergamum was the city where Satan had his throne. In this city, people followed his demonic orders. Antipas may have been their first martyr, but he was not to be the last. History records that later on in Pergamum, men named Carpus,

Papylus and Agathonike also shed their blood as martyrs for Christ.[3]

Your church may not have physical martyrs for Christ, but it may well have people who have burned out, given up or been blown away. Your leaders may ache over good people who have chosen to go to other churches and left the burdens of ministry to an overworked few. Your church may have sorrowful memories of accidents or death that took out an effective leader just when things seemed to be moving in the right direction. Or it may have painful memories of a more destructive kind—false teachers, selfish controllers, power-hungry leaders, immoral hypocrites or critical gossips.

One relatively healthy and growing church was going through the Setting Your Church Free process. The participants were praying individually, forgiving those who hurt their church. During the silence between spoken prayers, a man began to shake and weep. This man was a leader, a supporter, a server, a teacher and a pillar. But deep inside his soul, old hurts festered like open sores. Strong personalities in the past had abused their power and influence in the church. He was among those who had dealt with the offenders, but it was never easy.

For a minute or two, he quietly sobbed. This was not a cry of regret or the tears of confession, but simply a time of release. It was a tender moment as the pain of church leadership surfaced, perhaps for the first time in years. The pain ebbed away. The rest of the group simply waited silently and prayerfully. It was a healing moment.

Church in a Coma

The church in Sardis looked alive, but was dead (see Rev. 3:1-6). Jesus commanded it to wake up, saying it had a little strength left. Maybe it was in a coma. This church had a great reputation. Others thought it was alive, and it was vibrant at one time. But now most of the people had dirtied their clothes with sin. What little strength it had was almost gone. Its life was slipping away.

The Lord Jesus wrote to the church at Sardis, recalling a good memory—the memory of the gospel that brings life to the dead, alertness to the sleeping, consciousness to the comatose:

> *Remember*, therefore, what you have received and heard; obey it, and repent (Rev 3:3, emphasis added).

> *Remember* the teaching that you were given and that you heard. Hold firmly to it and turn from your sins (Rev 3:3, *CEV*, emphasis added).

Some of the best memories of a church are of the gospel being preached and taught. When the whole counsel of God is proclaimed, believed and obeyed, sometimes those in a coma come to life! David A. Seamands gives some helpful insight into what the Bible means when it calls us to remember:

> Memories include feelings, concepts, patterns, attitudes, and tendencies toward actions which accompany the pictures on the screen of the mind. This is the way the Bible uses the concept of remembrance, or stirring us up to remember something. When Scripture commands us to "remember the Lord," it does not mean to simply have a mental picture of God. It is a command to whole persons to orient all our thoughts and actions around God.[4]

You can't fix the past, but you can free yourselves from it by facing it, forgiving others and seeking forgiveness. Keeping this biblical background in mind, let's focus on the actual procedure for step 3 of Setting Your Church Free.

DEALING WITH MEMORIES

In step 3, you are asking the Lord to remind you of the best memories, as well as the traumatic events in your church's past. Make two lists for step 3, one titled "Good Memories" and the other titled "Painful Memories."

Good Memories

List all of the good memories first. They provide an occasion for thanksgiving to God for His blessings upon your church. Participants enjoy this step and the emotional tone of the group sometimes lifts noticeably. This is good in itself. It also provides a cushion of support for the pain that goes with the second part of this step.

If your church has been around for several years, consider it decade by decade, beginning with the earliest recalled past. What happened in the 1950s, '60s, '70s, '80s or '90s? Some churches may want to do some research or talk with longtime members. If anyone in the congregation has written a history for a church anniversary, read it and, if possible, talk with the author. The patterns that emerge are often eye-opening to the participants.

If your church is younger, you may want to divide its history in half or into thirds. What happened in the first five years, or in the last five years? Although the lists may be shorter for a younger church (especially a brand-new church), both good and painful memories exist. This is the time to capture the good memories.

The Steps to Setting Your Church Free give a printed prayer for good memories. Some people object to written prayers, but this process allows us to move out of the ordinary for a distinct purpose. When we seek the Lord—who never changes—in fresh ways, we sometimes catch fresh glimpses of His goodness, and then we are changed. As one participant commented, "The Setting Your Church Free seminar requires you to open your heart and let go of painful memories, but this allows more room to let Jesus *completely* into your heart!"

Once again, follow the group prayer with a time of silent prayer. The facilitator should then ask two of the participants to close the time of silence with spoken prayer. The facilitator and recorder (secretary) will once more move into action. The people who have grown up in the church, or have been there the longest, often do most of the sharing for the earliest decades, because they are the only ones who remember.

Good opening questions from the facilitator are, "Who remembers the furthest back? Was anyone here during the 1950s (or whatever decade seems to fit the age of the participants)?" Other questions might include, "Did anyone do any reading or research on this church's early history? What did you find?" To keep the process from bogging down, the facilitator simply needs to list memories in a few words. Beware of storytellers who want to reminisce in detail.

A typical good-memories list might include all-church activities and social events, youth groups that were strong and helpful, the tenure of an outstanding pastor, special meetings in which fresh commitments to God were made, major programs that required teamwork, people accepting Christ, periods of growth and building, sports teams, musical groups and much more. When the list of good memories is complete, the facilitator then asks the participants to lift them before the Lord in thanksgiving and praise. Encourage everyone to pray aloud, beginning with the words "Lord, I thank You for (name the good memory)."

Painful Memories

After thanking the Lord for the good memories, make another list of painful memories. Every church has its own history of pain, although some more than others. If not addressed, these painful memories will continue to have a chokehold on those who feel the pain, as well as on the church's present ministry. Again, use the decade-by-decade method of recall. This allows the participants who have the most longevity in the group to speak first, which is a disarming move. Their sharing will drop defenses and give permission for others to talk about the pain of more recent years. The more recent the conflict, the more likely it is to be a point of tension between members of the group.

Neil was once leading a Christian corporation through the Steps. When they came to forgiveness, nobody would share. Finally, the second-highest-ranking person said, "I know of two people who should be on the list, but I am not going to share their names." He was speaking for most of the others. Neil recessed for lunch, because there was no good reason to go on. He met with the top-ranking member of the group, and they both discerned what was wrong. Past leadership had created a climate of fear and nobody wanted to share for fear of reprisal. The leader came back and set the tone by saying, "If God has put me on your mind and you don't share that, you are disobeying God, and we cannot accept that if we want to be right with God. Nothing will leave this room, and I promise that there will be no reprisals for sharing the truth." The power block was broken and people began to share freely. Later, they identified corporate sins that resulted in a corporate bondage to fear. Neil handed out a small sheet of paper and asked them to complete the following statements:

- If I spoke honestly at staff meetings, I (what you believe would happen).
- If I disagreed with the pastor or team leader, I (what you believe would happen).
- If I shared my mind with the leadership above me, I (what you believe would happen).

The present leadership was nothing like the previous leadership, but the staff who had been trained (conditioned) under the old leadership were still believing and living the same way as they had been taught in the past. This is why simply eliminating poor leadership does not always lead to issues being resolved.

In another instance, the board came to a point of tension that led to a confrontation. Both of those who disagreed were mature and respected by the group. It was a healthy time of asking one another "why?" without anger or accusations. The issue was resolved and the two felt greater respect and closeness to one another. The one who first challenged the other later wrote,

The personal relationship that became more open has become one of the important blessings in my life. Without the seminar, that relationship would likely still be closed. This openness has led to more cooperation and greater good for our movement.

Real Names

The facilitator will ask the group to use the real names of those involved in painful memories. It is nearly impossible to get in touch with the inner emotional core of pain without using people's names. However, in order for the participants to feel comfortable in using actual names, confidentiality must be assured. No person will be permitted to share this confidential information outside the group. The facilitator should say, "This is the leadership of the church. Everything said here must be kept with the strictest confidentiality. This information is not even to be shared with husbands or wives who are not here today. Let's be careful in this section not to place blame or make disparaging remarks. We're here to heal the pain, not spread the gangrene."

The recorder is not to write down the painful memories section (at the conclusion of the whole event, you will want to destroy the large sheet up front). The group will then pray together, following a similar procedure as before. As names come to mind, they should be written on the sheet of paper up front. The focus should be on what was done, rather than on analyzing why it was done. Analysis only leads to rationalizations, verbal excursions or problem solving. You are not trying to solve problems in this step. This is a freeing time. You will have plenty of time to solve problems later.

Problem Solving

Should anyone in this Setting Your Church Free event begin problem solving (which often happens), the facilitator should address it. Here is an example:

> "The problem with elders (board members, pastors) is that they keep acting like elders." (Laugh)

> "Every time we get together, we solve problems. This is not a problem-solving time. We are simply identifying them in this step. We will have plenty of time in future meetings to work on solving problems."

Once again, the group interacts and the facilitator writes the list on the sheets up front. Each person is then to lift the painful memories before the Lord, asking for courage to face the pain honestly and for grace to forgive fully. Releasing the offenses results in relieving the pain.

Silent Forgiveness

The group should now begin individually and silently forgiving each person who has ever hurt them or their church (when they were involved) and then release the offenses. The facilitator can suggest a similar prayer to the one used in the personal Steps to Freedom in Christ:

> Lord, I forgive (name the person) for (specifically name every painful memory), which made me feel (identify the emotional pain).

Do not hurry through this time of individual silent prayer. The facilitator should ask the participants to review the list, bow their heads and then lift them only when they are finished forgiving those who hurt them. This lets the facilitator know when everyone has processed this personal forgiveness. Often it takes longer than expected.

During this time of silent forgiveness, the group should prayerfully focus on each person until every remembered pain surfaces. What is to be gained is freedom, not necessarily reconciliation. Principal people on the list may be dead. Some who are alive may not be willing to reconcile. Neither our freedom nor our church's will depend on what we have no right or ability to control. Paul writes, "If it is possible, as far as it depends on you, live at peace with everyone" (Rom. 12:18). Let's face it, sometimes it does not depend on us.

If, during this process, participants recall that someone has something against them, they should commit to go and ask forgiveness at their earliest convenience. If it is someone in the group, they should take advantage of the next break to go to the person and ask his or her forgiveness. Not to do so would hinder the Lord's leading in their lives and the freedom of the church.

Therefore, if you are offering your gift at the altar and there remember that your brother has something against you, leave your gift there in front of the altar. First go and be reconciled to your brother; then come and offer your gift (Matt. 5:23-24).

The Joy of Reconciliation

One church finished the memories section and took a break. The pastor's wife, whom we will call Renea, and her former close friend Shirlee began talking while everyone else vacated the room. (Some churches invite spouses to participate in this process; some do not.) The other leaders did not hurry back, because they suspected what was going on.

The pastor had come under heavy criticism from Bev, a mutual friend of both Shirlee and Renea. It all started because Bev felt offended over a conflict between her husband and the pastor. What began as a misunderstanding escalated into criticism, charges and church meetings in private and in public. The person Bev confided in most was Shirlee, a good friend of Renea's. Shirlee loved the pastor and his wife. She also loved Bev, and her heart went out to her because of the misunderstandings and the pain. But the more she listened to Bev's complaints and criticisms, the more estranged she felt from Renea. A distance and coolness soon developed in their friendship.

Renea sensed the rift of tension between Shirlee and herself. She felt shunned. She felt like the innocent victim who was attacked for no good reason. She felt like she was dying on the inside. By the time of this meeting, Bev and her husband had left the church. The church leaders had done their best in the process of resolving the church issue, but not the personal one between the two women.

At the break time, Renea and Shirlee began talking, working out their misunderstandings and asking forgiveness of one another. When they finally showed up for refreshments with tears in their eyes and beaming faces, the other members of the group were ready to go back to work! It had been worth every minute of the wait. Months later, the pastor, a capable and godly man, reported that this healing of old hurts by the Lord was the highlight of the event for his family.

Blessing Enemies

Returning to the process of step 3, after the silent time of forgiveness, the group will then pray together following the printed guideline. The facilitator will alert the group to what is coming next. After praying the written prayer together, but before saying "Amen," all the participants will be encouraged to pray individually and audibly. As God leads them one at a time, they can lift spontaneous prayers before the Lord, beginning with, "We forgive . . . "; "We release . . . "; and "We bless . . . "

One church had a capable former pastor who fell into sexual immorality. His sin had a delayed effect upon the church. After the initial shock, the church seemed to recover well, but soon deep pain and disillusionment began to set in. Those who trusted him most felt the deepest sense of betrayal. After his divorce, his tardiness in paying child support further aggravated their feelings. Conflicts with his former wife, whom they also loved, intensified their pain. They had a righteous sense of indignation.

Forgiveness, however, was not the toughest issue. Most of these church leaders had chosen to forgive. To obey the teaching of Jesus—"Love your enemies, do good to those who hate you, bless those who curse you, pray for those who mistreat you" (Luke 6:27-28)—seemed far more difficult. As they approached the "We forgive . . . "; "We release . . . "; and "We bless . . . " prayers, the feeling of pain in the room intensified. One godly Christian woman prayed with shocking honesty: "Lord, I can't pray to bless him by myself. I'm not even sure I forgive him. But by faith I ask you to bless him, and I release him." Her honesty cut through the resistance, and others soon joined in with similar prayers of forgiveness and blessing.

Months later, another elder who was present that day reported that the most helpful part of the session for their church was "coming face-to-face with the issue caused by the former pastor. Many of our people have been healed."

Corporate Forgiveness

Although we will not put all the prayers of the Steps to Setting Your Church Free in this book, this one on corporate forgiveness needs your prayerful understanding:

Dear heavenly Father,

We forgive each and every person who has hurt us or our church. We forgive as the Lord forgave us.

We release our resentments and regrets into Your hands. You alone can heal our broken hearts and bind up our wounds. We ask You to heal the pain in our hearts and in the corporate memory of our church. We ask for Your forgiveness for allowing a root of bitterness to spring up and defile many. We also ask You to forgive us for the times we did not seek to resolve these painful memories according to Your Word.

We commit ourselves to think of these memories—whenever we may happen to recall them—from the vantage point of our union with Christ. We will recall our forgiveness and Your healing. May Your grace and mercy guide us as we seek to live out our calling as spiritual leaders. By the authority of the Lord Jesus Christ, who is seated at Your right hand, we assume our responsibility to resist the devil. In Jesus' all-powerful name, we retake any ground that Satan may have gained in our lives and in our church through these painful memories. Because we are seated with Christ in the heavenly realms, we command Satan to leave our presence, our ministries and our church. We ask You, heavenly Father, to fill us with Your Holy Spirit. We surrender full control of our church Body to our crucified, risen and reigning head.

We ask You to bring healing to those who have hurt us. Also bring healing to those who may have been hurt by us. Bless those who curse us, and give rich and satisfying ministries to all who belong to You but have gone away from us. We bless them all in the name of our Lord Jesus Christ, who taught us, "Love your enemies, do good to those who hate you, bless those who curse you, pray for those who mistreat you" (Luke 6:27-28). According to Your Word, we pray for those who have hurt us:

We forgive . . .	[Individually, as the Lord leads,
We release . . .	pray for people and situations,
We bless . . .	beginning with these phrases.]

In Jesus' name we pray. Amen.

Satan's Advantage

Is it really possible that Satan can take advantage of a church corporately because of painful memories? Can the evil one exploit pain or divisions or misunderstandings to create more strife and problems? Can the accuser of the brethren misuse the memory of church conflicts to stir up more trouble in a church? We believe he can. It is not the memory itself that gives the enemy an advantage over us, but rather the lack of forgiveness.

Let's expand upon the passage quoted earlier concerning the church in Corinth. The church was tolerating a man among them who was living in incest. He was sleeping with his father's wife (i.e., stepmother), a scandal even among the pagans. Paul wrote to them in 1 Corinthians 5 to expel the immoral brother—and they did (see 1 Cor. 5:1-13; 2 Cor. 2:1-11). After his expulsion from the church, the man apparently repented of his sexual immorality. In the second letter, the apostle Paul called the church to forgiveness and to show Christian love:

> The punishment inflicted on him by the majority is sufficient for him. Now instead, you ought to forgive and comfort him, so that he will not be overwhelmed by excessive sorrow. I urge you, therefore, to reaffirm your love for him (2 Cor. 2:6-8).

Of special interest to us is the spiritual reason Paul gives for both personal and corporate forgiveness:

> But one whom you forgive anything, I forgive also; for indeed what I have forgiven, if I have forgiven anything, I did it for your sakes in the presence of Christ, so that no advantage would be taken of us by Satan, for we are not ignorant of his schemes (2 Cor. 2:10-11, *NASB*).

Forgiveness is not primarily for the good of the offender; it is for the good of the people who forgive. It is especially important because refusing corporate forgiveness allows Satan to have access to the church. The word "schemes" (*noema* in the Greek) in the passage above is used elsewhere in

2 Corinthians. Satan has "blinded the minds (*noema*) of unbelievers" (2 Cor. 4:4); "We take captive every thought (*noema*) to make it obedient to Christ" (2 Cor. 10:5); and "I am afraid that just as Eve was deceived by the serpent's cunning, your minds (*noema*) may somehow be led astray form your sincere and pure devotion to Christ" (2 Cor. 11:3). This clearly reveals the spiritual battle for our minds if we fail to forgive from our hearts. We will have no mental peace if we fail to forgive. A root of bitterness will spring up by which many will be defiled (see Heb. 12:15). Like a hungry lion stalking prey, Satan will mentally torment those who fail to forgive, and God will turn us over to him, because He doesn't want us to live in the bondage of bitterness (see Matt. 18:34-35).

Past Patterns

Working through this step helps the leaders see patterns emerging from the past. One church discovered a repeated pattern of strong personalities joining their fellowship. Because of these individuals' natural forcefulness and ego strength, they were often put up front or given positions of responsibility. However, they also had character flaws that caused severe problems. Dealing with the strong personalities was painful and sometimes damaging to the church.

This happened not once but several times during different eras of one church's history. Believing that the evil one may instill a strong spirit of independence, the leadership at this church now takes more precautions in selecting their leaders. They have become alert to their tendency to put strong, outgoing personalities up front before these individuals' proven character from Christ is evident. The pastors and elders talk openly about this tendency when they see a problem arising. They have learned from the past how to deal with a problem before it becomes severe. They are more alert to where their church is vulnerable. How many churches do not have the foggiest idea about what patterns from the past might be repeated in the future? If they are ignorant of Satan's schemes, he can easily take advantage of them.

Months after the Setting Your Church Free event, one pastor wrote, "Sometimes we really don't know what our church may be facing. At those times it certainly is good to do something like this to see if our apathy, pain, anxiety or whatever is caused by giving footholds to Satan." For those who are reluctant to give credit for anything—even bad things—to the devil, let us reassure you that this process is psychologically healthy. It works on a human level even if there is no demonic activity in a church. However, it is more powerful when the church leaders know that Christ's Kingdom of light is taking back ground from Satan's kingdom of darkness. As Corrie ten Boom used to say, "Jesus is Victor!"

After working through the first three steps, the participants need a break. But first, the facilitator can close by asking the participants, "Is there someone you need to talk with right now?" Sometimes there is, and you will see a couple get together to patch up differences. Usually, they are asking for each other's forgiveness. When they come back, they will be ready to consider corporate sins and their effects on the church, which is the topic of the next chapter.

Notes

1. Oscar Wilde, "The Importance of Being Earnest," act 2, line 11.
2. David A. Seamands, *Healing of Memories* (Wheaton, IL: Victor Books, 1985), p. 186.
3. Robert H. Mounce, *The Book of Revelation: The New International Commentary on the New Testament* (Grand Rapids, MI: Eerdmans Publishing Co., 1977), p. 97.
4. Seamands, *Healing of Memories*, p. 15

DEALING WITH CORPORATE SIN

Chapter 9

(Step 4 in the Setting Your Church Free Event)

A friend of mine was sharing about a summer he spent in China. When the people there asked him about crime and divorce rates in the United States, he admitted that the press reports were true. The Chinese people replied that such terrible things were not allowed in their country. My friend felt ashamed for "Christian America."

I recall the astonishment of some Japanese students at the H. P. Haggard School of Theology at Azusa Pacific University. The counseling course was addressing the problem of sexual abuse of children. The students were aghast and said such things did not happen in Japan. Their explanation why was simple—adults are never alone with children. Everyone lives so close together that privacy is unknown and children are protected. I felt ashamed of our culture.

Think of the dismay we feel when we learn about other cultures' corporate sins. Abortion for the sole reason of gender selection is common in India and China. A few years ago, I visited Thailand. In the city of

Bangkok, the guides pointed out the "spirit houses" outside of the homes and hotels. They look like ornate birdhouses, and some are fairly elaborate. The people place offerings and sacrifices in them to appease the spirits. I was grieved. Every country, institution or social organization has corporate sins—churches included.

WHAT ARE CORPORATE SINS?

By "corporate sins," we mean patterns of behavior in a church that are displeasing to God and contrary to His revealed will. Corporate sins do not differ from individual sins in nature. Sin is still sin, whether practiced by an individual or a group. What sets corporate sins apart from individual sins is that they are held in common by the whole church or by a significant group within it. This pattern of sinfulness within the group life of the church calls for corporate action on the part of its leaders in order to deal with it.

"Lord, you are righteous, but this day we are covered with shame" (Dan. 9:7). Daniel was confessing corporate sin. He felt shame for the wickedness, rebelliousness and disobedience of "all Israel" (Dan. 9:7,11). He was in exile because his forefathers had sinned, but Daniel correctly said "we" because every generation shares in the guilt and has the responsibility to resolve it. Daniel knew the importance of confessing corporate sin—feeling the shame that goes along with it. Along with godly sorrow comes confidence in the power of Christ to forgive, cleanse and heal if we repent (see 2 Chron. 7:14; 2 Cor. 7:10).

If praying for the whole nation or all of Western culture seems too much, how about confessing the corporate sins of your family or your church? It is easy to blame our disintegrating culture for what is wrong and then forget that corporate sins touch our own families, churches and denominations. Concerning churches, what are their corporate sins? To answer that, look again at the letters to the seven churches in Revelation 2—3. Five of the seven churches were guilty of corporate sins:

Ephesus	For forsaking their first love.
Pergamum	For tolerating false teaching that approved of participation in non-Christian religious rituals, and for committing sexual immorality.
Thyatira	For the same reasons as Pergamum, in addition to tolerating people within the church who committed adultery with a false teacher.
Sardis	For deadness and incomplete works.
Laodicea	For being lukewarm and finding security in material things.

Corporate sins and the shame that goes along with them are not limited to biblical times. Congregations today often fall into sinful patterns practiced by the church as a whole or a significant group within it. After many Setting Your Church Free seminars, we are acutely aware that nearly all churches tolerate corporate sins. Sinful patterns can cause incredible pain and damage to our Christian fellowship. Worse yet, they can hold us back from experiencing Christ's blessings. Let's take gossip as an example.

Digging up Dirt

Why do so many people like to hear about others peoples' dirty laundry? One reason may be because we were created in the image of God, but as a result of the Fall and our own sinful choices, God's image within us is flawed. Consequently, we have a longing to feel good about ourselves.

One counterfeit way to heighten our sense of worth is to compare ourselves to others. When we learn something bad about a prominent personality or a personal acquaintance, we think, *I may have problems, but I'm not that bad!* It puts our weaknesses in a better light. Sometimes we compare our strengths with others' weaknesses, which is substitute satisfaction for genuine character building, giving a false sense of feeling better about ourselves. The Bible warns us about comparing ourselves with one another (see 2 Cor. 10:12).

If we feel depressed, we may take the opposite tack and compare our weaknesses with others' strengths. Self-pity thrives on this negative mind game. Digging up dirt, or any kind of evil for that matter, has a strange attraction, which is why the nightly news is dominated by the latest crime reports. "The words of a gossip are like choice morsels; they go down to a man's inmost parts" (Prov. 26:22).

The only right comparison is between ourselves and Jesus Christ. At first, this comparison humbles us (as it should), but as we realize our union with Him, He becomes our Savior, Lord, teacher, friend and hope. He restores a healthy self-image as we "put on the new self, which is being renewed in knowledge in the image of its Creator" (Col. 3:10). One practical result is that our words change. Instead of digging up dirt, we mine for gold in other people. "Therefore encourage one another and build each other up, just as in fact you are doing" (1 Thess. 5:11). (For more information, see Neil's book *Overcoming Negative Self-Image*, Regal Books, 2003.)

If we would memorize Ephesians 4:29 and put it into practice, half of our problems would disappear overnight: "Do not let any unwholesome talk come out of your mouths, but only what is helpful for building others up according to their needs, that it may benefit those who listen." When we build others up according to their needs, we never grieve the Holy Spirit, as the next verse warns against (see Eph. 4:30). It grieves God when we put down one another instead of building up one another. By our words, we can either give grace to the hearer or cut them low.

Poison in the Body

Suspicion, gossip, dissension, divisiveness, rebellion—these corporate sins are like garbage. Neil wrote earlier that demons are like flies. They feed on garbage. And this kind of fodder they like better than dessert. The devil constantly stirs up a spirit of independence that causes division. It happens in churches, and it poisons the Body.

When gossip is rampant, people lose their trust in one another. Divisiveness shows up in business and committee meetings. Hurt feelings lead some to leave the church. Formerly good people become part of the wrecking crew instead of the building crew. The desire to win, come out on top, maintain an image and other beneath-the-surface desires wrongly seem far more important than discerning and doing God's will.

Immorality and sins of the flesh are painfully obvious to those who love the Lord. However, corporate sins such as prayerlessness, apathy and disobeying the Great Commission are often overlooked. If you ask the Lord to show you the corporate sins of your church, be ready to have your eyes opened. You need to be ready to confess, renounce and forsake them. "Remember, therefore, what you have received and heard; obey it, and repent" (Rev. 3:3).

THE BIBLE AND CORPORATE SINS

In one seminar a man commented, "I don't believe in corporate sins. I believe we are each responsible for our own sins." However, after the Bible study, he was convinced. Let's look again at Daniel's experience. The people of Judah were in exile, captive in Babylon for nearly 70 years. Upon learning that Jeremiah the prophet had prophesied 70 years of captivity, Daniel recognized from the Scriptures that God's time for deliverance was at hand. Soon the people of Israel were going to become eligible for parole from their captivity and return to their homeland in Judah. What they lacked at that point was a righteous perspective on how to live.

Daniel's Confession
Daniel interceded before God and confessed their corporate sins and the sins of their ancestors. He confessed the wickedness, rebelliousness and disobedience of "all Israel." Here is his prayer, as recorded in Daniel 9:4-19, with certain words and phrases highlighted to reveal the corporate nature of their sins:

O Lord, the great and awesome God, who keeps his covenant of love with all who love him and obey his commands, we have sinned and done wrong. We have been wicked and have rebelled;

we have turned away from your commands and laws. We have not listened to your servants the prophets, who spoke in your name to our kings, our princes and our fathers, and to all the people of the land.

Lord, you are righteous, but this day *we are covered with shame*—the men of Judah and people of Jerusalem and *all Israel,* both near and far, in all the countries where you have scattered us because of *our unfaithfulness* to you. O LORD, *we and our kings, our princes and our fathers are covered with shame because we have sinned against you.* The Lord our God is merciful and forgiving, even though *we have rebelled* against him; *we have not obeyed* the LORD our God or kept the laws he gave us through his servants the prophets. *All Israel has transgressed your law and turned away, refusing to obey you.*

Therefore the curses and sworn judgments written in the Law of Moses, the servant of God, have been poured out *on us,* because *we have sinned* against you. You have fulfilled the words spoken against us and against our rulers by bringing upon us great disaster. Under the whole heaven nothing has ever been done like what has been done to Jerusalem. Just as it is written in the Law of Moses, all this disaster has come *upon us, yet we have not sought the favor of the LORD our God by turning from our sins and giving attention to your truth.* The LORD did not hesitate to bring the disaster *upon us,* for the LORD our God is righteous in everything he does; yet *we have not obeyed him.*

Now, O Lord our God, who brought your people out of Egypt with a mighty hand and who made for yourself a name that endures to this day, we have sinned, we have done wrong. O Lord, in keeping with all your righteous acts, turn away your anger and your wrath from Jerusalem, your city, your holy hill. Our sins and the iniquities of our fathers have made Jerusalem and your people an object of scorn to all those around us.

Now, our God, hear the prayers and petitions of your servant. For your sake, O Lord, look with favor on your desolate sanctuary. Give ear, O God, and hear; open your eyes and see the desolation of the city that bears your Name. We do not make requests of you because we are righteous, but because of your great mercy. O Lord, listen! O Lord, forgive! O Lord, hear and act! For your sake, O my God, do not delay, because your city and your people bear your Name.

Please note the major point we are making. Daniel is confessing the corporate sins of his people and of his ancestors. He is not confessing his own personal sins, although he includes himself in the group prayer. Also note that Daniel wrote this prayer down. (Sometimes written prayers are extremely helpful.) Corporate sins do exist, and responsible, godly leaders can seize the initiative and confess them to the Lord on behalf of themselves and all their people. The Lord heard and answered Daniel's prayer. In three waves of immigrants, a remnant of the people of Israel returned from Babylon to Judah.

Nehemiah's Confession

Just before the third immigration, Nehemiah called out to God, confessing his own sins and the corporate sins of his people:

> O LORD, God of heaven, the great and awesome God, who keeps his covenant of love with those who love him and obey his commands, let your ear be attentive and your eyes open to hear the prayer your servant is praying before you day and night for your servants, the people of Israel. *I confess the sins we Israelites, including myself and my father's house, have committed against you. We have acted very wickedly toward you. We have not obeyed the commands, decrees and laws you gave your servant Moses* (Neh. 1:5-7, emphasis added).

Nehemiah acknowledged God's justice in scattering his people among the nations for their sins. He also appealed to God's promises in Scripture to gather them back from the farthest horizons of exile if they returned to Him and obeyed His commands. He claimed their true identity as the redeemed people of God. Then he asked for favor before the king (see Neh. 1:8-11).

Because he was the king's cupbearer, Nehemiah planned to make an appeal to the king to lead the third wave of immigrants back to Jerusalem (see Neh. 2:1-9). The king heard his request and granted it. In time, Nehemiah became governor of Judah. He is famous for his leadership in rebuilding the wall of Jerusalem with a volunteer crew in a mere 52 days (see Neh. 6:15). The next task, which was to rebuild the people, took a little longer.

Ezra's Confession

The people of Israel assembled together and asked Ezra, the leading priest, to read from the book of the Law of Moses (see Neh. 8:1). As the people heard God's Word read and expounded, conviction of sin came upon them. They repented and abandoned their sins. What followed was rejoicing in the Lord and significant changes in their lifestyle. They committed themselves to obey God's Word.

It appears that the fires of confession and revival spread, because on the twenty-fourth day of the same month, the people of Israel assembled together again (see Neh. 9:1). It is possible that many more gathered this time, including many who were not present the first time. Once more they heard God's law read and confessed their sins, both individual and corporate, including the sins of their ancestors. "They stood in their places and confessed their sins and the wickedness of their fathers" (Neh. 9:2). Some of these corporate sins included some painful memories.

> But they, our forefathers, became arrogant and stiff-necked, and did not obey your commands. They refused to listen and failed to remember the miracles you performed among them. They became stiff-necked and in their rebellion appointed a leader in order to return to their slavery. But you are a forgiving God, gracious and compassionate, slow to anger and abounding in love. Therefore you did not desert them (Neh. 9:16-17).

But they were disobedient and rebelled against you; they put
your law behind their backs. They killed your prophets, who had
admonished them in order to turn them back to you; they committed awful blasphemies (Neh. 9:26).

But as soon as they were at rest, they again did what was evil in
your sight. Then you abandoned them to the hand of their enemies so that they ruled over them. And when they cried out to
you again, you heard from heaven, and in your compassion you
delivered them time after time. You warned them to return to
your law, but they became arrogant and disobeyed your commands. They sinned against your ordinances, by which a man
will live if he obeys them. Stubbornly they turned their backs on
you, became stiff-necked and refused to listen. For many years
you were patient with them. By your Spirit you admonished
them through your prophets. Yet they paid no attention, so you
handed them over to the neighboring peoples (Neh. 9:28-30).

In all that has happened to us, you have been just; you have acted
faithfully, while we did wrong. Our kings, our leaders, our
priests and our fathers did not follow your law; they did not pay
attention to your commands or the warnings you gave them.
Even while they were in their kingdom, enjoying your great
goodness to them in the spacious and fertile land you gave them,
they did not serve you or turn from their evil ways (Neh. 9:33-
35).

Like Daniel and Nehemiah before him, Ezra confessed the corporate
sins of the people of Israel, concentrating especially on the sins of their
ancestors. The elders and people were with him in this case. However,
they did more than point the finger of blame at past generations. They
also confessed their own sins:

Because of *our sins*, its abundant harvest goes to the kings you have placed over us. They rule over our bodies and our cattle as they please. We are in great distress (Neh. 9:37, emphasis added).

The people, including their leaders, Levites and priests and Nehemiah the governor made a binding agreement with God. This document committed them to strict obedience to the Law of Moses and its practical applications for their day. You might even call it something of a Prayer Action Plan (step 6). Our point here, however, is that corporate sins do exist, and they invite God's judgment. Leaders and people can confess corporate sins and turn away from them, which pleases God and brings His blessings upon leaders and people alike. These Old Testament examples were written for our good, and the principles apply to us as well (see 1 Cor. 10:11; 2 Tim. 3:16; 2 Pet. 1:20-21).

The Day of Atonement

Daniel and Ezra did not dream up the concept of corporate sins. God built it into the sacrifices of Israel as He prescribed in Leviticus. The Lord designed the Day of Atonement specifically for the corporate sins of Israel (see Lev. 16). Individual sins had precise sacrifices that were required by the person who committed the transgression. But confession of individual sins alone was not enough. "Make atonement for the sons of Israel *for all their sins* once every year" (Lev. 16:34, emphasis added, *NASB*). On the annual Day of Atonement, "Aaron [the high priest] is to offer the bull *for his own sin offering* to make atonement for himself and his household. *He shall then slaughter the goat for the sin offering for the people*" (Lev. 16:6,15, emphasis added). The purpose of the Day of Atonement was not for individual transgressions but for the uncleanness, rebellion and wickedness of all Israel (see Lev. 16:15, 16,21,24,30,34).

The good news is that our Lord Jesus Christ has made a better sacrifice than the blood of bulls and goats. He is the atoning sacrifice for both individual and corporate sins (see Heb. 9:22-28). Because of His grace and kindness expressed to us in the perfect sacrifice of the Cross, our task is to respond to Him with repentance and faith. In Revelation 2—3, Jesus gave sharp commands to His churches in regard to their corporate sins:

Ephesus	Remember, repent
Pergamum	Repent
Thyatira	Hold on
Sardis	Wake up! Strengthen what remains, remember, obey, repent
Laodicea	Be earnest, repent

RENOUNCE AND ANNOUNCE

"Renounce" is a helpful word that summarizes what Jesus commanded His churches to do about corporate sins. It is the first step in repentance; it carries a sense of completely rejecting and disowning sin (or any kind of demonic activity). According to Webster's dictionary, "renounce" means "to give up, especially by formal announcement." When a church renounces its corporate sins, it gives them up as their possession. It rejects and disowns them. It signs a quitclaim deed, handing them over to the Lord Jesus Christ, who died and rose to put away all sins, personal and corporate. Paul wrote in 2 Corinthians 4:1-3 (*NASB*):

> Therefore, since we have this ministry, as we received mercy, we do not lose heart, but we have renounced the things hidden because of shame, not walking in craftiness or adulterating the word of God, but by the manifestation of truth commending ourselves to every man's conscience in the sight of God.

In the Setting Your Church Free process, the participants renounce the sins of the churches in Revelation 2 and 3, as paraphrased and applied to life today. The participants then announce the positive biblical opposite. For the theologically minded, this amounts to repentance and faith, our biblical response to any kind of sin. Because renouncing lies and sins and announcing truth and righteousness will be important concepts later on, see the following list.

CHURCH RENUNCIATIONS

We renounce . . .

We renounce forsaking our first love.

We renounce tolerating false teaching.

We renounce overlooking non-Christian beliefs and practices among our members.

We renounce tolerating sexual immorality among some of our members.

We renounce our reputation of being alive when we are dead.

We renounce our incomplete deeds—starting to do God's will and then not following through.

We renounce disobedience to God's Word, including the Great Commandment and the Great Commission.

We renounce our lukewarmness—being neither hot nor cold for Christ.

We renounce our false pride in financial "security" that blinds us to our actual spiritual needs.

We announce . . .

We announce that Christ is our first love because He first loved us and gave Himself as an atoning sacrifice for our sins (see 1 John 2:2; 4:10; Rev. 2:4).

We announce that God's truth is revealed to us through the living and written Word of God (see John 17:17; 2 Tim. 3:15-16; Heb. 4:12).

We announce that Christ is our true identity and the only way to salvation and fellowship with God (see John 14:6; 2 Cor. 5:17).

We announce that our sexuality is God's gift, and sexual union is to be enjoyed only within the marriage of one man and one woman (see Gen. 2:24; 1 Cor. 6:18-20; 1 Thess. 4:3-8).

We announce that Christ alone is our resurrection and our life (see John 11:25-26).

We announce that Christ is the head of His Body, the Church, and as His members we find freedom and strength to finish the work He has given us to do (see Eph. 1:19-23; 2:10; Phil. 4:13).

We announce that God energizes us to desire and to do His will so that we can obey Christ (see Phil. 2:13).

We announce that Christ is our refining fire who disciplines us for our own good so that our faith may prove genuine (see Mal. 3:1-3; Heb. 12:10,29).

We announce that Christ is our true wealth, purity and insight, and outside of Him we are wretched, pitiful, poor, blind and naked (see Col. 2:1-3; Rev. 3:17-18).

Corporate Sins Today

Every church needs to examine its spiritual health in response to the living Christ. In Chuck's tradition, the Friends Church, there is a practice called a "Meeting for Clearness." It is a time set aside with significant leaders to discern God's will on a matter through prayer, discussion and the leading of the Holy Spirit. In one such meeting on a denominational level, the subject of corporate sins was explored. Among many possibilities, there were three that seemed to stand out as especially applicable: rebellion, arrogance and self-righteousness. Those who know Friends history will recognize that these corporate sins lie embedded in its spiritual genes. These sins are its heredity handed down from its spiritual ancestors. What is fascinating is that each one is the demonic opposite of one of its greatest strengths.

Rebellion, for example, is the flip side of the strength of standing up for truth and speaking that truth with power to those in authority. Friends, formerly called Quakers, were among the first to win the right of religious freedom in both England and the American Colonies. It did not come easy. Many of the forefathers and foremothers were imprisoned; some were martyred. (Three men and one woman were hung in Boston Common for preaching the Friends' understanding of the gospel.)

Arrogance, as another example, is the exact opposite of the Christlike humility that cannot tolerate sin. Friends, led by John Woolman, was the first Christian movement to free nearly all its slaves in America, 75 years before the Civil War. Separated from Christ, however, humility vanishes and intolerance for God's truth (when it differs from our perception of it) becomes a real temptation.

In a similar way, self-righteousness is a distorted form of genuine righteousness. It is no accident that Friends, motivated by a true righteousness, produced several classics of devotion. Those who enjoy the devotional masters may recognize names such as George Fox, John Woolman, Stephen Grellet, Hannah Whithall Smith, Thomas Kelly, Douglas V. Steere and Richard J. Foster.

Renouncing Rebellion

How does a movement or any given church renounce corporate sins such as rebellion, arrogance and self-righteousness and replace them with the positive biblical opposite? One way is to do it in prayer, preferably in public. The following three declarations or prayers are useful for making such a break with our old sins. They also serve as illustrations of what corporate sins might look like today. In the Setting Your Church Free seminars, we use these as prayers and as teaching tools.

We renounce rebellion as one of our corporate sins. We have so often rejected authority from any source that displeases us—government, church officials, Scripture, critics of other theological persuasions and especially our own chosen leaders. We have so often given responsibility without authority. We have so often set ourselves up as judges of the actions and attitudes of our pastors, elders and leaders. At times, we have valued our own traditions above God's truth, rebelling against the very Holy Spirit we profess to obey. We rebel against evangelism because it embarrasses us. We rebel against holiness because it makes us distinct from the world around us. We blindly deny the works of Satan and his demonic forces, clearly taught in Scripture, because they do not neatly fit into our own understanding of reality. We admit that we are guilty, and we repent of our rebellion.

We announce that in Christ we have godly submission to our living Lord and His called and gifted human leaders. In Christ, we submit ourselves to every authority He has placed over us—government, church officials, Scripture, whatever is true from critics of other theological persuasions and especially our own chosen leaders. We submit to the spiritual authority of our pastors, elders and leaders, especially in the responsibilities we have given to them.

We submit ourselves to the Holy Spirit and the Scriptures, including the clear commands regarding evangelism, holy living and continuous prayer. We humbly ask for the renewing, reviving work of the Holy Spirit as we love, trust and obey the Word of God.

Renouncing Arrogance

We renounce arrogance as one of our corporate sins. Pride in ourselves and in our past spiritual insights and achievements have become an idol in our hearts. We have wrongly believed that the distinctives the Holy Spirit revealed to us were superior to the distinctives the Holy Spirit revealed to others. Some of us have prided ourselves more on belonging to our denomination than on belonging to Jesus Christ. We have even taught that what we emphasize is so special that it comes across as spiritually superior—as if somehow we were God's ultimate work, His pet project, His specially chosen vessel of truth above and beyond His other children. In our arrogance, we believe that we are better than others, that we have a corner on knowing God in the most intimate way. We admit that we have been deceived, and we repent of our arrogance.

We announce that we have authentic humility in living union with our Lord Jesus Christ. We humbly confess that Jesus Christ is the only way to salvation and fellowship with God. Our confidence is in Him and in Him alone. We cherish what the living Christ has revealed to us through God's Spirit, God's Word, God's works and God's people. Yet we humbly declare ourselves needy of His searching light in our lives today. We gladly acknowledge that the same Lord Jesus—crucified, risen, reigning and returning—who gave insights to our founders is present to teach us Himself. We humble ourselves before God—heavenly Father, Lord Jesus Christ and Holy Spirit—who alone teaches us to understand and practice His truth unveiled to us through Scripture, sound reason and the spiritual gifts of His people.

Renouncing Self-Righteousness

We renounce self-righteousness as one of our corporate sins. Many of us have believed that "what's right for me" is okay, even if it contradicts the clear teaching of Scripture. Many of us consider satisfying our own needs as more important than obeying God's Word. Many of us have made up our own rules and feel content in our self-made righteousness. As a corporate Body, and as individuals, we often tolerate these false ideas in one another and refuse to confront non-scriptural behavior, especially if we are comfortable with it.

While ignoring biblical righteousness, we too quickly judge one another for not conforming to the non-scriptural expectations of our group such as appearance, social fit and religious vocabulary. We too easily believe gossip and rumor about people instead of loving and forgiving them in Christ.

We excuse ourselves and judge others, which is the heart of self-righteousness. We admit that we are guilty of setting up our own rules instead of God's, and we repent of our self-righteousness.

We announce that in Christ we have the righteousness of God that comes by faith alone. We gladly acknowledge His righteousness as a free gift of grace, which we can never earn or deserve. We announce that in Christ we increasingly are made right before God in our daily conduct. We affirm that being a Christian includes a way of life intent on obeying all that Christ commands us in His written and living Word.

We announce that in Christ we have genuine love for all people, even if they do not seem to fit into our group. Among our own members, we announce the gracious accountability that encourages one another to love, to do good deeds and to practice biblical, holy living.

These examples apply to more than one denomination or grouping of churches. Parts of them, at least, fit others as well. Wherever they fit you, please use them. More important for our purpose in this book is for you to understand what corporate sins are like. If you are not yet convinced that corporate sins really exist for churches, consider one more point: Corporate sins include tolerating open sins within the church and neglecting to do anything about them.

To the church in Thyatira, Jesus wrote, "Nevertheless, I have this against you: You tolerate that woman Jezebel, who calls herself a prophetess. By her teaching she misleads my servants into sexual immorality and the eating of food sacrificed to idols" (Rev. 2:20). Current equivalents of Thyatira's problems might be tolerating false teachers, sexual immorality by leaders, or non-Christian rituals such as the New Age use of crystals or channeling. Tolerating sins can only be done by those in authority, even if they themselves are not involved. This clearly is a corporate sin distinct from an individual sin.

PROCEDURE FOR STEP 4

The procedure for step 4 (dealing with corporate sins) in the Setting Your Church Free process follows a similar format to the other steps. The participants pray a group prayer and then follow with a few moments of silent prayer. They ask the Lord to help them discern all sins of commission and omission by present and past leadership, as well as the church as a whole. This is necessary because spiritual leaders represent the Body of believers, and their decisions affect the whole church. The facilitator then asks the group to share the church's corporate sins.

The facilitator will seek discernment from the group. From this step onward, group discernment is vital, rather than only listing each person's ideas. This builds unity and ownership of the problem. It creates balance, sharpens discernment and removes a potential cause of criticism. By this time, the trust level in the group is usually high and the communication open. Because of the nature of corporate sins, this step starts slowly but gradually gains momentum. Be patient and wait for general agreement.

The actual list will vary from church to church, but all groups so far have come up with an agreed-upon list of corporate sins. Here are actual examples compiled from several different churches, using their own words:

- Complacency and passivity
- Apathy
- Critical spirit
- Self-pride ("My way is best," not humbling ourselves before the Lord)
- Unwillingness to forgive
- Poor stewardship
- Believing gossip and rumor
- Power struggles
- Allowing sins to continue, being unwilling to confront
- Accepting of unacceptable behaviors—not challenging each other, not keeping each other accountable
- Unwillingness to evangelize

In this step (and the next one) an opportunity is given to pray together against each specific sin. The suggested prayer is as follows:

Heavenly Father,
   We confess (specifically name each corporate sin) *as sinful and displeasing to our Lord Jesus Christ. We turn from it, forsake it and renounce it. We thank You for Your forgiveness and for You purifying our lives and our church.*

In the case of our example church, this short prayer is prayed through once with "complacency and passivity" filling the blank. Then it is prayed through again, out loud and together, for "apathy," and so on through the corporate sins. It should be repeated again for each item on the list. Although this sounds redundant, in practice it is quite powerful for the leaders to renounce, one by one, the corporate sins of their own church. When this is completed, the leaders then join together in a group prayer that biblically deals with corporate sins and their consequences, which petitions God to grant His cleansing, renewal and filling. Spiritual warfare is obvious in this prayer (see appendix A).

At this point, the facilitator will invite everyone to search their own hearts, asking the Holy Spirit to reveal each person's participation in the church's corporate sins. Each individual, as directed by the Holy Spirit, should then pray out loud, confessing personal involvement in these corporate sins. The facilitator should alert everyone that it is off-limits to confess someone else's sins. (The participants will usually laugh when the facilitator says this, but it prevents a big mistake from happening.)

It is not uncommon for nearly all the participants to confess out loud in spontaneous prayer their own personal involvement in the corporate sins of the church. The sense of sincerity is transparently clear to all who are present. The moving of the Holy Spirit in the leaders' hearts and minds is evident as His cleansing takes place. The participants' ownership of the church's corporate sins and confession of them openly seals the unity of the group as few other activities will. The facilitator may want to encourage people to talk during the break with anyone in the room with whom they need to reconcile, make amends or ask forgiveness.

In one church, an older gentleman had never prayed out loud in a spontaneous way in front of any group in the church. He passed on praying anything aloud with his group except reading the printed prayers. But during this step, he too prayed out loud in front of the group. He confessed his own sins, just as the others did. The Holy Spirit works in marvelous ways when we become biblically obedient in confessing corporate and personal sins.

SENSE OF RELEASE

The sense of release that comes from honest confession can be incredibly refreshing. Some church leaders were not aware of all of the corporate sins. Others had felt one or two of these sins weighing on their conscience. Although every church is different, many leaders have left board meetings feeling spiritually defeated. They may have struggled with thoughts such as *We covered over it again, I didn't want to be a troublemaker by bringing it up,* or *I must be the only one feeling this way.* Their spirit was troubled, but they did not want to be negative. In some cases, they might have lacked the leadership or the understanding to resolve the problem.

This step in the Setting Your Church Free process establishes an environment in which it is safe and acceptable to name corporate sins and to resolve them through repentance. The church leaders have acknowledged their corporate sins and confessed them to God. Further, the participants have acknowledged their own personal involvement and also have repented.

St. Francis of Assisi was a true spiritual leader who lived around the twelfth and thirteenth centuries. The following story from his experience illustrates our vulnerability, the necessity of repentance and the fact that nothing is really new on planet Earth:

One day in Portiuncula while at prayer alone in his cell, St. Francis saw a vision of the whole house surrounded and besieged by devils. They were like a great army surrounding the place, but none of them could gain entrance to the house. The brothers were so disciplined and devoted in their lives of sanctity that the devils were frustrated without a host upon whom they might find a way in.

It happened, in the days soon after Francis's vision, that one of the brothers became offended by another and he began to think in his heart of ways to revenge the slight. While the scheming brother was devising vengeful plans, entertaining wicked thoughts, the devil, finding an open door, entered Portiuncula upon his back.

Francis, the watchful shepherd of his flock, saw that the wolf had entered, intending to devour his little sheep. At once, Francis called the brother to him and asked him to disclose the hatred that had caused this disturbance in his house. The brother, frightened that Francis knew the content of his heart, disclosed to him all of the venom and malice that consumed him, acknowledging his fault and begging humbly for forgiveness.

Loving his sheep as does the Father, the shepherd soon absolved the brother, and immediately, at that moment, before his very face, Francis saw the devil flee from his presence.

The brother returned to the flock and the wolf was gone from the house.[1]

Note

1. Paul Sabatier, *The Road to Assisi: The Essential Biography of St. Francis* (Brewster, MA: Paraclete Press, 2003), p. 167.

DEFEATING SATAN'S ATTACKS

Chapter 10

(Step 5 in the Setting Your Church Free Event)

Whenever Neil and I do conferences, we often ask the participants, "How many here have been awakened, either terrorized or alertly awake, at precisely 3:00 A.M.?" In North America, at least one-third of the audience will respond that they have. The percentage is often much higher for Christians leaders. These individuals are likely being targeted by the enemy. Just as the Lord sends angels as messengers and guardians, Satan sends demons to tempt, accuse and deceive. Neil once worked with a couple who both were subjected to satanism by their parents, but who both were now marvelously saved and serving God. He asked the couple, "What is going on at 3:00 A.M.?" They replied without hesitation that 3:00 A.M. is "prime time" spiritually—the time when people are targeted spiritually. Summoning and sending demons is part of satanic rituals.

The idea that Satan may attack a corporate church Body came to me rather slowly as my worldview became more biblical. I had served as a denominational leader for several years and observed many churches firsthand. Some were healthy and happy; others were diseased and unhappy. Many simply seemed to hold their own, serving quietly and well. But in a couple of churches, I saw strange patterns that defied rational explanation.

Main Street Church (a fictitious name) was one of these two congregations. For 40 long years, the people in this church had fought with each other. Their fights did not seem to occur over any one issue or between two groupings of people, but they did follow a predictable pattern, distorted though it was.

Their pattern of conflict went something like this: an issue arose, big or small, and people chose sides for the church fight. They inflicted verbal and emotional pain on each other. In time, the winning side ran the "problem person"—the one who led the losing opposition—out of the church. Everyone breathed a sigh of relief that, with the problem producer gone, everything would be better. After all, the rest of that person's group remained in the church and life seemed to get back to normal.

A new problem soon emerged, however. Instead of returning to the same groupings from the last church fight, new coalitions formed. Former enemies became allies, and former friends became foes. When it was all over, another problem person had been run off. (The church attendance slowly declined for years.) The time of peace did not last long before yet another conflict popped up. The same pattern repeated itself again and again, with still new groupings of good guys and bad guys. What was going on?

DENOMINATIONAL REBELLION

Another congregation had a different scenario. Small Town Church—again, a fictitious name—had a repeated pattern of rebellion against denominational leaders for the past 80 years. Then there was an interesting turn of events. An aggressive new pastor came to Small Town Church. He was brash, but too quick for the leaders to nail him to a wall. Talk about fireworks! It went from light show to light show or, to change the analogy, from Round 9 to Round 10. Within a few years, new people had all but replaced the original members of the church. The total attendance, however, was somewhat larger than when the pastor first came.

In time, this pastor accepted a call to serve in another church that was more than a thousand miles away. His replacement came from a different denominational background in another state and knew nothing about the history of this church. Both the new pastor and the church were doing well when a denominational issue arose. It stirred up some heated controversy in many congregations, as these sorts of things often do. The other churches in the district seemed to take it in stride, but not Small Town Church. The pastor called me and reported, "Our people are talking about leaving the denomination."

How could a church that had a new pastor and almost 100 percent different people fall right back into their historic pattern of rebellion against denominational authority? How could they so overreact to this issue when they handled other kinds of problems in a more normal way? This pattern went beyond any predictable group behavior and did not fit any typical group pathology.

Spiritual Attacks upon Churches

I began to suspect that Satan may be targeting churches. I already knew that if the leaders indulged in gross personal sin and the church committed and tolerated corporate sins, demonic forces would take advantage of their vulnerability. But could they just be under attack because of who they were and what they represented, not because they were doing something wrong? Maybe they were under attack because they were doing something right. If evil forces followed predictable patterns in causing trouble in a congregation, it would repeat itself over and over. An outsider like myself could observe it, and it could last as long as the church existed.

I began to share my findings with other denominational leaders. They were in a position to observe many churches firsthand and were often involved in problem solving. So I shared my observations both within our denomination and outside of it. To my surprise, I found a sweeping sense of agreement. Others also had observed irrational patterns that repeated themselves in the same churches. Most of my colleagues believed these patterns had no rational or natural explanation. Real evil was involved. Many believed as I did that it was spiritual and demonic.

Before you dismiss this proposition as ridiculous and unbiblical, consider the following questions: Is it not a fact revealed in Scripture that Satan exists? Doesn't the Bible say, "Our struggle is not against flesh and blood, but against the rulers, against the authorities, against the powers of this dark world and against the spiritual forces of evil in the heavenly realms" (Eph. 6:12)? Is it not true that these evil powers in the heavenly realms are fallen angels under Satan's command? Is it possible, even theoretically possible, that Satan might target Christians and churches with some of his fallen angels to disrupt what they are doing?

The Bible does not tell us with any precision how Satan organizes his kingdom of darkness. Some passages clearly give different names and titles to evil powers. Some suggest ranks and assignments, implying a hierarchy of demons. We have to admit that our biblical knowledge of Satan's organization is pretty sketchy—and for good reason. If God told us precisely how Satan organized his troops, the evil schemer would change it. Then the Bible would be full of errors. God is too wise to fall into that trap.

Discerning Satan's Schemes

Neil mentioned earlier that the devil will try to divide our minds, marriages and ministries. He will take advantage of any weak soul, but if he is clever, he will go after those people and churches bearing the most fruit. To capture a private in the army is a small victory, but to capture a commanding general is a huge victory.

If I were the enemy, I would target governments and their leaders. I would assign some of my workers to the courts, the legislative bodies, the military and the educational systems. I would assign some to criminal warlords, organized crime and all kinds of street gangs. I would assign some to the media and some to the entertainment and music industries. I would attack institutions such as marriage and family.

Being the father of lies, I would especially attack the Church, which is the pillar and support of truth (see 1 Tim. 3:15).

If I (trying to play Satan) could slow down, immobilize, distract or derail the churches of Jesus Christ, there would no longer be salt or light. If people remain blind to the gospel, they remain in the kingdom of darkness. The only human institutions that pray for God's light to dispel the darkness and proclaim the gospel are churches and Christian organizations. I would therefore assign at least one fallen angel to every church. My point is this: Satan is more clever, more intelligent and a better strategist than any mortal who walked on Earth. Only Jesus is vastly superior in power and wisdom.

Vulnerable Churches

According to the Bible, the evil one snatches away some of the good seed of the gospel that is preached in our churches (see Matt. 13:19). He sows weeds among the wheat in our fellowships (see Matt. 13:27-28,38-39). Someone as close to Jesus as Peter can sometimes speak Satan's words (see Matt. 16:23). Is it possible that the "rulers of this world" might attack the followers of his archenemy (see 1 Cor. 2:6-8)? We have been warned about the dangers of Christians participating with demons (see 1 Cor. 10:20-21). Deceitful people in your church could be masquerading as Christ's representatives, just as Satan masquerades as an angel of light (see 2 Cor. 11:13-14).

There is ample scriptural evidence to show that churches are in some ways vulnerable to Satan's deception and attacks, just like individuals. New Testament scholar Clinton E. Arnold writes, "The powerful supernatural work of the devil and his powers sets itself against individual Christians *and the church as a whole.*"[1]

SEEING WITH JESUS' EYES

Having this vulnerability in mind, let's look at our key passages in Revelation 2 and 3 once more. Keep in mind that what people see in perplexing problems and what Jesus sees are quite different. People see

other people causing trouble; Jesus sees Satan and his henchmen causing trouble.

> **To Smyrna:** "I know the slander of those who say they are Jews
> and are not, but are *a synagogue of Satan*. Do not be afraid of what
> you are about to suffer. I tell you, *the devil* will put some of you in
> prison to test you, and you will suffer persecution for ten days"
> (Rev. 2:9-10, emphasis added).

What people saw were Jews who slandered the Christians in the Smyrna
church. What Jesus saw was "a synagogue of Satan." What people saw
were Roman rulers who threw Christians in jail. What Jesus saw was the
devil who put some of them in prison. Not all synagogues were demonized, but this one was. Not all authorities believed lies about Christians,
but in Smyrna the Roman overlords did. These enemies of the gospel
were doing the devil's work by attacking the church in Smyrna.

> **To Pergamum:** "I know where you live—*where Satan has his throne*.
> Yet you remain true to my name. You did not renounce your
> faith in me, even in the days of Antipas, my faithful witness, who
> was put to death in your city—*where Satan lives*" (Rev. 2:13,
> emphasis added).

What people saw was a city on a hill with major temples in it. What Jesus
saw was Satan's throne. What people saw was the center of emperor worship in Asia. What Jesus saw was the city where Satan lived. This place
was oppressive to Christians. It killed some of them and threatened the
others. This was a dangerous place for a church. The "roaring lion" actually devoured people in this city (see 1 Pet. 5:8). Satan does not actually
headquarter in certain cities today, does he? Or could it be that his
strategies have not changed that much?

> **To Thyatira:** "Now I say to the rest of you in Thyatira, to you
> who do not hold to her teaching and have not learned *Satan's so-*

called deep secrets (I will not impose any other burden on you):
Only hold on to what you have until I come" (Rev. 2:24-25,
emphasis added).

What people saw was a prophetess who taught that, since grace covered
every sin, it was okay to indulge in the pagan temple feasts. What
Thyatira church members might have heard was, "'Once saved, always
saved,' and so what consenting adults do in a company party or in the
privacy of their own bedrooms is not anyone's business." What Thyatira
believers might have heard was, "Experimenting with New Age rituals
and rites helps you understand non-Christians better so that you can
witness to them intelligently." What Jesus saw was Satan's deceptive
secrets for indulging in sexual sin and satanic rituals. What Jesus said
was that church members were about to be struck dead for their sins (see
Rev. 2:21-23).[2]

> **To Philadelphia:** "I will make those who are of *the synagogue of
> Satan*, who claim to be Jews though they are not, but are liars—I
> will make them come and fall down at your feet and acknowl-
> edge that I have loved you" (Rev. 3:9, emphasis added).

What people saw were two religious groups who had different interpretations about their beliefs. What Jesus saw was a demonized synagogue.
What people saw was deep animosity that had religious roots. What
Jesus saw was a pack of liars who were about to be proved wrong. What
people saw were allegations of the dangerous practices and beliefs of
Christians. What Jesus saw was a church wrongly accused and a faithful
band of people to whom He was about to prove His love, even to their
deceived enemies.

What people often see today are circumstances, group dynamics and
various points of view. What Jesus sees is the Church under attack by
Satan and his henchmen. What people see are groups who act in a way
that can be explained by the culture, religion, politics, economy or one of
the behavioral sciences. Jesus reveals a Christian, supernatural worldview

of the Church and its enemies. Dr. Timothy Warner, former missions professor at Trinity Seminary and currently on staff with Freedom in Christ Ministries, makes a telling comment in his lectures to missionaries around the world: "If our worldview does not allow for spirit activity in daily life, we will be easy targets for the enemy's deception, and we will not reach out by faith to receive the resources available to us as God's children."

Corporate sins in a church are not the same as Satan's attacks, but they do give the deceiver an advantage over us. Corporate sins give him a place to attack. He may deceive us into tolerating false teaching and then use its lies to weaken our faith and lead us into heresy. He may dull our senses into tolerating some of our unmarried members living together and then use that "ground" to cause our youth to rationalize all kinds of sexual sins. He may distract us with many little things that leave us with little time for prayer and the teaching of God's Word. The next thing you know, we are lukewarm believers.

THE REST OF THE STORY

There is more to the story of Main Street Church and its repeated pattern of church fights. Several people retired and moved out of the community. The attendance continued to decline. As a last-ditch effort toward renewal, the denomination found an experienced interim pastor for one year, whom we will call Pastor Joe. He was followed by a new pastor, whom we will call Pastor Ed.

After arriving on the scene, Pastor Ed launched some research into the church's past, including its painful memories. The official minutes recorded some stormy sessions in detail. Forty years earlier, the people were deeply divided about changing locations to the present site. Infighting and a gradual decline in attendance had occurred ever since. But that was not all. One of the former pastors reportedly died of syphilis. Another had to leave the church because of an adulterous affair. Although the church had many faithful pastors and good people, it appeared that the enemy had taken advantage of many sins.

In recent years, a church plant rented Main Street Church's facilities in off-hours. Some of the members of Main Street Church did not like the new church's brand of theology or its growth, because it constantly needed more and more space. Some of the members became fed up and began an effort to oust them from the facility. In time, they succeeded.

Needing to replace the income, however, Main Street Church quickly rented the facilities to a non-English speaking church, which had ethnic roots in another country. Tragedy of tragedies, it turned out to be a cult that denied the deity of Christ and distorted the Christian understanding of the Trinity. Pastor Joe, the one-year interim pastor, strongly objected to the heresy being taught in the church building, but he found heavy resistance to canceling the renter's lease. Yet he did not give up. The local leaders of the cult group were interviewed about their false beliefs. After a stormy meeting or two among the church leaders, the renters were asked to vacate. Later, as Pastor Ed did his research, he wondered if the cult group left any lingering openings for the evil one.

Although the church had good memories, as well as painful ones, several of the recent pastors sensed a spiritual darkness and a gloom in the facility. Pastor Joe sensed it and led several people to pray from the four corners of the property. A series of special meetings with a guest speaker soon followed, which bore fruit. The pastors of the first church that rented the facility also had sensed the same oppressive darkness. They had, in fact, confirmed it to their own satisfaction through one of their trusted visiting evangelists. Pastor Ed felt the same spirit of darkness too, a sense of depression and despair. He began to read and study on the subject of spiritual warfare and became convinced that the place needed a more thorough spiritual cleansing. He and a few others prayed through every room of the place but did not yet sense any full release.

Pastor Ed called for a Setting Your Church Free conference. The process seemed to go well. The participants were honest in their evaluations and sincere in their prayers. But a fascinating story emerged the next morning. Pastor Joe, a godly man of prayer, phoned from 1,500 miles away to say that he had been praying the day before. The Lord whispered to his heart, "Something powerful is happening today at

Main Street Church." He phoned to confirm his sense of discernment from the Lord. When he learned that the Setting Your Church Free event was underway during the same time he was praying, he praised the Lord.

Pastor Ed soon sensed the effectiveness of the spiritual cleansing. A new freedom was felt in the facility. The old oppressiveness was gone. Gone, too, were the former patterns of conflict. Decisions, even tough decisions that did not please everyone, were made and implemented. Pastor Ed also began to make restitution on the church's behalf. He contacted the leadership of the church that had been ousted, seeking forgiveness. The sense of Christian fellowship was graciously restored. After this meeting, Pastor Ed felt a tremendous sense of release. He sensed that the old debts were canceled; the church was free and clear.

By this time, however, the church was depleted. The remaining leaders sensed that the best strategy was to close the church and plant a new, completely different congregation in the same facility after a reasonable period of time. Pastor Ed did not believe his calling was church planting, and the church officially closed.

The spiritual cleansing of the facility, the restoration of ruptured relationships and the physical upgrades in the building itself prepared the way for a fresh start. A new church emerged with healthy relationships. It has a strong missionary vision and has planted a daughter church.

WHAT'S GOING ON?

Having a case history before us, we can now analyze the situation. Different people may reach various conclusions, but Neil and I saw a pattern of demonic influence at work in Main Street Church. The principle of Exodus 20:4-6 applied here:

> You shall not make for yourself an idol in the form of anything in heaven above or on the earth beneath or in the waters below. You shall not bow down to them or worship them; for I, the LORD your God, am a jealous God, punishing the children for

the sin of the fathers to the third and fourth generation of those who hate me, but showing love to a thousand generations of those who love me and keep my commandments.

In the New Testament, the apostle Peter writes, "Knowing that you were not redeemed with perishable things like silver or gold from your futile way of life *inherited from your forefathers*" (1 Pet. 1:18, *NASB*, emphasis added). Spiritual strongholds can be passed on from one generation to the next if not dealt with. Nobody is guilty because his or her forefathers sinned; however, because of their sin, Satan may gain access to you, your family or your church. Nature (genetics) and nurture also contribute to this cycle of abuse. All three conditions can predispose an individual or a church to a particular sin.

We have noted how Old Testament leaders confessed their sins and the sins of their fathers (see Neh. 1:6; 9:2; Jer. 14:20; Dan. 9:10-11). In the early sixth century, the prophet Ezekiel had to correct a misunderstanding of the generational "curse":

> The word of the LORD came to me: "What do you people mean by quoting this proverb about the land of Israel: 'The fathers eat sour grapes, and the children's teeth are set on edge'? As surely as I live, declares the Sovereign LORD, you will no longer quote this proverb in Israel" (Ezek. 18:1-3).

The popular proverb was neither from the book of Proverbs nor from the mouth of God. The problem Ezekiel was trying to correct was a fatalistic response to the Law and the abdication of personal responsibility. Children are not guilty because of their parents' sins, and they will not be punished for their parents' iniquities, which are visited upon them, if they are diligent to turn away from the sins of their parents. The book of Proverbs says, "Like a fluttering sparrow or a darting swallow, an undeserved curse does not come to rest" (Prov. 26:2). But scholars have taught the necessity of individual and group repentance for corporate sins:

The corporate involvement of sin deeply impressed itself upon the people, however. The prophets proclaimed that it was not only a few wicked individuals but the whole nation that was laden with sin (see Isa. 1:4). Generation upon generation treasured up wrath. Thus it was easy for those who were finally forced to bear the painful consequences to protest that all the effects of corporate guilt were being visited upon them. The exiles lamented: "Our fathers sinned and are no more, and we bear their punishment" (Lam. 5:7). They even had a proverb: "The fathers have eaten sour grapes, and the children's teeth are set on edge" (Jer. 31:29). Against this both Jeremiah and Ezekiel protested (see v. 30; Ezek. 18:10-20). No son was to be held accountable for his father's crimes: "The soul who sins is the one who will die" (Ezek. 18:4). In saying this, they did not mean to deny corporate sin; this was beyond dispute. Their purpose was to accentuate individual responsibility, which was in danger of becoming submerged in a consciousness of overpowering national calamity. Even though the nation was now suffering a bitter corporate punishment, there was hope for the individual if he or she repented.[3]

Main Street Church opened doors to the evil one through the scandal of sexual sin on the part of some of its former pastors. The church people repeatedly engaged in the corporate sin of divisiveness, disrupting unity within the fellowship. The refusal to forgive was evident to any objective observer. The evil powers did not lack opportunity to undermine this fellowship in corporate terms. Other than the sins of the pastors, no attempt was made to investigate the possible sinful practices of some of the members. They were "submerged in a consciousness of overpowering national calamity." Repentance came too late to save the former church, but a new healthy church of the same denomination emerged in the same facility.

The practice of praying from the four corners of the property, and again through each room in the building, appeared to be of some help.

However, it did not give full or lasting relief. Resisting the devil loosens his grip, but if the resistance does not include repentance of the personal and corporate sins as well as a commitment to obey Christ, it is unlikely that freedom will last (see Luke 11:24-25). It is fine for pastors to pray for the church, but it is much more powerful when all the responsible leaders renounce their sins, announce their resources in Christ, claim God's promises and commit themselves to replace the sin with positive action. When they follow through on their commitment, the shield of faith is held firmly in place. It extinguishes the flaming arrows of the evil one (see Eph. 6:16).

CHRIST'S JUDGMENTS

Christ's judgments fall upon Christians *in this life* who fall into obvious sin and refuse to do anything about it. His judgments come upon churches that indulge in corporate sins or even tolerate them. Consider the following passages in Revelation 2—3:

> **To Ephesus:** "If you do not repent, I will come to you and remove your lampstand from its place" (Rev. 2:5).

> **To Pergamum:** "Repent therefore! Otherwise, I will soon come to you and will fight against them with the sword of my mouth" (Rev. 16).

> **To Thyatira:** "I have given her time to repent of her immorality, but she is unwilling. So I will cast her on a bed of suffering, and I will make those who commit adultery with her suffer intensely, unless they repent of her ways. I will strike her children dead. Then all the churches will know that I am he who searches hearts and minds, and I will repay each of you according to your deeds" (Rev. 21-23).

> **To Sardis:** "But if you do not wake up, I will come like a thief,

and you will not know at what time I will come to you" (Rev. 3:3).

To Laodicea: "So, because you are lukewarm—neither hot nor cold—I am about to spit you out of my mouth" (Rev. 3:16).

Those whom I love I rebuke and discipline. So be earnest, and repent (Rev. 3:19).

The good news is that warnings of judgment are not the end of the story. Every church can turn around and follow Jesus. Every Christian can overcome his or her sins and past and become a winner. The Spirit is speaking to the churches, and the risen Jesus walks among His people and knows what they do and teach. He is the living, powerful Christ revealed in the vision of Revelation 1. He has authority, power, splendor and strength to lift His people from personal and corporate sins into the joy of holy living and effective witnessing. What is more, He promises great rewards to every church that obeys Him.

CHRIST'S REWARDS

It is not the purpose of this book to become a commentary that tries to explain all the symbolism of the rewards promised in Revelation 2 and 3. The lesson here is that Jesus does reward each Christian and every church that "overcomes." Every letter to the seven churches has a reference to overcoming and a promise for those who share the victory of Christ's death, resurrection and reign. In the New Testament, "overcomes" (*nikaó*) is a spiritual warfare word. *The New International Dictionary of New Testament Theology* states that *nikaó* always assumes the conflict between God or Christ and the opposing demonic powers.[4] Like Jesus, believers sometimes win by losing. They become martyrs, prisoners or the targets of slander and lies, but they overcome by following Jesus' instructions to repent, remember, hold fast and obey.

CHURCH	PROMISED REWARD
Ephesus	"To him who overcomes, I will give the right to eat from the tree of life, which is in the paradise of God" (Rev. 2:7).
Smyrna	"Be faithful, even to the point of death, and I will give you the crown of life" (Rev. 2:10). "He who overcomes will not be hurt at all by the second death" (Rev. 2:11).
Pergamum	"To him who overcomes, I will give some of the hidden manna. I will also give him a white stone with a new name written on it, known only to him who receives it" (Rev. 2:17).
Thyatira	"To him who overcomes and does my will to the end, I will give authority over the nations. . . . I will also give him the morning star" (Rev. 2:26,28).
Sardis	"He who overcomes will, like them, be dressed in white. I will never blot out his name from the book of life, but will acknowledge his name before my Father and his angels" (Rev. 3:5).
Philadelphia	"Him who overcomes I will make a pillar in the temple of my God. Never again will he leave it. I will write on him the name of my God and the name of the city of my God, the new Jerusalem, which is coming down out of heaven from my God; and I will also write on him my new name" (Rev. 3:12).
Laodicea	"To him who overcomes, I will give the right to sit with me on my throne, just as I overcame and sat down with my Father on his throne" (Rev. 3:21)

Do you recall Small Town Church and its pattern of rebellion against denominational authority? The church hosted a Setting Your

Church Free event. It was one of the early ones, when the process was still in primitive form. Nevertheless, the people in the church identified several problem areas and dealt with them by prayer and action. Within a year, things began to happen. The church sold its facility. Demonstrating their loyalty to God and to the denomination, the people in the church tithed their income from the sale. Most of the funds went to denominational missions, church planting and ministry projects designated by the church.

The pastor of Small Town Church, who was from another church background, did a fine job, but he sensed the Lord leading him to go back to his old denomination. After a careful search, Small Town Church called a new pastor who had experience in relocating a congregation. They changed the church name and moved to a nearby community to start over. The new start was treated like a church planting project. The church found freedom from bondage and was marked by loyalty.

Not every Setting Your Church Free event is a quick fix or a cure-all. It simply opens the way spiritually for godly, hardworking leaders to do their tasks. As Neil pointed out in the earlier chapters, leadership abilities and practices hold a remarkable influence upon the ongoing life of the Church. But even the best of leaders still find themselves the target of Satan's attacks. The Christian life was never designed for luxury and ease. Christ built His Body to overcome and to win the spiritual battle!

SATAN'S ATTACKS

We need to make a distinction between spiritual attacks from the evil one and the place we give Satan because of personal and corporate sins. Corporate sins give the devil a foothold to do his dirty work. Satan's attacks are something else. They are the enemy's attempts to disrupt the work of God. We are under attack because of what we do right. When churches or individual Christians love their neighbors, do good works, witness for Christ and glorify God, they can expect some opposition.

How does the enemy attack churches and its people? Consider

something that happens to almost every Christian family. More family hassles take place getting ready for church than at any other time. Compared to work or school, church usually starts later, ends sooner and requires less effort. So why the bickering and arguments on the way to church? Why is it so much harder going to church than it is going to Little League, or McDonald's, or a school program? Have you ever noticed that when you get back into the car after church the tension is gone? No more abnormal hassles. No big arguments. Just normal family talk. Is the enemy trying to disrupt worship and distract from the study of God's Word?

Neil had a skeptical Doctor of Ministry student who reported after the class that Sunday mornings before church were the worst periods of their lives. Every Sunday morning, he and his wife would get into an argument and go off to church mad, where they would then attempt to preach and teach God's Word! He never would have guessed that Satan was behind it. Since the class, he and his wife became aware of the spiritual battle and started to pray when they first woke up every Sunday morning. Sunday morning hassles stopped, and they could sense the difference in their preaching and teaching.

Why don't you give it a try? For the next few Sundays, ask everyone in your family to pray something similar to the following when you first get up:

Dear heavenly Father,

We love You and thank You for all the rich blessings You bestow upon us. We deserved hell, but you gave us eternal life. We set aside this day to worship and honor You. We yield ourselves and our home to You and ask You to fill us with Your Holy Spirit. Enable us to speak the truth in love with one another and to be receptive to the instruction we are to receive today. Empower us for ministry as we seek to meet the needs of one another. By the power and authority of the Lord Jesus Christ, we command Satan and all his demons to leave our presence, our home and our transportation to church, and we ask that you would put a hedge of protection around our home and our family. In Jesus' name we pray. Amen.

Consider the problem of falling asleep during a church service. People generally have more time to sleep Sunday morning, so they come to church more rested than they do to work or school, and most sermons are shorter than the 50-minute lectures given at school or elsewhere. One of Neil's students couldn't keep her eyes open for most of his class, and Neil is not a boring teacher. She waited for three weeks after the class was over before she came to see him. She said, "I have always had trouble staying awake in church, and I blamed it on boring preachers, but I have attended church the last three Sundays alertly awake. I would never have considered that the problem could be spiritual before your class, but now I know it is."

Why do some people never sing in church—not even a joyful noise? Some, of course, have perfectly normal reasons. They may not know the words or the tune, or some may be tone deaf or feel socially inhibited. But others are being spiritually inhibited from singing hymns and choruses of praise to God. When Neil was pastoring, he had an elder in his church who made life miserable for him. The man never sang in church. This phenomenon is more evident in counseling the spiritually oppressed. The evil one does not like praise music. David played the harp and the evil spirit departed from Saul.

Leadership Attacks

One of the most common attacks identified in the Setting Your Church Free seminars is the harassment of Christian leaders. Satan knows that Christian leaders hold strategic value to the progress of the Church, so he focuses his attacks on them.

When we effectively bear fruit, we sense more opposition. When a church actively engages in evangelism accompanied with intercessory prayer, expect the enemy to stir up opposition. Neil would experience a spiritual attack the night before he started a Living Free in Christ conference, which continued for the first five years he held the conferences. We never sense any spiritual opposition in personal counseling unless we are trying to resolve something. That is why many counselors never experience any demonic interference if all they do is listen, explain and help others cope with their difficulties.

What the Devil Hates

Those involved in evangelistic events, church planting and pioneer missions have learned to expect some spiritual resistance to their work. Veteran missionaries are prayerfully cautious when they invade Satan's strongholds. Some of the most effective strategists send intercessory prayer teams into the area first, followed by evangelists and church planters (see Rom. 15:30; Eph. 6:18-20). The opposition often shows up in team relationships if the members have not been established alive and free in Christ. We strongly encourage missionary groups to help their missionary candidates resolve their personal and spiritual conflicts before they go on the field.

The last thing the devil wants us to know is who we are in Christ. The accuser of the brethren has kept many Christians living well below their potential, believing that they are no-good failures. Many have been falsely led to believe that they have committed the unpardonable sin, which no Christian can do. Most Christians struggle with a negative self-image and are ignorant of their spiritual heritage.

Neil and I routinely experience the adversary's opposition before our conferences and when we seek to resolve personal and spiritual conflicts. If the Lord lays it on your heart, pray for your spiritual leaders, your colleagues and Neil and I according to Ephesians 6:18-20:

> And pray in the Spirit on all occasions with all kinds of prayers and request. With this in mind, be alert and always keep on praying for all the saints. Pray also for me, that whenever I open my mouth, words may be given me so that I will fearlessly make known the mystery of the gospel, for which I am an ambassador in chains. Pray that I may declare it fearlessly, as I should.

Attacks on Ministry

The Bible reveals that Satan can hinder the direction and progress of Christian leaders. Paul wrote, "For we wanted to come to you—certainly I, Paul, did, again and again—but Satan stopped us" (1 Thess. 2:18). (For other examples of Satan's activity, see Matt. 4:1; Acts 10:37-38; 2 Cor. 11:3.)

The point is that the evil one can and will attack us when we are obedient and faithful. In Revelation 2—3, the two great threats to the Church are from within (compromise and corporate sin) and from without (harassment and persecution). In the previous chapter on corporate sins we talked about the threat from within, but the attacks described in this chapter are from without. They come from pressure and persecution of a hostile culture, which tries to muzzle the public testimony of God's faithful people. They also come from harassment and hindrances as the evil one attacks the faithful followers of the Lamb. "Then the dragon [Satan] was enraged at the woman [the people of God] and went off to make war against the rest of her offspring [us]—those who obey God's commandments and hold to the testimony of Jesus" (Rev. 12:17).

PROTECTION OR PERSEVERANCE?

In the context of spiritual warfare, Paul admonishes us to pray in the Spirit on all occasions, with all kinds of prayers and requests for all the saints (see Eph. 6:18). How should God's people pray about Satan's attacks? Do we pray for protection? Do we pray that we will avoid pain and be exempt from hardship? Do we pray for a trouble-free church? Do we pray that we will avoid pressure and persecution at all costs? Is protection our ultimate goal?

On the other hand, suffering for the sake of righteousness is part of the sanctification process. Should we then pray for perseverance and strength to endure suffering and pain? Should we take up our cross, rejoice in the midst of evil and put up with the enemy's attacks? The quick answer is that we should pray *both* for protection and for perseverance—but this requires a little explanation.

Certainly Christians pray for protection from Satan and his evil forces. The Old Testament descriptions of God as our rock, refuge, sword, shield, strong tower and fortress all suggest protection. The armor of God is for our protection (see Eph. 6:10-20; 1 Thess. 5:8-9). Jesus petitioned the Father for our protection: "My prayer is not that you take them out of the world but that you protect them from the evil one" (John 17:15). He taught us to pray, "Deliver us from the evil one" (Matt.

6:13). Paul asked others to pray for him and promised God's protection upon them: "And pray that we may be delivered from wicked and evil men, for not everyone has faith. But the Lord is faithful, and he will strengthen and protect you from the evil one" (2 Thess. 3:2-3).

On the other hand, trials and tribulations produce proven character (see Rom. 5:3-5). Paul also taught, "For it has been granted to you on behalf of Christ not only to believe on him, but also to suffer for him" (Phil. 1:29). Peter writes that Christians are not to be surprised when they suffer: "But rejoice that you participate in the sufferings of Christ, so that you may be overjoyed when his glory is revealed" (1 Pet. 4:13; see vv. 12-19). Christians have been tortured and martyred for their steadfast faith: "They overcame him by the blood of the Lamb and by the word of their testimony; *they did not love their lives so much as to shrink from death*" (Rev. 12:11, emphasis added).

Two Exemptions

Obedient Christians will not have to endure the wrath of God (see 1 Thess. 1:10; 5:9; Rom. 5:9), nor do they need to suffer from the accusations, temptations and harassments of Satan, except by the perfect will of God. The Lord may use Satan and his demons for His purposes, which may be necessary for the sake of discipline, but know that God disciplines His children for their own good (see Heb. 12:5-11). The apostle Paul was given a "messenger [literally angel] of Satan" to torment him for a disciplinary purpose—to keep him from becoming conceited (2 Cor. 12:7). When sufferings come to faithful Christians who have taken their stand in Christ, they need to persevere (see Heb. 10:32-36).

Praying for Protection

After the Setting Your Church Free sessions, some pastors report intensified spiritual battles. The implementation of what they have learned is often the hardest step. The opposition comes when they seek to resolve the conflicts, but not so much when they only are gaining clarification as to what those conflicts are. Those who experience no opposition to their ministry probably are not accomplishing much. Woe to us if all men speak well of us. We should expect some resistance if we're bearing fruit.

Based on Romans 12:1-2, Ephesians 6:10-18 and James 4:7, Neil strives for personal balance with the following prayer and declaration:

Prayer

Lord, I submit myself to You and yield my body as a living sacrifice. I ask You to fill me with Your Holy Spirit. If what I'm experiencing is in accordance with Your will, I gladly submit to this time of testing in order that my faith may be strengthened and my character may be made more like Yours. I believe that Your will is good, acceptable and perfect. I pray for Your protection. In Jesus' name. Amen.

Declaration

In the name and authority of the Lord Jesus Christ, I refuse and renounce any assignments by Satan that are directed at me, my family or my ministry, which are not according to God's will. I command Satan to leave my presence. Since I bear the responsibility of being the head of my home, I lift the shield of faith over my family.

Church Protection Prayer

Although it is not part of the Setting Your Church Free process, the following is a prayer and declaration of mine for your church's protection and perseverance. It claims Christ's resources and stands fast against the adversary:

Prayer

Dear heavenly Father,

Thank You that our Lord Jesus disarmed the evil powers and authorities at the Cross. You made a public spectacle of them (see Col. 2:15). Guide us in enforcing Your victory.

Lead us to remove the "high places" that the enemy gains in our lives through our personal and corporate disobedience. Reveal to us our corpo-

rate sins, that we may renounce, repent and reject them. Flood us with biblical truths that replace them. We confess our lack of faith and trust in You. We confess our lack of time in prayer and our disbelief in Your present, active power in response to prayer. Cleanse us of complacency and make us healing and refreshing, not lukewarm and putrid.

We confess holding back costly love and giving only what costs us nothing. We now forgive one another from our hearts for the times we have hurt or lied to one another.

Heal the pain left by the attacks of Satan—and the damage caused—on our churches and leaders. Open our eyes to see the adversary's attacks and cause us to use the sword of the Spirit to stand against them in His power. Weaken whatever positions the enemy may have left.

Release Your angels to accomplish for us and for our church everything You send them to do. Remove the enemy's interference so that Your angels can minister unhindered to our church and our people.

Fill us afresh and anew with the fullness of the Holy Spirit. Lead us to live in Him and keep in step with Him. As head of our church, Lord Jesus Christ, direct us, guide us and protect us. As Bridegroom of Your Bride, purify us, nourish us and satisfy us. As architect and builder, design us, build us and develop us. As author and finisher of the faith, teach us, instruct us and disciple us. Make us the beautiful Church in Your sight that You intend us to be.

Stimulate us to respond to You with revolutionary repentance and also with genuine faith, hope, love, obedience and holy living, and thank You that in Christ we are forgiven.

In the precious and powerful name of our Lord Jesus Christ. Amen.

Declaration

As shepherds of God's flock under our care, we stand our ground as overseers and examples (see 1 Pet. 5:1-4). We offer ourselves and our bodies to God as living sacrifices, holy and pleasing to Him, which is our spiritual worship (see Rom. 12:1-2). As servants of Christ and as those entrusted with the secret things

of God, we fulfill the requirement that is entrusted to us so that
we may prove faithful (see 1 Cor. 4:1-2). We submit our ministries, our programs, our classes and groups, our activities, our
facilities, and all our members and attendees to God. In full
union with our Lord Jesus Christ, including His protection and
power, we now command Satan and all evil powers targeting
our church to leave us and everything under our care. In the
name and authority of Christ, we remove any advantage the
adversary has gained. We forbid the evil one or his henchmen
from attacking us. We accept only what is within our heavenly
Father's will to accomplish His sovereign purposes. We declare
that Satan and his forces are defeated through the death, resurrection and present reign of Christ at the right hand of the
Father. We claim the promise of Jesus when He said, "I will
build my church, and the gates of Hades will not overcome it"
(Matt. 16:18).

STEP 5: IDENTIFYING AND RESISTING ATTACKS

We turn now to the procedure used in the Setting Your Church Free
event to identify and resist the enemy's attacks. The facilitator will want
to remind the group that this step has a different focus from the one on
corporate sins. The last step dealt with the advantage gained by Satan
because of what your church or its people did wrong. The attacks you
will identify in this step come because of the things that your church,
your pastors and your leaders *are doing right.*

Satan will harass the pastors, leaders and people in your church at
their points of greatest vulnerability. Not only are Christ's faithful followers being individually harassed, but also deceived people are used
skillfully by the adversary to cause disunity within the churches.

During the Setting Your Church Free event, the group prays a written prayer together, followed by silent prayer, asking the Lord to help
them discern accurately the nature of Satan's attacks upon the church.
Group discernment is necessary once again. The facilitator may ask
something like, "Do we agree that this is a spiritual attack? Does anyone

see it differently?" Many Western Christians have been taught that every effect has a natural explanation. Others want to see a demon as the cause of everything. It requires spiritual maturity to discern the truth. "But solid food is for the mature, who by constant use have trained themselves to distinguish good from evil" (Heb. 5:14). It takes a little longer to reach group consensus, but it is far better than listing only the ideas of one person.

Sample Attacks

The following examples of attacks are from conferences in several churches, with their own actual wording used:

- On leadership—stress, division, burnout, marriage problems, anger against people
- On families—divorce, problems with children, financial difficulties, unemployment, abuse, death, broken relationships
- Deception that we're doing good enough
- Attacks on pastors (and former pastors)
- Stimulate anger over false perceptions and assumptions
- Creating apathy toward good things so they die
- Distraction from spiritual disciplines
- The spirit of deception
- Things look right but are not
- Believing rumors
- Situations exaggerated
- Christians have no problems, not like me

Similar themes will come up in the various steps of the seminar, such as weaknesses, painful memories, corporate sins and attacks. This will happen naturally and will prove helpful in the next step, the Prayer Action Plan (we will discuss this repetition more in the next chapter). At this point, it is enough to say that duplication is okay; in fact, it is good. By this time, a collective pattern begins to become obvious when the weaknesses, corporate sins and spiritual attacks are seen together.

Christian leaders must actively take their place in Christ and stand against the spiritual opposition rather than passively withdraw. God instructs us to test the spirits (see 1 John 4:1-6), and He gives us assurance of power to overcome every spirit that fails to acknowledge Jesus, "because the one who is in you is greater than the one who is in the world" (1 John 4:4). Notice the active participation on our part when Paul discusses the armor of God in Ephesians 6:10-20:

- Be strong (v. 10)
- Put on the full armor (vv. 11,13)
- Stand your ground (v. 13)
- Stand firm (v. 14)
- Take up the shield of faith (v. 16)
- Take the helmet of salvation (v. 17)
- [Take] the sword of the Spirit (v. 17)
- Pray in the Spirit (v. 18)

John instructs us to "overcome" (see 1 John 2:13-14; Rev. 2:7,11,17). James and Peter admonish us to "submit to God" and "resist the devil" (see Jas. 4:7; 1 Pet. 5:8-9). We should renounce Satan's attacks and come against them in Jesus' powerful name. Christians have greater authority and power in Christ than Satan and his demons. There are no instructions given in Scripture to fear the devil. God is our only legitimate object of fear. You don't want to take on the devil in the flesh, but in the Spirit he is no match for any child of God who knows the truth. Christians are instructed in Scripture to stand firm and resist. In this step, that is exactly what the group does with the evil attacks it discerns.

When the list is complete, renounce each attack one by one, as follows:

In the name and authority of our Lord Jesus Christ, we renounce Satan's attacks [list each one of the identified attacks]. We resist them and stand firm against them in Jesus' powerful name. Together we declare, "The Lord rebuke you, the Lord bind you" from any present or any future influence upon us.

Points of Caution

Testimonies of some former satanists and cult members indicate that certain deceived or wicked people are deliberately out to destroy effective Christian ministries. Sometimes blood sacrifices are made to claim false ownership of Christian leaders or ministries. At other times, satanic assignments are placed upon God's people or their leaders. In the past, this type of activity was more open in animistic cultures in which belief in evil spirits is accepted by everyone. Western Christians have tended to dismiss the activity of witch doctors or shamans as mere superstition. Committed Christians are now taking a second look.

Satanists are becoming bolder. We know of one church (it can't be named because the court wisely ordered a media lid) where people from a satanic cult took children out of the nursery during worship, abused them and then brought the little kids back before worship was over. Some of the accused were church members considered to be infiltrators from the cult. In this court case, two people were convicted of child abuse and are now serving time.

On the other hand, we have seen true spiritual leaders falsely accused of incest and satanism. In turn, the small percentage of false accusations cause the less informed to conclude wrongly that all memories are false. The point of caution is to make a thorough investigation before bringing any allegations. Such allegations should not be dismissed out of hand but checked out first by church officials and then, if necessary, by civil authorities.

During the Setting Your Church Free seminar, the group will use the following declaration to stand against these attacks:

Declaration

As leaders of this church and members of the Body of Christ, we reject and disown all influence and authority of demonic powers and evil spirits that cause resistance to Christ's work. As children of God, we have been delivered from the power of darkness and brought into the kingdom of God's dear Son.

Because we are seated with Christ in the heavenly realms, we renounce all satanic assignments that are directed toward our church and our ministry. We cancel every curse that deceived or that wicked people have put on us. We announce to Satan and all his evil forces that Christ became a curse for us when He died on the cross.

We renounce any and all sacrifices by satanists or anyone else who claims false ownership of us, our ministry, our leaders or our people. We announce that we have been bought and purchased by the blood of the Lamb. We accept only the sacrifice of Jesus, whereby we belong to Him.

This step concludes with a prayer for protection and dedication to God of the leaders, people and church facilities. This is more than a mere formality. Something of genuine spiritual significance takes place when we dedicate our facilities to God. My former pastor, C. W. Perry of Rose Drive Friends Church, used to unlock all the doors and turn on the lights on Sunday mornings. (This was before the church became too large for him to continue.) As he turned on the physical lights, he prayed that God would turn on the light of Christ. He prayed for God's Word to flow freely from the Sunday School leaders and children's church leaders. God answered his prayers and the church built an effective Christian education ministry to people of all ages.

After the retreat, participants may want to walk through every room in their church facility, rededicating it and all who use it to Christ. During this step, however, there will not be the time or the energy to do this. Instead, the following prayer can be used for protection and dedication of the leaders, people and church facilities:

Prayer

Dear heavenly Father,

We worship You and You alone. You are the Lord of our lives and the Lord of our church. We offer our bodies to You as living sacrifices, holy and pleasing to God. We also present our church Body to You as a sacrifice of praise.

We pray for Your protection of our pastors, leaders, members, families, attendees and all of our ministries. Grant us the wisdom and grace to deal with heretics and spiritual wolves. We pray for discernment in order to judge between good and evil.

We dedicate all of our facilities to You and all the property that You have entrusted to us, including our sound system, audiovisual equipment, kitchen and transportation. We rededicate our sanctuary, classrooms, offices and every part of our facility and property.

Lord Jesus Christ, You are the head of this church, and we exalt You. May all that we do bring honor and glory to You. In Jesus' holy name we pray. Amen.

The next step is the most challenging. It involves discerning God's will in order to synthesize all the input from the first five steps into a short, manageable Prayer Action Plan. This is what we have been building up to.

Notes
1. Clinton E. Arnold, *Powers of Darkness: Principalities and Powers in Paul's Letters* (Downers Grove, IL: InterVarsity Press, 1992), p. 213. Emphasis added.
2. See the major commentaries for the interpretations that lead to this modern-day application.
3. Francis Brown, S. Driver and Charles Briggs, *Hebrew and English Lexicon* (Peabody, MA: Hendrickson Publishers, 1996), n.p.
4. Walther Günther, *The New International Dictionary of New Testament Theology*, vol. 1, p. 650.

THE PRAYER ACTION PLAN

Chapter 11

The conclusion of the Setting Your Church Free event is summarized in the Prayer Action Plan. Hopefully, the group has now heard from God through His conviction and guidance as discerned by the leadership. The leadership is now in a better position to focus their prayers and make plans for action. From the patterns that have emerged, they should know what they need to confess and renounce. However, turning away from that which is sinful and unfruitful is not enough. In keeping with the spirit of repentance, the leadership also must announce their decisions, claim their resources in Christ and affirm the promises of God. The final step is to overcome strategically that which is wrong and advance that which is right.

In 1 and 2 Chronicles and the book of Psalms, the emphasis is upon God's splendor rather than the splendor of nations, royalty or creation. The Lord is robed with splendor and majesty, and He calls us to worship Him in Spirit and in truth.

Splendor and majesty are before him; strength and glory are in his sanctuary. Ascribe to the LORD, O families of nations, ascribe to the LORD glory and strength. Ascribe to the LORD the glory due his name; bring an offering and come into his courts. Worship the LORD in the *splendor* of his holiness; tremble before him, all the earth (Ps. 96:6-9, emphasis added).

God is calling the "families of nations" and "all the earth" to ascribe to the Lord the glory due His name. This is not for the nation of Israel alone, but for God's people everywhere. God intended for Israel to serve as a magnet to draw others to Himself, and Christ commissioned the Church to take His message to all the nations.

DISPLAY OF SPLENDOR

It is God's intent to display His splendor among all the nations by means of His people. To glorify God means to manifest His presence, and this can only happen in churches and in children of God who are living in a righteous relationship with Him. Perhaps this is why the seven churches of Revelation are pictured as lampstands. They hold the true light that gives light to everyone (see John 1:4,9). They radiate the splendor of God's glory. "For God, who said, 'Let light shine out of darkness,' made his light shine in our hearts to give us the light of the knowledge of the glory of God in the face of Christ" (2 Cor. 4:6). Liberated churches fulfill God's eternal purposes of revealing His glory and displaying His splendor.

Surely you will summon nations you know not, and nations that do not know you will hasten to you, because of the LORD your God, the Holy One of Israel, for *he has endowed you with splendor* (Isa. 55:5, emphasis added).

Then will all your people be righteous and they will possess the land forever. They are the shoot I have planted, the work of my hands, *for the display of my splendor* (Isa. 60:21, emphasis added).

And provide for those who grieve in Zion—to bestow on them a crown of beauty instead of ashes, the oil of gladness instead of mourning, and a garment of praise instead of a spirit of despair. They will be called oaks of righteousness, a planting of the LORD *for the display of his splendor* (Isa. 61:3, emphasis added).

Some of this prophecy will be fulfilled when Christ comes again and gathers His people to Himself, but are we not called to glorify God in our bodies and in His Body, the Church? Where is the church that God has endowed with splendor? Where are the people who glorify God in their bodies? Could it not be your church? Could it not be your people? Don't you want the presence of the Lord to be glorified in you and your church?

Jesus said, "Let your light shine before men, that they may see your good deeds and praise your Father in heaven" (Matt. 5:16). Does the goal of displaying God's splendor in your church and your community seem too high too reach in this adulterous generation in which we live? What is our witness if God isn't glorified, if there is no change taking place for the better in our people, if church is little more than a social gathering of like-minded people? If there is no vision of God being glorified in your church, the people will perish.

LISTEN TO THE LORD OF SPLENDOR

The Lord Jesus gave some sharp commands to His churches in Revelation about their weaknesses, memories, corporate sins and evil attacks. Let's review His commands before we consider our response:

Ephesus	Remember, repent
Smyrna	Be faithful
Pergamum	Repent
Thyatira	Hold on

Sardis	Wake up; strengthen what remains, remember, obey, repent
Philadelphia	Hold on
Laodicea	Be earnest, repent

The Prayer Action Plan is our response to these commands. It makes four declarations: "We renounce . . . "; "We announce . . . "; "We affirm . . . "; and "We will . . . " These declarations constitute our response to what our leaders have discerned from God's guidance, as follows:

- *We renounce* is our response to Christ's command, "Repent."
- *We announce* is our response to Christ's command, "Remember."
- *We affirm* is our response to Christ's command, "Hold on."
- *We will* is our response to Christ's command, "Obey."

It is important that all the church leaders know what they are doing in the Prayer Action Plan. Let's examine these four commands and our responses.

REPENT AND RENOUNCE

Again and again, Jesus commands His churches to repent. No playing politics. No delays. No excuses. It is time to change and it is time to change now. Jesus wants decisive action. He shouts, "Stop! Don't do that anymore! Change your attitude! Change your lifestyle!" He wants His churches to make a clean break with their personal and corporate sins.

What you have discerned does not require six committees bogged down for a year resulting in a two-inch-thick environmental impact report on your church. Jesus is talking about sin, which is offensive to Him and damaging to His people. He wants His churches to abandon their sinful ways right now.

We respond by *renouncing* that which displeases God. We plead guilty and openly admit that we are and have been wrong—but we do more. We repudiate, reject, disown and disavow any and all sin. We don't rationalize or defend ourselves. We change our thinking and change our ways.

"We Renounce . . . "

"I renounce you, Satan, and all your works and all your ways" is one of the oldest declarations of the Church. It is in the *Book of Common Prayer* as part of the baptismal ritual, and many liturgical churches still use it. Just choosing to believe the truth is not enough if we are still holding on to past practices and beliefs. Paul wrote in 2 Corinthians 4:1-2:

> Therefore, since we have this ministry, as we received mercy, we do not lose heart, but we have renounced the things hidden because of shame, not walking in craftiness or adulterating the word of God, but by the manifestation of truth commending ourselves to every man's conscience in the sight of God (*NASB*).

What do churches renounce in the Setting Your Church Free process? The following is a representative list taken from various churches, again using their own wording:

- We renounce complacency and contentment.
- We renounce a critical and judgmental spirit.
- We renounce our passivity in spiritual disciplines.
- We renounce gossip and pettiness.
- We renounce moral failure.
- We renounce factions in the church that separate us from the love and unity of Christ.
- We renounce lukewarmness and weariness in doing the Lord's work.
- We renounce our distrust of God's chosen and faithful leaders.
- We renounce our sinful pride that keeps us from confessing our sins and receiving salvation and healing.
- We renounce our poor stewardship of time, talent and treasures.

- We renounce our selfish pride that says "We're good enough."
- We renounce our self-focus that produces apathy to the lost.

Although church leaders most often renounce corporate sins, many do not stop there. Some renounce Satan's attacks, painful memories and weaknesses. The following are more examples:

- We renounce attacks of the devil in stimulating doubts and disagreements.
- We renounce ungodly values that the world imposes on our families.
- We renounce the spirit of darkness and heaviness that seeks to destroy our church.
- We renounce the spirit of fear that paralyzes open sharing, involvement, service and evangelism.
- We renounce attacks on leadership.
- We renounce any footholds gained by the evil one through past hurts and traumas.
- We renounce the spirit of criticism that divides rather than unites.
- We renounce Satan's use of discouragement as a tool against us.
- We renounce a spirit of division and defeat.
- We renounce the "destroyer" spirit and all his attacks on our church and community.

Keeping the "repent and renounce" declaration in mind, let's turn to the second response to Christ's commands. He commands us to remember, and we respond by announcing the riches we have in Christ.

Remember and Announce

It is our fallen human nature to be absorbed in our problems instead of being conscious of Christ's presence and power. We tend to be problem-centered instead of solution-centered. We must keep in mind who we are in Christ, what He has done on our behalf, and the spiritual power and authority we have to do His will. This is more than a mental exercise; it is a spiritual discipline. It is affirming every day our God-given riches in Christ. John Stott wrote:

> So, in practice we should constantly be reminding ourselves who we are. We need to learn to talk to ourselves, and ask ourselves questions: "Don't you know? Don't you know the meaning of your conversion and baptism? Don't you know that you have been united to Christ in His death and resurrection? Don't you know that you have been enslaved to God and have committed yourself to His obedience? Don't you know these things? Don't you know who you are?" We must go on pressing ourselves with such questions, until we reply to ourselves: "Yes, I do know who I am, a new person in Christ, and by the grace of God I shall live accordingly."[1]

We respond to Christ's call to remember by *announcing* our resources in Christ, declaring them together. In so doing, we focus on our riches in Christ rather than on our poverty without Him. We recall our position in Christ rather than the pain from our past. We claim our resources in Christ, rather than relying on our own strength and resources. We proclaim the positive biblical opposite of what we renounced. To illustrate, let's look at part of our former list, along with the positive biblical opposites. Again, these are actual declarations from real churches.

- *We renounce complacency and contentment.*
- We announce that in Christ we have vision, boldness, freedom and confidence.
- *We renounce a critical and judgmental spirit.*
- We announce that in Christ we have love and acceptance for one another.
- *We renounce our passivity in spiritual disciplines.*
- We announce that in Christ we have spiritual hunger for intimacy with God.
- *We renounce gossip and pettiness.*

- We announce that in Christ we have the Holy Spirit who brings unity.
- *We renounce moral failure.*
- We announce that in Christ we have moral fidelity.
- *We renounce factions in the church that separate us from the love and unity of Christ.*
- We announce that we are one in Christ Jesus.

With the renounce and announce pattern in mind, we are now ready to consider the third declaration. Jesus commands us to hold on, and we respond by saying, "We affirm." What we announce focuses on our resources in Christ; what we affirm focuses on God's promises. In the affirmations, we look for biblical and motivational truths that encourage us to use the riches we have in Christ.

Hold On and Affirm

Affirming the living truth of the gospel helps us to appropriate the promises of God. We hold on so we can hold up. When life is tough, we hold on to what Christ has given us so that we can hold up under the crushing burden of hard times. When life is easy, we must resist turning loose of our riches for the glitter of a cheap substitute. Whatever happens, hold on and keep standing firm in your faith!

Another closely related command from Christ is "Be earnest" (Rev. 3:19) or "Be zealous" (*NASB*). Motivated Christians are passionate as well as disciplined. They are obedient, steadfast in their faith, enthusiastic about Jesus, glowing with the Holy Spirit and sincere in worship. Hold on to what you know to be true and affirm what motivates you to use your God-given resources for Christ.

Let's consider some of our declarations with the affirmation statement added:

- *We renounce complacency and contentment.*
- We announce that in Christ we have vision, boldness, freedom and confidence.

- *We affirm that we are children of God and have all His resources* (see John 1:12; Rom. 8:16-17; 2 Cor. 5:17; Gal. 3:26-29).
- *We renounce a critical and judgmental spirit.*
- We announce that in Christ we have love and acceptance for one another.
- *We affirm that Christ brings unity and peace among us* (see 1 Cor. 12:12-13; Eph. 4:3; Phil. 2:1-2).
- *We renounce our passivity in spiritual disciplines.*
- We announce that in Christ we have spiritual hunger for intimacy with God.
- *We affirm that we were created for fellowship with God* (see 1 John 1:3,7).
- *We renounce gossip and pettiness.*
- We announce that in Christ we have the Holy Spirit who brings unity.
- *We affirm that Christ can teach us to bridle our tongues and show us how to resolve problems* (see Matt. 18:15-17; Eph. 4:29; Jas. 1:26)

The announce and affirm declarations can be easily intertwined. We have found it helpful to keep the "we affirm" statements centered on the promises of Scripture. Here are a couple of examples:

- *We renounce acting independently of God.*
- We announce that in Christ we have God and all His resources.
- *We affirm that we can do all things through Christ who strengthens us* (see Phil. 4:13).
- *We renounce our lack of commitment to and practice of spiritual disciplines.*
- We announce that in Christ we have continual opportunity to commune with God.
- *We affirm that Christ is knocking at our heart's door, longing for intimacy with us* (see Rev. 3:20).

The Will to Obey
With the first three declarations in mind—renounce, announce, affirm—

we are ready for the fourth. Jesus does not give us orders and commands without expecting us to obey them.

A pastor asked his junior and senior high school youth to be aware of his vocabulary while he was preaching. He was asking for honest feedback because he did not want to use words that were out of date or that did not communicate his meaning. After listening for some time, the youth reported that "obey" was not a word in their regular vocabulary. Living under the grace of God doesn't negate our need to obey.

The Prayer Action Plan calls for prayer plus action. In response to Christ's call to obey, we respond that *we will* do what He desires. Notice that each of the declarations are connected. When you are completing the "we will" stage, start by looking back at what was renounced in the first declaration. In light of that renunciation, what does Jesus want us to do to obey Him? What action can we take to counter the corporate sins or spiritual attacks that we have renounced?

Consider our examples once more with the fourth action step added:

- *We renounce complacency and contentment.*
- We announce that in Christ we have vision, boldness, freedom and confidence.
- *We affirm that we are children of God and have all His resources.*
- We will step out in faith from our comfort zone.
- *We renounce a critical and judgmental spirit.*
- We announce that in Christ we have love and acceptance for one another.
- *We affirm that Christ brings unity and peace among us.*
- We will accept our differences as strengths.
- *We renounce our passivity in spiritual disciplines.*
- We announce that in Christ we have spiritual hunger for intimacy with God.
- *We affirm that we were created for fellowship with God.*
- We will teach, preach and regularly practice the spiritual disciplines.
- *We renounce gossip and pettiness.*

- We announce that in Christ we have the Holy Spirit who brings unity.
- *We affirm that Christ can bridle our tongues and show us how to resolve problems.*
- We will speak the truth in love.

STEP 6 OF THE SETTING YOUR CHURCH FREE PROCEDURE

The Prayer Action Plan (step 6) synthesizes the information gathered in the earlier steps and condenses them in a one-page format. The facilitator should place four large sheets of paper side by side on the wall. All of the previous sheets should be visible as well. On the first sheet, the facilitator should write "We renounce . . . " On the next three sheets he or she should jot down in order "We announce . . . ", "We affirm . . . ", and "We will. . . " The group is now ready to combine everything discerned so far in short, summary declarations.

The facilitator will next briefly review what the group is summarizing.

1. We will want to *renounce the evil* (attacks, corporate sins, conflicts, weaknesses). For example, "We renounce division among us."
2. We will *announce the positive biblical opposite of what we renounced,* worded in terms of our resources in Christ. For example, "We announce that in Christ we have the unity of the Spirit."
3. We will *affirm in emotional language a scriptural promise or truth that encourages and motivates us* in regard to the same item. For example, "We affirm that in the depths of our hearts we are all one in Christ Jesus" (see Gal. 3:26-28).
4. We will *commit to an action step that we will take.* For example, "We will talk to the right person in the right spirit when conflicts arise."

The first item on the list should be worked out following the order of "We renounce," "We announce," "We affirm" and "We will." The group can then go on to the next item, and so on.

The goal is to make the shortest list possible without leaving out any major weaknesses, sins and spiritual attacks that were discerned by the leadership. This list, along with the greatest strengths of the church, becomes the Prayer Action Plan. (See appendix B for an example.) The process should begin with group prayer, followed by quiet contemplation in which each individual asks for the Holy Spirit's guidance, discernment, sense of unity and the right words for the Prayer Action Plan. Fatigue may be a factor by now, so the group should call upon God for divine energy and wisdom to make sense out of all the lists on the sheets.

MAKING SENSE OF IT

By this time in the Setting Your Church Free day (or evening by now), the task of making a clear summary will seem challenging. Be encouraged. In our experience, every group has come up with an intelligible Prayer Action Plan. The facilitator and some key leaders may take the initiative in suggesting wording, yet it is important to seek mutual agreement for how to word the items.

This part of the process is extremely valuable to the participants, capturing on paper the sense of discovery as the group interacts with one another. Creating an environment for honest communication is a valuable experience for church leadership. Many are relieved that these issues are now out on the table. What is helpful is that the group neither argues nor problem solves, but simply comes to consensus. For one participant, this feature of the seminar was the most helpful:

My best memory from the hours the elders and pastors spent together was all the communication that finally took place. The people need an opportunity to communicate instead of gossip to share their feelings. It was difficult to talk about some issues, but they needed to be brought up! I believe a lot of people felt good about finally being able to share their feelings. I've always known how important communication is, but I really didn't realize how important it is to set an environment for people to be able to talk. It is important to help people feel free to open up. I will try to be aware of this now!

The typical group will discard some suggestions and modify many others. What they state will fit the theology, concerns and style of their own church, because they, not the facilitator, will be discerning the declarations. Each list is unique, stated in a way that only the specific church and group of leaders can describe. Group participation enhances a sense of ownership and unity.

When the process lags, the facilitator may ask, "Is there any other major theme that we have not addressed?" or "What else do you see?" or "Do we have it?" It is not necessary to cover every item on the sheets from previous steps, but rather the major patterns that have emerged. There are usually five to eight items for each of the four declarations.

BINDING AND LOOSING

When the declarations are finished, the group should stand and position themselves so that they can read the four sheets. They should then hold hands and pray the Prayer Action Plan aloud. *This prayer is essential.* All the authority of heaven stands behind church leaders who fully agree and unite in prayer about a matter that they discern in the presence of God. When they declare it together, they are exercising the power of binding and loosing:

> I [Jesus] will give you the keys of the kingdom of heaven; and whatever you bind on earth shall have been bound in heaven, and whatever you loose on earth shall have been loosed in heaven (Matt. 16:19, *NASB*).

Binding and loosing is not manipulating God or making up our minds about something whereby God must respond to us. The *New*

International Version and most other modern translations of the Bible often have a footnote indicating an "alternative reading" of this passage that agrees with the *New American Standard* translation quoted above. Look carefully at the wording again: "Whatever you bind on earth *shall have been* bound in heaven, and whatever you loose on earth *shall have been* loosed in heaven" (emphasis added). The task of church leaders is to discern what has already been bound or loosed in heaven and then announce it on Earth. In the Prayer Action Plan, we bind by *renouncing* and loose by *announcing*. We never ask the Lord to capitulate to our will; we gladly surrender to His will.

The above verse in Matthew follows Peter's declaration that Jesus is the Christ, the Son of the living God (see Matt. 16:16). In response, Jesus promises, "I will build my church, and the gates of Hades will not overcome it" (Matt. 16:18).

R. E. Nixon writes, "The gates suggest the picture of a fortress or prison which lock in the dead and lock out their rescuers. This would imply that the church is on the offensive, and its Master will plunder the domain of Satan."[2] Note the spiritual warfare reference in this passage and in Matthew 12:29. In the Prayer Action Plan, we renounce the efforts of the "gates of Hades" to hold people captive and hinder the building of Christ's Church. We then announce our resources in Christ by which our Lord builds His Church.

CHURCH DISCIPLINE

The same teaching is found in Matthew 18, but the context gives instructions for church discipline. The need for church discipline may surface during the Setting Your Church Free process. We are on safe biblical grounds using our God-given authority in Christ to bind and loose (renounce and announce) what we discern as Christ's will for our local churches.

Authorized by Christ
Let's consider what the Church is authorized by Christ to do.

The Church has prayer authority. What we have discerned together about each issue in our Prayer Action Plan we can pray and announce with spiritual authority based on what Jesus said about two or more gathering in His name (see Matt. 18:18-20). The two or three do not decide amongst themselves what they believe or want. They collectively discern God's will.

The Church has teaching authority. We have the God-given right and responsibility to teach and preach what we scripturally discern as Christ's will for our church.

The Church has disciplinary authority. If we find that members, and especially leaders, of our church are living in defiance of clear scriptural teachings and we agree about our discernment of Christ's direction for what we must do, He gives us the authority to take appropriate action within our church.

Church discipline is always a painful and touchy subject. Yet we dare not ignore what the Bible teaches. We are not to judge one another's character, especially when we have not taken into account the plank in our own eyes (see Matt. 7:1-5). However, the Church must discipline those who are living in sin for their sake (see Matt. 18:15-17; 1 Cor. 5:3-13; 6:1-6; 1 Tim. 5:19-20). Discipline is not punishment for wrong done, nor is it retroactive. Discipline must be based on observed behavior by one or more witnesses, with the intention of helping the people live righteous lives in the future:

> For they [fathers] disciplined us for a short time as seemed best to them, but He [God] disciplines us for our good, so that we may share His holiness. All discipline for the moment seems not to be joyful, but sorrowful; yet to those who have been trained by it, afterwards it yields the peaceful fruit of righteousness (Heb. 12:10-11, *NASB*).

If you ignore church discipline, you may suffer public scandal. Non-Christians use church sins as an excuse for rejecting Christ, and the media loves to exploit church scandals. Christian leaders falling prey to sexual abuse or financial fraud fuels the media fire. In addition, immature Christians often follow the example of fallen leaders in disobeying the Lord Jesus.

A Biblical View

For years, Neil taught biblical principles of church discipline in his seminary classes. As a denominational official, I have experienced my share of personal pain, not to mention the pain I have witnessed of others involved in disciplinary processes. Church leaders will feel the tension between protecting the church from scandal and confronting sin. The Catholic Church recently tried to do the former, but failed in the end. Secret sin on Earth is open scandal in heaven. Jesus said there is nothing concealed that will not be revealed. When Paul states that "those who continue in sin, rebuke in the presence of all, so that the rest also will be fearful of sinning" (1 Tim. 5:20, *NASB*), he was not being vindictive but was confronting sin in such a way so that people can have a way of resolving issues. When sin is tolerated or covered up, people can't process the problem, and it becomes divisive in their homes and churches. The person confronted can repent, and others can forgive and learn from the experience.

Discipline is the proof of Christian love (see Heb. 12:5-11) and is essential for the health of the church. To pray passively, asking God to do what He has commanded church leadership and parents to do, is to fail in our responsibility as church leaders and as parents. The purpose of discipline is to carry out the ministry of reconciliation and to restore a Christian brother or sister caught in a sin (see Gal. 6:1). The goal is not to expose the sin, but to win back the offender and to enhance the purity of the church.

It is essential to base discipline upon prior instruction and observed behavior. If there is no standard, there is no sin. If reputable witnesses observe sinful behavior, there is no judgment taking place. The person is "caught in a sin" (see Gal. 6:1). Discipline is related to behavior, whereas judgment is related to character. When all attempts at reconciliation have failed, Scripture teaches a breaking off of fellowship, and the nature of the sin is to be told to the church (see Matt. 18:15-20; 1 Tim. 5:19-20).

Who decides when breaking this fellowship is required? Does knowledge on the part of the elders or church board constitute telling the church? *A word to the wise: Always honor the procedures of your church's polity in disciplinary matters. In a lawsuit-oriented society, following due process saves much grief.* However, no church polity or lack of it can nullify the commands given to church leaders in Scripture. (In addition to the passages already cited, see 1 Thess. 5:14; 2 Thess. 3:14-15; Titus 3:9-11.)

Risking Lawsuits

Civil courts usually don't hear cases involving internal church disputes, but they may if slander, libel, invasion of privacy or economic disaster are involved. Church discipline toward members living in defiance of Scripture raises some important questions: What is the basis of a lawsuit against a church in a discipline case? How can a church protect itself and still obey the commands of Jesus? What precautions can a church take to stay out of legal trouble? What are the limits of the law that everyone, including church leaders, must abide by?

The Bible tells us, "Be wise in the way you act toward outsiders" (Col. 4:5; also see 1 Thess. 4:12; 1 Tim. 3:7; 1 Pet. 3:16-17). People who win lawsuits against churches usually base their case on the violation of one or more sensitive legal issues, and we recommend that you confer with a Christian attorney for legal counsel. However, every church leader should be aware of the following three pitfalls:

1. *Slander, libel or defamation of character is illegal.* Slanderous statements are those that are untrue or that may be true but are intended to damage a person's reputation. For the matter to be considered slander, it must be published to a third party. It is not slander or libel for the pastor, elders or the official board to confront a church member about sexual immorality or any overt sin. It is slander if they publish it to others in a way that damages the person's reputation.

2. *Invasion of privacy is illegal.* This provision is difficult for churches because legitimate privacy rights are sometimes used as a cover for private sin. However, churches cannot legally take a private relationship and make it public in a harmful way. Church discipline by the pastor, elders or church board is not invasion of privacy if these standards are previously published and known by the offender. Any public censure or excommunication proceedings must use fairly general terms. All statements, written and oral, need to be prepared carefully and fall in line with Scripture and official church polity.

3. *Inflicting a detrimental effect on a person's economic status is illegal.* One church took disciplinary action against a member who worked as an insurance salesman. Most of his customers were also members of the same church. The church leaders advised the people not to aid him in any way. Many of the church members dropped the insurance policies that they purchased from him, and his business declined dramatically. The man sued. The caution here is for churches not to go beyond the biblical limits of discipline. Dropping a person from membership and fellowship is legal; inflicting economic harm on that person is not.

For more information on the ministry of reconciliation, see our book *Blessed Are the Peacemakers* (Regal Books, 2002). This book lists the steps that can be taken to help believers be reconciled with God and each other.

Some Precautions

The following points describe what churches can do to protect themselves from a lawsuit:

1. *A church can publish its standards of conduct and church discipline and communicate them to all members.* The membership class is the

ideal place to explain Scripture relating to church discipline. In a positive way, the leaders can explain why those in the church care so much about each other that they resolve conflict early and privately. Public discipline is a last resort that will be imposed only under the conditions stated in the church's standards of conduct and church discipline. Disciplinary matters in the Church should never be settled in public courts (see 1 Cor. 6:1-11). Independent Christian mediation organizations often are helpful in resolving disputes between church members.

2. *A church can communicate what steps of disciplinary action it may take and in what kinds of cases it will take that action* (see 1 Cor. 5:1-5; 6:9-11; 2 Thess. 3:14-15; 1 Tim. 1:20; 2 Tim. 2:17-18; Rev. 2:14-16). All church staff members should be notified in writing in advance of their hiring that immediate dismissal is the consequence of sexual immorality, financial fraud or any scandalous sin. After making the basic knowledge known, it is better to act than to talk. In other words, do not make threats. The church must follow its stated polity and procedures explicitly and use due diligence. Counseling and restoration procedures should be part of the process so that the offender does not repeat the same sins in the next church.

3. *A church needs to limit the number of people who are part of the process and give only general information to others.* This is both gentle and wise (see Gal. 6:1; Eph. 5:15-16). Any communication with the offenders should explain the biblical basis for the actions taken and avoid anything that might be construed as slander. In most cases, it is wise to keep everything, including church minutes, out of print or in general terms. Written documents provide the kind of evidence attorneys will use in court.

PRAYING IN UNITY

Let's return now to the Prayer Action Plan that the participants have just prayed through. In prayer, they bind what has been bound in heaven and loose what has been loosed in heaven. They have discerned Christ's will for their church and responded in prayer.

A sense of accomplishment and joy is felt by the group as they join together in declaring their Prayer Action Plan to God. The sense of unity is what participants remember the most. One pastor wrote, "My best memory from the Setting Your Church Free seminar was the sense of unity with which everyone responded. Although each person had unique insights and comments, when it came to the *big* issues, there was unity and agreement, and a sense of working together."

The Prayer Action Plan becomes a tangible way to submit to God and resist the devil on behalf of the whole church. "Submit yourselves, then, to God. Resist the devil, and he will flee from you" (Jas. 4:7). One pastor commented, "I didn't realize this was like a letter from Jesus. That would have added a lot of power to it!" It is helpful to think of your Prayer Action Plan as a letter from Jesus, or at the very least, think of it as your discernment of what Jesus would write in a letter to your church.

The process is eye-opening for many of the leaders. Most arrive for the event having only hazy ideas about their own corporate sins and attacks from the evil one. Now they are in unity about the actual spiritual health of their church and have a plan that calls for prayer plus action. One person wrote, "Since completing the Setting Your Church Free seminar, we have a concrete understanding of our strengths and weaknesses, areas where God is blessing and areas where the enemy has strongholds. We now have the ability to pray and work specifically to be completely free."

Recall that each of the seven letters of Revelation contains the exhortation "He who has an ear, let him hear what the Spirit says to the churches" (Rev. 2:7,11,17,29; 3:6,13,22). Hearing with the intention of obeying is the proper idea of this passage. Little children often procrastinate or stall when their parents ask them to do something, to which the parent often responds, "Did you hear me?" The children have heard with their physical ears, but what the parent is really asking is "Are you going to obey me now?" Your heavenly Father is saying, "Did you hear Me? Are you willing to obey?" A strategy for putting the message of this book into action is the subject of our last chapter.

Notes

1. John Stott, *Romans: God's Good News for the World* (Downers Grove, IL: InterVarsity Press, 1994), p. 187.
2. R. E. Nixon, "Matthew," *The New Bible Commentary: Revised* (Grand Rapids, MI: Eerdmans Publishing Co., 1970), p. 837.

A LEADERSHIP STRATEGY

Chapter 12

---

*Whether Christianity can be adequate to the moral leadership of our
civilization today and tomorrow depends on whether it can capture that
"first fine, careless rapture" of its earliest days.*

KIRBY PAGE

A young Canadian pastor attended one of Neil's conferences and discovered what it meant to be a child of God, and through repentance, he
experienced his own freedom in Christ. He planted a new church along
with a core group of leaders, and they agreed that anyone joining their
church would also be given the opportunity to be established alive and
free in Christ. They wanted new members to join their church with a
fresh start, leaving their unresolved baggage from the past behind. New
members were taught how to forgive as Christ forgave them, how to
walk by faith in the power of the Holy Spirit, and how to win the battle
for their minds. This led to remarkable growth in the new church. In six
months, the fellowship grew to 250 people. A year later, there were over
800 in attendance, with a high percentage of conversion growth. The

people in the church were bearing fruit because they were established alive and free in Christ through genuine repentance and faith in God.

New churches don't have any history, so there are no corporate issues to be dealt with. Establishing new members alive and free in Christ can do a lot to prevent future problems from developing. Established churches can't start from scratch with a clean slate, but they can clean the slate, and that is what we are attempting to do with this process. Hopefully, you have heard from God and made a commitment to take appropriate action, which we will consider next.

COMMON STRATEGIES

The first and foremost strategy for implementing the Prayer Action Plan is personal prayer. Encourage all the participants to pray through the Prayer Action Plan on a daily basis and appropriate the message in their own lives. By doing so, the leaders sensitize themselves to the corporate sins and common attacks from the enemy. These same patterns tend to re-emerge weeks or months later, but the leaders should be able to discern them. It is not uncommon to hear comments such as, "We are about to repeat one of our old corporate sins" or "We just did one of the things we renounced." This kind of alertness to old flesh patterns and spiritual attacks is essential in bringing about lasting change.

From experience, we have observed that many will not follow through on this daily prayer commitment without accountability. We suggest that you appoint someone besides the pastor or a paid staff member to remind the group about their prayer commitment. This person also could take responsibility for leading the group regarding the other strategies. Pastors and staff members must do their part in implementing this last step.

The second strategy is to pray through the Prayer Action Plan together at each of your regular meetings. This reinforces the commitment to lead the church in obedience to Jesus. Pray through the Prayer Action Plan until all of the action points are fulfilled and the items renounced no longer reappear. This will likely take between 6 and 18 months.

Sermon Series

The third strategy is for the pastor to preach through the Prayer Action Plan in a sermon series. The congregation has not been a part of the process as yet, and the leadership should bring them along carefully. The pastor and/or leaders can collectively present their findings with sensitivity and care so that the congregation does not feel judged, condemned or overwhelmed. However, as leaders, we can't move any faster than we can educate, and we must lead by example. The best way to call the church to repentance is to demonstrate our own repentance. It is important that the congregation knows that they are not being asked to do anything the leaders aren't already doing.

The sermon series seems to work best if one issue is addressed each week. Start with a positive biblical truth such as "We announce" and "We affirm," and then follow with what needs to be renounced. Affirming the church for its greatest strengths prepares the way for facing up to its weaknesses. You can and probably should omit the items that apply only to the leaders of the church.

At the close of the first sermon, lead the congregation in declaring together the four statements that relate to the subject. At the end of the second week, have them declare both the first week's statements and the second week's statements. By the end of the series, they will declare most, if not all, of the Prayer Action Plan. It does not work to slip parts subtly into other messages or preach one sermon as an overview of the whole Prayer Action Plan. Beating around the bush leaves the bush intact, and superficially addressing problems leaves them unresolved.

Involving Other Leaders

A fourth strategy is having other groups of leaders in your church process the Steps to Setting Your Church Free. In larger churches, specialized levels of leadership (men, women, youth) may not have participated in the Setting Your Church Free event. In one large church, the college and youth pastor were so impressed by the humility of their leadership that they wanted to do the same with their ministries. So they purchased the first edition of this book, had all their leaders read it, and then scheduled a weekend for setting their ministry free with exciting results. Some have used this process with their families and businesses.

Subministries should include all the leadership in their unique area of responsibility. Each group needs to process the personal Steps to Freedom in Christ first and then require full participation at the Setting Your Ministry Free event. The renounced and announced items will differ from the session by the church board and pastoral staff, but they should fit each unique ministry or organization.

We have led denominations, seminaries, missionary groups and parachurch ministries through the process. Following up the event for such groups will vary considerably. Regardless of the group or ministry, the primary key is to effect a change in the leadership and the spiritual atmosphere of the ministry. One denomination had to renounce a non-Christ-centered cultural climate and a corporate bondage to fear.

Two Buckets

Those who experience the Setting Your Church Free process will have the greatest appreciation for it. Hopefully, all the leaders in your church have experienced their personal freedom in Christ and participated in the sermon series on the Prayer Action Plan. Teaching through this series is a good time to introduce the "two-bucket" principle. Every church leader carries two buckets—one full of water and the other full of gasoline. It makes all the difference in the world which one is used.

A church problem can flare up like a fire, and often others hear about it before the pastor does. If a leader pours gasoline on the problem, it will explode into a raging fire. If the leader douses it with water, it will die down or go out. The fire may have started with a misunderstanding, gossip, jealousy, a critical spirit or some corporate sin. If an elder, deacon, committee chairperson or longtime member dumps gasoline on the problem, the fire will attract lots of misguided attention. Just the right amount of water, however, puts out the fire and hopefully extinguishes the problem.

A big fire needs attention immediately. Instead of one bucket of water, it needs a fire department. Call for help! Phone the pastor or elders. Call in reinforcements if needed, but don't ignore the problem. No one in authority can deal with a problem that he or she does not know about. On the other hand, use some discernment. Minor conflicts are a part of the growing process. Don't become a smoke detector or start looking for minor character defects that mar everyone.

It usually is harder to light a good fire under your congregation than it is to put one out. Paul wrote, "Do not put out the Spirit's fire" (1 Thess. 5:19). The fire of the Holy Spirit may come when a young believer experiences a dramatic answer to prayer, new freedom in Christ or a personal surprise from God's sovereign hand. The pessimist hears, yawns and changes the subject. He or she uses the wrong bucket and drenches the Holy Spirit's fire. A godly leader uses the other bucket and fans the flame of revival.

The fire of the Holy Spirit comes when a new Christian discovers a key Scriptural passage for the first time. Those who quench the Spirit say, "I've known that one for years," having a tone of voice that implies, "You mean you didn't know that!" The encourager, however, gets excited, listens to why it is so meaningful and shares a personal story of how God used the same verse in his or her life. The fire of the Holy Spirit may be a desire to start a new ministry to the disadvantaged, to abused children, to cocaine users or to any new group. It might be something a particular church has never done before. The leader can douse the idea or fan the flames.

Use the water bucket to extinguish church problems, but not to quench the Holy Spirit. Use the gasoline bucket to feed the fires that come from God; never use it to feed the egos of problem-producing personalities. Every church leader carries two buckets. Use each one wisely!

Prayerful Discussion
A fifth strategy is for the participants to discuss specific ways to obey each action point. This may happen in a series of regular meetings of the staff and church board. Another option is to call a special session to think prayerfully through the church's purpose, strategies, goals, ministries and specific actions. The greatest danger is to consider the Setting Your Church Free event as simply one more seminar, file the notes, and then go back to doing church as usual.

You can use the following questionnaire or something similar as a starting point for these discussions. We suggest that you customize it to fit your Prayer Action Plan and add specific questions that fit your church and retain some of the general questions that apply to all churches and leaders. Pastors and staff members may be especially adept at writing questions that will stimulate good thinking about follow-through. Ask the participants to fill out the questionnaire before the meeting. Advance thinking and praying will help your discussion.

STRATEGY QUESTIONNAIRE
PRAYER ACTION PLAN

Please remember to pray through the Prayer Action Plan daily. Before our next meeting, please fill out this questionnaire. It will serve as our basis for discussion. Thank you for taking time to prepare in advance.

1. What must we do to become the leaders God has called us to be?
2. How can we keep Christ as the center of all we are and do as a church?
3. What must we do to ensure that our people are living free and productive lives in Christ?
4. Including prayer, what steps can we take to ensure that our people are spiritually alive, free and protected?
5. As a letter from Jesus, what parts of His Prayer Action Plan must we act on at once?
6. Which parts of the plan require only alertness and prayer?
7. Who should we designate as leaders to implement various parts of the plan?

LETTING LEADERS LEAD

Some people are born to be strong natural leaders. Assuming such people are spiritually qualified, the church hierarchy should let them lead.

This person or persons may not always be the senior pastor or part of the ordained staff. If we are secure in Christ, we will let such people lead and rejoice in their accomplishments. They don't have to have an official title, position or degree, but they must be respected and accepted by the congregation. It is tragic when such gifted, talented and personable people are not recognized and encouraged to lead. Nehemiah wasn't a priest, but he was a great leader. Our Western concept of professionalism can kill the Church. We must see the need to equip the layperson to do the work of ministry, which includes letting gifted, talented, personable, godly people rise to the top.

The Holy Spirit has gifted some to lead, and to this person Paul wrote, "If it [the spiritual gift] is leadership, let him govern diligently" (Rom. 12:8). The gift of administration, which Paul mentions in 1 Corinthians 12:28, refers to organizational ability, which is a managerial task. Both gifts are essential, but one person cannot effectively do the role of the other, and usually the leadership knows which person should present the program and which one should manage it. If both individuals are secure in Christ, there are no egos involved and they gladly let one lead, one manage and others follow. Above all, leaders should model what Scripture teaches concerning elders:

> All of you, clothe yourselves with humility toward one another, because, "God opposes the proud but gives grace to the humble." Humble yourselves, therefore, under God's mighty hand, that he may lift you up in due time. Cast all your anxiety on him because he cares for you. Be self-controlled and alert. Your enemy the devil prowls around like a roaring lion looking for someone to devour. Resist him, standing firm in the faith, because you know that your brothers throughout the world are undergoing the same kind of sufferings (1 Pet. 5:5-9).

Followers' Responsibilities

Those who are chosen to represent and lead the people should be supported. No leader can survive disloyalty. Those who have been delegated responsibility must have the authority to do what they have been called to do. Scripture admonishes all of us to "Obey your leaders and submit to their authority. They keep watch over you as men who must give an account. Obey them so that their work will be a joy, not a burden, for that would be of no advantage to you" (Heb. 13:17).

Leaders' Responsibilities
The best leaders listen to wise and godly counsel. They especially need those who have spiritual discernment, and for male leaders, this is often their wives. We both routinely say to male leadership, "Men, listen to your wives." Most wives can detect a wrong spirit in another woman, especially if it is related to sexual matters. Christian leaders must learn to be spiritually discerning. "For everyone who partakes only of milk is not accustomed to the word of righteousness, for he is an infant. But solid food is for the mature, who because of practice have their senses trained to discern good and evil" (Heb. 5:13-14, *NASB*). If you are part of a board or committee meeting and sense that something is wrong, don't continue on with business as usual. Stop and pray. For more instruction on discernment, read Neil's book *Finding God's Will in Spiritually Deceptive Times* (Harvest House, 2003).

Pastoral staff and lay leaders will more likely lead the church in making the changes and fulfilling the challenges of the Prayer Action Plan if they feel the prayer support of intercessory prayer partners. Encourage every leader to have his or her own intercessory prayer team and give the leader a copy of Neil's book *Praying by the Power of the Spirit* (Harvest House, 2003).

Why don't more pastors and Christian leaders call for prayer partners? Some may not recognize the potential blessing available. Some may feel as though it is a selfish request or think their ministry is not significant enough. The ministry of every child of God is significant enough to invite others to pray for them! For others the problem may be pride, but all pastors need to take this significant step and be more vulnerable to those who can hold them up in prayer.

Several years ago, I prayed for a couple to intercede on my behalf.

God answered, and two prayer warriors lifted me before the throne of grace. Then I appealed, on a somewhat lower commitment basis, for a prayer team. Today, more than 25 people regularly hold me and my ministry before the Lord in intercessory prayer. My own ministry took a turn for the better once this started. Before seminars, speaking engagements and important meetings, I write or phone my intercessors and request special prayer. The result is that the events almost always have a greater sense of God's blessing and power than before. Neil has a prayer team that receives his schedule and regular reports of his ministry.

A Setting Your Church Free conference takes one or two days in the life of your church. Skeletons may continue to emerge from carefully concealed closets. We hope you now know how to deal with them when they do emerge. We suspect that some churches have such a long history of bondage that the Lord may peel off one layer at a time. This certainly has been the case in personal counseling.

The moment you take your freedom for granted, you will lose it. Remember what Jesus taught: "If you hold to my teaching, you are really my disciples. Then you will know the truth, and the truth will set you free" (John 8:31-32). The Lord wants you and your ministry to experience the freedom He purchased for you. "It is for freedom that Christ has set us free" (Gal. 5:1). May the Lord grant you repentance and knowledge of the truth that will set you free and equip you to be the spiritual leader He created you to be. We close with the following encouraging letter from a pastor whose church experienced the Setting Your Church Free process:

Since the Setting Your Church Free mini-retreat, I have noticed significant healing and growth in the church as an organization and as an instrument. I know that I may be a bit naive being so young, but I am constantly amazed to find skeleton after skeleton in this church's closet.

The good news is we are bringing old issues and deep hurts out into the open. People say our church is laid back, friendly and very relational. This assessment seems fair on the surface. I am learning, however, that if you dig beneath the surface, you begin to see incredible pains that have not been resolved.

Having an outside person, who is qualified to deal with spiritual issues, do what you did in that retreat has offered us hope. Our corporate sins are enough to close this place down. They have already severely stunted our growth and effectiveness to do God's work.

You have helped us to start a tremendous and often very painful healing process. We have been faithful in following through with the six steps listed in our Prayer Action Plan. I am guessing that before this retreat we wouldn't have finished any of them. God has used you to bless us. We are truly thankful.

APPENDIX A

Steps to Setting Your Church Free

It is imperative that each participant read *Extreme Church Makeover* before attempting this corporate conflict resolution process. The biblical basis for the process and directions for the facilitator are in the book. *Extreme Church Makeover* also answers practical questions such as when to schedule the event, how to set up the room, how the facilitator conducts the process and what the participants actually do.

All of the participants should process the personal Steps to Freedom in Christ before they attempt corporate conflict resolution. Each participant should also have his or her own copy of the Steps to Setting Your Church Free. (This appendix can be used or copies of the Steps can be purchased from Freedom in Christ Ministries.) We recommend a day of fasting and prayer by the participants and their prayer partners prior to the event. Encourage prayer partners to intercede before and during this time together.

All of the elders or board members and all full-time pastoral staff should be present for the process. You should consider postponing the event if even one member cannot attend. We recommend that an unbiased outside facilitator lead your leadership through these steps. The pastor and staff members need to be part of the process. The process can take up to 10 hours, so some schedule the event over two days.

DAY OF RETREAT

Begin the event by praying the following personal renewal prayer—once silently and then out loud together:

> *Dear heavenly Father,*
> *Open my eyes to understand Your truth. Give me ears to hear and a desire to respond in faith to what the Lord Jesus Christ has already*

accomplished for me and is now doing in and through me.

I confess Jesus Christ—crucified, risen and reigning—as my one and only Lord and Savior. I renounce any past involvement with non-Christian religions or experiences. I announce that Christ died on the cross for my justification and rose again bodily from the dead for my salvation and new life in Christ.

I choose to believe that the Lord Jesus Christ rescued me from the dominion of darkness and transferred me into His Kingdom of light. I announce that Jesus Christ is my Lord, Savior, teacher and friend. I choose to obey everything that He commanded. I yield myself fully to Christ to do whatever He wants me to do, to be whatever He wants me to be, to give up whatever He wants me to give up, to give away whatever He wants me to give away, to become whatever He wants me to become.

I confess, reject, renounce and disown every sin in which I have ever been involved. I renounce Satan and all his works and all his ways. I announce that in Christ I have received redemption, the forgiveness of sins. Because of the finished work of Christ and my faith in Him, I choose to believe that I am now reconciled with You, my heavenly Father, and am at peace with You.

Knowing that I have been forgiven of all my sins, I choose to forgive every person who has ever hurt, abused or taken advantage of me. I yield my right to seek revenge and choose to let You be the final judge who metes out perfect justice.

I submit myself and my body to You as a living sacrifice, and ask You to fill me with Your Holy Spirit. Having the mind of Christ within me, I pray for the renewing of my mind that I may prove that the will of God is good, acceptable and perfect. I desire to conform to Your image from this day forward until I stand before the judgment seat of Christ and hear my name read from the Lamb's Book of Life.

In Jesus' powerful name I pray. Amen.

After you have prayed the above prayer together, continue in group prayer as the Lord leads and conclude together with the Lord's Prayer.

BIBLE REVIEW

Read the letters to the seven churches in Revelation 2–3, with seven individuals reading one letter apiece while all the participants pay attention to the following:

- Note the love of the risen Lord Jesus for His churches and His encouragement to them. Christ wants all His children and churches to experience their freedom in Christ. Notice how many times "I" (Christ) occurs in each letter. The major emphasis in these seven letters is on the presence of the living Christ among the churches.
- Note that each church has an angel. Two common functions of angels in the book of Revelation are (1) to praise and worship God, and (2) to carry out the promises and judgments of Christ. The angel assigned by Christ to your church may do these very things.
- Note the corporate sins of the churches in Revelation 2–3.
- Note the phrases that indicate Satan's attacks or opposition to the churches.
- Note the Lord's judgments for disobedience and promises for obedience.
- Note the repeated phrase "To him who overcomes." In the New Testament, "overcomes" is a word most often used for the Christian's battle against the world, the flesh and the devil.

During this process of corporate conflict resolution, each person needs to be sensitive to God's leading. To each of the churches in Revelation 2 and 3, John concludes by writing, "He who has an ear, let him hear what the Spirit says to the churches." If the Lord Jesus wrote a letter to your church, would you obey Him? What would keep you from reading the letter and responding appropriately?

Pray together the following prayer and then read aloud the "Church Renunciations" that follow:

Dear heavenly Father,

Open our eyes to see Your truth and our ears to hear what Your Holy Spirit is saying to our church. We acknowledge that the Lord Jesus Christ is the head of our church, and we renounce any claim of ownership on our part. This is Your church, not ours, and You are the head. We renounce any personal and independent spirit, and declare our full dependence upon You.

We come together to discern Your will for our church. We renounce any and all desires or attempts to exert our own wills through arguing, manipulating or intimidating. You are light, and in You there is no darkness at all. We choose to walk in the light in order to have fellowship with You and with one another. We ask You to fill us with Your Holy Spirit and grant us repentance so we can glorify You in our church Body.

Because we are seated with Christ in the heavenlies, and because the Church is commissioned to go into all the world and make disciples of all nations, we take our stand against the evil one and all his forces. We gladly submit to You, heavenly Father, and obey Your command to resist the devil. We ask You to protect us from the evil one so that we will be free to know Your will and choose to obey it.

In Jesus' precious name. Amen.

Read aloud the following church renunciations. The first one is an ancient declaration of the Early Church. The others are based on Revelation 2—3. Although they may not precisely fit your church, they represent corporate sins that all churches should avoid.

CHURCH RENUNCIATIONS

We renounce . . .

We renounce you, Satan, in all your works and in all your ways.

We renounce forsaking our first love.

We announce . . .

We announce that Christ is Lord of our lives and choose to follow only His ways.

We announce that Christ is our first love because He first loved us and gave Himself as an atoning sacrifice for our sins (see 1 John 2:2; 4:10; Rev. 2:4).

We renounce tolerating false teaching.

We announce that God's truth is revealed to us through the living and written Word of God (see John 17:17; 2 Tim. 3:15-16; Heb. 4:12).

We renounce overlooking non-Christian beliefs and practices among our members.

We announce that Christ is our true identity and the only way to salvation and fellowship with God (see John 14:6; 2 Cor. 5:17).

We renounce tolerating sexual immorality among some of our members.

We announce that our sexuality is God's gift, and sexual union is to be enjoyed only within the marriage of one man and one woman (see Gen. 2:24; 1 Cor. 6:18-20; 1 Thess. 4:3-8).

We renounce our reputation of being alive when we are dead.

We announce that Christ alone is our resurrection and our life (see John 11:25-26).

We renounce our incomplete deeds—starting to do God's will and then not following through.

We announce that Christ is the head of His Body, the Church, and as His members we find freedom and strength to finish the work He has given us to do (see Eph. 1:19-23; 2:10; Phil. 4:13).

We renounce disobedience to God's Word, including the Great Commandment and the Great Commission.

We announce that God energizes us to desire and to do His will so that we can obey Christ (see Phil. 2:13).

We renounce our lukewarmness—being neither hot nor cold for Christ.

We announce that Christ is our refining fire who disciplines us for our own good so that our faith may prove genuine (see Mal. 3:1-3; Heb. 12:10,29).

We renounce our false pride in financial "security" that blinds us to our actual spiritual needs.

We announce that Christ is our true wealth, purity and insight, and outside of Him we are wretched, pitiful, poor, blind and naked (see Col. 2:1-3; Rev. 3:17-18).

If the Lord Jesus wrote a letter to your church, what would He commend? What would He rebuke? Although you will not likely draft a letter with the same authority as Scripture, you can ask the Holy Spirit to help you discern how the Head of the Church views your ministry.

DISCERNING THE LORD'S VIEW OF YOUR CHURCH

If you have not already done so, appoint a recorder to write down all the compiled lists of the group.

Step 1: Our Church's Strengths

In this first step, you are seeking to discern the strengths of your church. Pray together the following prayer and then follow with a few moments of silent prayer. Allow the Lord to impress upon your heart what you are doing right. The facilitator, or those appointed, will close the time in prayer.

> *Dear heavenly Father,*
>
> *Thank You for calling and choosing us as shepherds of the flock and servant leaders in Your Church. Thank You for this church and what You have done through it. Thank You for the people who worship and serve You here.*
>
> *Show us what the living Lord Jesus commends in our church. Remind us of what we are doing right and the strengths You have given to our church. As we wait silently before You, show us our good works that glorify You in heaven [see Matt. 5:16]. In Jesus' name. Amen.*

This step has two parts. First, the facilitator asks the group to list the church's strengths as the Holy Spirit brings them to mind. Encourage all the participants to identify as many strengths of the church as possible.

Second, the facilitator asks the group to summarize the greatest strengths God has given to their church. Questions to consider include: What are the things we always do best? What works for us every time? How has God uniquely gifted us as a church Body? Keep this list short, having only the greatest strengths identified, normally five to seven items.

The facilitator writes on the poster paper the greatest strengths, beginning each one with, "We thank God for . . . " These should be stated in complete sentences and saved for the final summary in the Prayer Action Plan (step 6).

Conclude this step by praying in unison the following prayer:

Dear heavenly Father,

Thank You for the strengths You have given to us and to our church.
Thank You for gracing us with Your presence and for working through the
gifts, talents and service of Your people. We bow in gratitude for the ways
that You have ministered through our church. We know that apart from
Christ we can do nothing. So we gladly acknowledge that every good and
perfect gift is from above.

Continue to equip us to be good stewards of these strengths, as well as
responsible managers of our resources and relationships You have given to
us. In the name of our Lord and Savior Jesus Christ we pray. Amen.

Step 2: Our Weaknesses

In step 2, the group will ask the Holy Spirit to help discern the weaknesses of the church. You will be considering your shortcomings, faults and failures. What are you not doing well? What should your church be doing that is not being done?

Pray together the following prayer. Then spend a couple of minutes in silent prayer, allowing the Lord to impress upon your hearts the weaknesses of your church.

Dear heavenly Father,

We have not fully utilized the gifts, talents and strengths that You
have made available to us. We have chosen patterns of thinking and act-
ing that displease You. We fall short of Your best and of all that You intend
for us to be. We ask You to open our eyes so that we may see our weak-
nesses as You do. We wait silently before You in the powerful name of
Jesus. Amen.

The facilitator will ask the group to list the weaknesses that the Holy Spirit brings to their minds. Participants should feel free to express their own opinions, whether others agree or not. Don't object to another person's perspective or be defensive of the church or others.

Absolute accuracy is not essential this early in the process. You are not trying to identify your greatest weaknesses (as with the strengths in step 1), but are simply listing them for future reference. Don't be discouraged. Most ministries will identify more weaknesses than strengths. Leave the weaknesses posted for review later.

When you have finished listing your church's weaknesses, pray the following prayer together.

Heavenly Father,

You know our weaknesses as well as our strengths, and Your love for us remains steadfast. We have placed our confidence in ourselves instead of in You and relied upon our own strengths and resources. Thank You that in Christ we are forgiven. We choose to put no confidence in our flesh and declare our dependence upon You. We believe the good work You have begun in us will be completed.

Show us how we can improve on our weaknesses and live with our limitations. May Your power be made perfect in our weakness. In Jesus' strong name we pray. Amen.

Step 3: Memories

In this step, you are asking the Lord to remind you of your good and bad church experiences. If your church is older, consider it decade by decade, beginning in the earliest recalled or researched past. What happened in the 1950s, '60s, '70s, '80s, '90s and so on? If your church is younger, you may want to divide its history into halves or thirds. What happened in the first five years and the last five years?

Make two lists for this step, one titled "Good Memories" and the other titled "Painful Memories." List all of the good memories first. The good memories are fun to recall and are an occasion for thanksgiving to God for His blessings upon His people.

Begin with the following prayer:

Dear heavenly Father,

Thank You for the wonderful experiences we have shared together that have built such special memories. We thank You for Your blessings upon us and for all the good times You have given us. With joy and thanksgiving, we ask You to bring the good memories of our church into our minds. With grateful hearts, we pray in the name of Jesus. Amen.

When the list of good memories is complete, the facilitator will ask the participants to lift them before the Lord in thanksgiving and praise. Encourage everyone to pray aloud spontaneously, beginning with the following words:

Lord, I thank You for (name the good memory).

After thanking the Lord for the good church memories, pray together the following prayer. Then follow with a few moments of silent prayer, allowing the Lord to bring to your memories the painful experiences of your church's past.

Dear heavenly Father,

We thank You for the riches of Your kindness, forbearance and patience, knowing that Your kindness has led us to repentance. We acknowledge that we have not extended that same patience and kindness toward those who have offended us. We have not always acted gracefully and wisely in all our past dealings.

Sometimes pain has come to others even when we used our best judgment in following You. Sometimes the actions and attitudes of others have deeply wounded us. Show us where we have allowed a root of bitterness to spring up, causing trouble and defiling many. As we wait silently before You, bring to our minds all the painful memories of our church's past. In Jesus' compassionate name we pray. Amen.

Make another list of painful memories. Use real names. It is nearly impossible to get in touch with the emotional core of pain without using people's names. Everything said here is to be spoken with respect. Carefully avoid placing blame or making disparaging remarks. Absolute confidentiality must be assured. No person will be permitted to share this confidential information outside the group. Ask the recorder *not* to write down the painful memories section. After the process is finished, you should destroy the list of names.

You can't fix the past, but you can free yourself from it by facing it, forgiving others and seeking forgiveness. Once again, as the group shares the facilitator writes the names associated with painful memories on the sheets up front. Then each person prays silently about the painful memories, asking for courage to face the truth and pain honestly and for the grace to forgive fully and from the heart. Individually and silently, forgive each person you recall and release the offenses as follows:

Lord, I forgive (name the person) for (specifically name every painful memory).

Prayerfully focus on each person you know until every remembered pain has surfaced. Each person should acknowledge God's forgiveness of himself or herself as needed. Proceed when every head is lifted from this time of silent prayer.

In unison, release these painful memories to the Lord in the following declaration and prayer. At the end of the group prayer, there is an opportunity for all the participants to pray individually and audibly. This is a powerful time when individuals can pray: "We forgive . . . "; "We release . . . "; and "We bless . . . " This personalizes the prayer. Usually, those most affected by the painful memory are the ones the Lord prompts to pray.

Declaration
By the authority of the Lord Jesus Christ who is seated at Your right hand, we assume our responsibility to resist the devil. In Jesus' all-powerful name, we retake any ground that Satan may have gained in our lives and in our church through these painful memories and lack of forgiveness. Because we are seated with Christ in the heavenly realms, we command Satan to leave our presence, our ministries and our church.

Prayer

Dear heavenly Father,

We forgive each and every person who has hurt us and our church Body. We forgive as You have forgiven us.

We release our resentments and regrets into Your hands. You alone can heal our broken hearts and bind up our wounds. We ask You to heal the pain in our hearts and in the corporate memory of our church. We have allowed a root of bitterness to spring up and defile many. We have not properly sought to resolve these painful memories according to Your Word.

Should we happen to recall these painful memories in the future, we do so from the vantage point of our union with Christ and choose to acknowledge Your forgiveness and Your healing.

May Your grace and mercy guide us as we seek to live out our calling as spiritual leaders. We ask You, heavenly Father, to fill us with Your Holy Spirit. We surrender full control of our church Body to our crucified, risen and reigning head.

We ask You to bring healing to those who have hurt us. Also bring healing to those who may have been hurt by us. Bless those who curse us, and give rich and satisfying ministries to all who belong to You but have gone away from us. We bless them all in the name of our Lord Jesus Christ who taught us, "Love your enemies, do good to those who hate you, bless those who curse you, pray for those who mistreat you" (Luke 6:27-28). According to Your Word, we pray for those who have hurt us.

Now, individually as God leads you, say out loud:

We forgive (name).
We release (name).
We bless (name).

This is a good time to take a break and ask yourself, "Is there someone I need to talk with right now?"

Step 4: Corporate Sins

In this fourth step, you will identify corporate sins. Individual sins that do not corporately affect the Body will not be a part of this process. They must be dealt with individually. Corporate sins need not involve the whole church, but they must involve a significant group within the church.

Pray together the following prayer. Then follow with a few moments of silent prayer. Ask the Lord to impress upon your minds the past and present corporate sins of your church or of any significant group within it.

> *Dear heavenly Father,*
>
> *As we seek Your face, bring to our minds all the corporate sins that we, or any significant group within our church, have committed. Like Ezra and Daniel, we stand before You, ready to repent of the sins of our spiritual ancestors in this church. We also ask for your discernment to identify and renounce our own sins. As we wait silently before You, bring to our minds all the corporate sins that we, and the spiritual leaders before us, have tolerated or not adequately dealt with. Then grant us the grace that we may confess, renounce and forsake them. In Jesus' forgiving name we pray. Amen.*

The facilitator will now ask you to share your church's corporate sins. Usually this step starts slowly but gradually gains momentum. The facilitator will seek discernment from the group. Write on the sheets up front only those corporate sins that have group consensus. From this step onward group discernment, rather than individual perspectives, is vital. Be patient and wait for general agreement.

Pray the following prayer aloud together for each corporate sin you have listed on the large sheet on the wall:

> *Heavenly Father,*
>
> *We confess (name one sin each time) as sinful and displeasing to You, and we renounce it.*

When every corporate sin has been confessed and renounced, pray the following prayer together:

Heavenly Father,

As spiritual leaders in our church, we acknowledge that these corporate sins are unacceptable to You. We renounce every use of our corporate Body as an instrument of unrighteousness by ourselves and by those who have gone before us. We reject and disown all the sins of our ancestors. We cancel out all advantages, schemes and other works of the devil that have been passed on to our church from them.

By the authority of Christ, the head of His Body, the Church, we demolish every satanic foothold and stronghold in our church gained because of our own corporate sins. We retake all ground given to the adversary in our church, in our related organizations and in our life together as a congregation. We release control of that territory to the Holy Spirit.

We invite the Holy Spirit to cleanse us, renew us, fill us and lead us into all truth. Enable us to turn from this sin and lead us to make all the necessary changes we need to make in order to live righteously together.

We submit ourselves and our church to the sovereign ownership of our heavenly Father, the Lordship and fullness of Christ, and the presence and power of the Holy Spirit. By Your grace and according to Your Word, we acknowledge that we are fellow citizens with all the saints, and we belong to God's household. We affirm that we have been built upon the foundation of the apostles and prophets, Christ Jesus Himself being the chief cornerstone. We praise our Lord Jesus Christ for His headship of our church, and we see ourselves as His Body, Bride and dwelling place.

"Now to him who is able to do immeasurably more than all we ask or imagine, according to his power that is at work within us, to him be glory in the church and in Christ Jesus throughout all generations, for ever and ever! Amen" (Eph. 3:20-21).

At this point, the facilitator will invite everyone to search his or her own heart. Ask for the Holy Spirit to reveal each person's participation

in the church's corporate sins. Each person, as directed by the Holy
Spirit, should then pray out loud, confessing personal involvement in
these corporate sins. It is off-limits to confess someone else's sins. After
this prayer time, you may want to talk during the break with anyone in
the room with whom you need to seek reconciliation.

Step 5: Attacks of Spiritual Enemies

The last step dealt with the ground given over to Satan because of what
your church or its people have done wrong. This step has a different
focus. The attacks you will identify in this step come because of the
things that your church, your pastors and your leaders are *doing right*.

Pray together the following prayer, and then engage in moments of
silent prayer. Ask the Lord to help you discern accurately the nature of
Satan's attacks upon your church, its leaders and its people because
of what you are doing right.

> *Dear heavenly Father,*
>
> *We thank You for our refuge in Christ. We choose to be strong in the
> Lord and in His mighty power. In Christ Jesus, we put on the full armor
> of God. We choose to stand firm and be strong in our faith. We accept the
> truth that our struggle is not against flesh and blood, but against the spir-
> itual forces of evil in the heavenly realms.*
>
> *We don't want to be ignorant of Satan's schemes. Open our eyes to
> the reality of the spiritual world that we live in. We ask You for the abili-
> ty to discern spiritually so that we can rightly judge between good and evil.*
>
> *As we wait silently before You, reveal to us the attacks of Satan
> against us, our pastors, our people and our ministries in order that we
> may stand against them and expose the father of lies. In Jesus' discerning
> name we pray. Amen.*

Once again, the group needs to discern the spiritual attacks, not just
list people's ideas. It takes a little longer to reach group consensus, but
it is far better than listing only the ideas of one person.

When the list is complete, renounce each attack one by one as follows:

In the name and authority of our Lord Jesus Christ, we renounce Satan's attacks (list each one of the identified attacks). We resist them and stand firm against them in Jesus' powerful name. Together we declare, "The Lord rebuke you, the Lord bind you" from any present or any future influence upon us.

Testimonies of former satanists and cult members claim that deceived and wicked people are deliberately out to destroy effective Christian ministries. Sometimes blood sacrifices are made to claim false ownership of Christian leaders or ministries. Satanic assignments are placed upon God's people and their leaders. Use the following declaration to break the influence of any of these attacks against your church, its leaders or its people:

Declaration
As leaders of this church and members of the Body of Christ, we reject and disown all influences and attacks of demonic powers and evil spirits that cause resistance to Christ's work. As children of God, we have been delivered from the power of darkness and brought into the kingdom of God's dear Son.

Because we are seated with Christ in the heavenly realm, which is the spiritual location of authority, we renounce all satanic assignments that are directed toward our church and our ministry. We cancel every curse that deceived or wicked people have put on us. We announce to Satan and all his forces that Christ became a curse for us when He died on the cross.

We renounce any and all sacrifices by satanists or anyone else who would claim ownership of us, our ministry, our leaders or our people. We announce that we have been bought and purchased by the blood of the Lamb. We accept only the sacrifice of Jesus whereby we belong to Him.

Conclude this step with the following prayer for protection and as an act of dedication of yourselves and your facilities to God:

Dear heavenly Father,

We worship You and You alone. You are the Lord of our lives and the Lord of our church. We offer our bodies to You as living sacrifices, holy and pleasing to God. We also present our church Body to You as a sacrifice of praise.

We pray for Your protection of our pastors, leaders, members, families, attendees and all of our ministries. We put on the Lord Jesus Christ and claim all the protection we have in Him. He is our sanctuary, and it is by His armor that we stand protected. Grant us the wisdom and grace to deal with heretics and spiritual wolves. We pray for discernment in order to judge between good and evil.

We dedicate all of our facilities to You and all the property that You have entrusted to us, including our sound system, audiovisual equipment, kitchen and transportation. We rededicate our center of worship, classrooms, offices and every part of our facility and property to You.

Lord Jesus Christ, You are the head of this church, and we exalt You. May all that we do bring honor and glory to You. In Jesus' holy name we pray. Amen.

Step 6: Prayer Action Plan

Place four large sheets of paper side by side on the wall. All of the previous sheets also should be visible. On the first sheet write, "We renounce." On the next three sheets jot down in order, "We announce," "We affirm" and "We will." Turn to the last page of this appendix for an example of how the wording begins for each item.

You are now ready to synthesize everything you have discerned in the last five steps. Look for recurring patterns that can be put together.

You will want to renounce the evil (attacks, corporate sins, conflicts, weaknesses). For example, "We renounce division among us."

Next, you will announce the positive biblical opposite of what you renounced, worded in terms of your resources in Christ. For example, "We announce that in Christ we have the unity of the Spirit."

You will then affirm a scriptural promise or truth that encourages and motivates you in regard to the same item. For example, "We affirm that in the depths of our hearts we are all one in Christ Jesus."

Finally, you will commit to an action step you will take. For example, "We will talk to the right person in the right spirit when conflicts arise."

Your goal in this crucial statement is to make the shortest list possible without leaving out any major issues discerned about your church. Pray the following prayer together and spend a few moments silently seeking God's wisdom. Ask for the Holy Spirit's guidance and for wisdom to have group consensus on the right words.

Dear heavenly Father,

We thank You for opening our eyes to see the strengths, weaknesses, good memories, painful memories, corporate sins and spiritual attacks of the enemy. Thank You for helping us understand and overcome our problems and enemies.

Provide us with discernment into the true condition of our church. We want to see our church the way You see it. Give us Your plan of action and teach us to respond appropriately in prayer and obedience.

We ask for Your divine guidance in formulating this Prayer Action Plan. We thank You that the Holy Spirit helps us in our weakness, because we don't really know how or what to pray. Give us unity. Grant us wisdom. Supply us with the right words and Your order of subjects for us to list.

Open our eyes to the truth of Your Word. Convict us of the need to follow through with what You cause us to see. In Jesus' all-wise name we pray. Amen.

For each subject, work across the four sheets—we renounce, we announce, we affirm, we will—before going on to the next item. Fatigue may be a factor, so call upon the Holy Spirit for divine energy to sort out all the lists on the sheets (see Col. 1:29).

When you have finished the list, ask all the participants to stand, face the four sheets and pray the Prayer Action Plan aloud. This prayer is essential.

Treat your Prayer Action Plan as a letter from Jesus to your church. In it, He calls you to repent ("We renounce"), to remember ("We announce"), to hold on ("We affirm") and to obey ("We will"). With this view of your church, how does the Lord want you to implement the Prayer Action Plan? Pray together the following prayer, followed by moments of silent prayer. Ask the Lord to impress upon your minds and hearts what you as leaders should do.

> *Dear heavenly Father,*
>
> *We come before You in worship, adoration and thanksgiving. Thank You for revealing to us Your perspective of our church. Show us if there is anything else that is keeping our church in bondage. We commit ourselves to renounce it, stand against it in Christ, hold fast to Your promises and obey Your will.*
>
> *We ask You to reveal what we should do with our Prayer Action Plan. Unveil to us the practical steps that You want us as leaders to take. Make Your will for us known in order that we may fully obey Your direction for our church. In Jesus' powerful name we pray. Amen.*

Some strategies for implementing the Prayer Action Plan are as follows:

- Pray through it on a daily basis.
- Pray through it together in each of your regular meetings.
- Preach through it in a sermon series.
- Take other groups of leaders in your church through the Setting Your Church Free process.
- Recruit committed intercessors to pray for the leadership.

Implementation works best if the leaders and pastors pray the Prayer Action Plan until it becomes a part of their lives and their thinking. Think of it as a letter from Jesus—not new revelation, but conviction and guidance from the Holy Spirit that your church must obey. The facilitator will again list on the paper sheets up front the action points reached by group consensus. Select one person besides the pastor or a paid staff member to hold the group accountable for following through on this Prayer Action Plan. Conclude the session by praying together the following prayer:

Heavenly Father,

Thank You, Lord, that we can call You our heavenly Father. Thank You for Your love and acceptance of us. Thank You for all You have done for us today. Thank You for hearing our prayers, forgiving our corporate sins and setting us free from the damaging influence of Satan's schemes against our church.

Thank You for opening our eyes to see and our ears to hear. Give us a heart to obey. We commit ourselves to follow through on the Prayer Action Plan You have given us. Teach us to pray and apply this plan as You have directed.

We praise You for uniting us with the Lord Jesus Christ. We praise You that the Son of God came to destroy the works of the devil. We ask for Your protection for our marriages, our families, our ministries and our church. Keep us from scandal. We love You and commit ourselves to become the people that You have called us to be. Empower us to walk in the light and to speak the truth in love.

"Now to the King eternal, immortal, invisible, the only God, be honor and glory for ever and ever. Amen" (1 Tim. 1:17).

AFTER COMPLETING THE STEPS

Make sure you destroy the sheet for step 3—"painful memories." Ask the recorder or a church secretary to compile all the other lists for the participants in this retreat. Compile the Prayer Action Plan on a single sheet for easy use by the participants. Place the strategy steps on the reverse side of the sheet. Use the following format.

OUR GREATEST STRENGTHS

1.

2.

3.

OUR PRAYER ACTION PLAN

We renounce . . .	We announce . . .	We affirm . . .	We will . . .
1.	1.	1.	1.
2.	2.	2.	2.
3.	3.	3.	3.

APPENDIX B

Greatest Strengths and Prayer Action Plan

OUR GREATEST STRENGTHS

1. We have a strong unity in Christ that creates a close family feeling and loving relationships.
2. We preach the truth and desire to live it out in holiness and righteousness.
3. We pursue unity, humility and the Holy Spirit's direction.
4. We have leadership with a servant's heart.
5. We encourage personal participation in Christ.
6. We have a strong and active children's ministry.
7. We have a Christ-led vision for health, growth, reproduction and optimism.

OUR PRAYER ACTION PLAN

We renounce

1. We renounce acting independently of God.
2. We renounce acting independently of one another.
3. We renounce our lack of commitment to and practice of spiritual disciplines.
4. We renounce our self-focus that produces apathy to the lost.
5. We renounce inappropriate dependence on the pastor that excuses us from our God-given ministries.
6. We renounce sexual immorality in all its forms.

We announce

1. We announce that in Christ we have God and all His resources.
2. We announce that in Christ we have mutual dependence on and submission to one another.
3. We announce that in Christ we have continual opportunity to commune with God.
4. We announce that in Christ alone we have the freedom and power to love the unsaved as ourselves.
5. We announce that in Christ we are each equipped for the ministries to which He calls us.
6. We announce that in Christ we have freedom from the power of sin.

We affirm

1. We affirm that we can do all things through Christ who strengthens us.
2. We affirm that we are united as one Body in Christ.
3. We affirm that Christ is knocking at our heart's door, longing for spiritual intimacy with us.
4. We affirm that Christ so loved the lost that He died for their sins to bring them to God.
5. We affirm that it's a high privilege and honor to serve the living God.
6. We affirm that there is no sin that is worth breaking our communion with Christ.

We will

1. We will be diligent in prayer, seeking to obey the will of God.
2. We will be sensitive to one another and yield our rights to one another, seeking the Lord's best for the Body.
3. We will renew our commitment to the spiritual disciplines by cutting out or giving up less important things in order to practice them.
4. We will set aside our fear and inconvenience to prayerfully and actively share the love of Christ.
5. We will make ourselves available to exercise our gifts, strengths and abilities as the Holy Spirit leads us.
6. We will hold each other accountable and pray for one another's purity.

ABOUT DR. NEIL T. ANDERSON

Dr. Neil T. Anderson was formerly the chairman of the Practical Theology Department at Talbot School of Theology. In 1989, he founded Freedom in Christ Ministries, which now has staff and offices in various countries around the world. In 2001, Dr. Anderson stepped down as President of Freedom in Christ Ministries and officially retired in May 2005 in order to start Discipleship Counseling Ministries. The purpose of this new ministry is to give greater focus to his personal speaking and writing ministry, and to allow him more flexibility to serve others without financial constraints. For more information about Dr. Anderson and his ministry, visit his website at www.discipleshipcounselingministries.org.

CORE MESSAGE AND MATERIALS

Victory Over the Darkness with study guide, audiobook and videocassettes (Regal Books, 2000). With over 1,000,000 copies in print, this core book explains who you are in Christ, how to walk by faith in the power of the Holy Spirit, how to be transformed by the renewing of our minds, how to experience emotional freedom, and how to relate to one another in Christ.

The Bondage Breaker with study guide and audiobook (Harvest House Publishers, 2000). With over 1,000,000 copies in print, this book explains spiritual warfare, what our protection is, ways that we are vulnerable, and how we can live a liberated life in Christ.

Breaking Through to Spiritual Maturity (Regal Books, 2000). This curriculum teaches the basic message of Discipleship Counseling Ministries.

Discipleship Counseling with videocassettes (Regal Books, 2003). This book combines the concepts of discipleship and counseling and teaches the practical integration of theology and psychology for helping Christians resolve their personal and spiritual conflicts through repentance and faith in God.

Steps to Freedom in Christ and interactive videocassette (Regal Books, 2004). This discipleship counseling tool helps Christians resolve their personal and spiritual conflicts.

Beta: The Next Step in Your Journey with Christ (Regal Books, 2004) is a discipleship course for Sunday school classes and small groups. The kit includes a teacher's guide, a student guide and two DVDs covering 12 lessons and the Steps to Freedom in Christ. This course is designed to enable new and stagnant believers to resolve personal and spiritual conflicts and be established alive and free in Christ.

The Daily Discipler (Regal Books, 2005). This practical systematic theology is a culmination of all of Neil's books covering the major doctrines of the Christian faith and the problems they face. It is a five day per week, one year study that will thoroughly ground believers in their faith.

VICTORY OVER THE DARKNESS SERIES

Overcoming a Negative Self-Image, with Dave Park (Regal Books, 2003).
Overcoming Addictive Behavior, with Mike Quarles (Regal Books, 2003).
Overcoming Doubt (Regal Books, 2004).
Overcoming Depression, with Joanne Anderson (Regal Books, 2004).

BONDAGE BREAKER SERIES

Praying by the Power of the Spirit (Harvest House Publishers, 2003).
Finding God's Will in Spiritually Deceptive Times (Harvest House Publishers, 2003).
Finding Freedom in a Sex-Obsessed World (Harvest House Publishers, 2004).
Unleashing God's Power in You, with Dr. Robert Saucy (Harvest House Publishers, 2004).

SPECIALIZED BOOKS

God's Power at Work in You, with Dr. Robert Saucy (Harvest House Publishers, 2001). A thorough analysis of sanctification and practical instruction on how we grow in Christ.

The Seduction of Our Children, with Steve Russo (Harvest House Publishers, 1991). This book explains what teenagers are experiencing and how parents can be equipped to help them.

Released from Bondage, with Judith King and Dr. Fernando Garzon (Thomas Nelson, 2002). This book has personal accounts of defeated Christians with explanatory notes of how they resolved their conflicts and found their freedom in Christ, and how the message of Discipleship Counseling can be applied to therapy with research results.

Daily in Christ, with Joanne Anderson (Harvest House Publishers, 2000). This popular daily devotional is also being used by thousands of Internet subscribers every day.

Who I Am in Christ (Regal Books, 2001). In 36 short chapters, this book describes who you are in Christ and how He meets your deepest needs.

Freedom from Addiction, with Mike and Julia Quarles (Regal Books, 1997). Using Mike's testimony, this book explains the nature of chemical addictions and how to overcome them in Christ.

One Day at a Time, with Mike and Julia Quarles (Regal Books, 2000). This devotional helps those who struggle with addictive behaviors and how to discover the grace of God on a daily basis.

The Christ Centered Marriage, with Dr. Charles Mylander (Regal Books, 1997). This book explains God's divine plan for marriage and the steps that couples can take to resolve their difficulties.

Freedom from Fear, with Rich Miller (Harvest House Publishers, 1999). This book explains anxiety disorders and how to overcome them.

Christ Centered Therapy, with Dr. Terry and Julie Zuehlke (Zondervan Publishing House, 2000). A textbook explaining the practical integration of theology and psychology for professional counselors.

Getting Anger Under Control, with Rich Miller (Harvest House Publishers, 1999). This book explains the basis for anger and how to control it.

Freedom in Christ Bible (Zondervan Publishing House, 2002). A one year discipleship study with notes in the Bible.

Blessed Are the Peacemakers, with Dr. Charles Mylander (Regal Books, 2002). This book explains the ministry of reconciliation and gives practical steps for being reconciled with others.

The Biblical Guide to Alternative Medicine, with Dr. Michael Jacobson (Regal Books, 2003). This book develops a grid by which you can evaluate medical practices, and then applies the grid to the world's most recognized philosophies of medicine and health.

Breaking the Strongholds of Legalism, with Rich Miller and Paul Travis (Harvest House Publishers, 2003). An explanation of legalism and how to overcome it.

Free, with Dave Park (Regal Books, 2005): A forty-day devotional on sanctification.

CONTACT INFORMATION

For more information regarding these materials, contact:

In the U.S.A.:
Freedom in Christ Ministries
    9051 Executive Park Drive, Suite 503
    Knoxville, TN 37923
    Telephone: (865) 342-4000
    E-mail: infor@ficm.org
    Website: www.ficm.org

In Canada:
    FIC Canada
    Box 33115
    Regina, SK S4T7X2
    Canada
    Telephone: (306) 546-2522
    E-mail: FreedominChrist@sasktel.net

In the United Kingdom:
    P.O. Box 2842
    Reading, UK RG29RT
    Telephone: (118) 988-8173
    E-mail: info@ficm.org.uk

For more information regarding the youth editions of Dr. Anderson's books coauthored by Dave Park, contact:

    One Passion Ministries
    P.O. Box 23495
    Knoxville, TN 37933-1495
    Telephone: (865) 966-1153
    E-mail: DavePark@integrity.com
    Website: www.onepassionministries.com